The Remediation of Learning Disabilities

A HANDBOOK OF PSYCHOEDUCATIONAL RESOURCE PROGRAMS

Second Edition

Robert E. Valett, Ed. D.

Professor of Education
California State University, Fresno
and Consulting Psychologist

Fearon Education
a division of
PITMAN LEARNING, INC.
Belmont, California

Designer: Richard Kharibian

Editor: Carol L. King

Illustrated by Jim M'Guinness

ISBN-0-8224-5851-9

Library of Congress Catalog Card Number: 67-26847

Printed in the United States of America.

Contents

Preface

The purpose of this book is to aid teachers, psychologists, and other specialist working with pupils with learning disabilities. Additional developmental learning tasks, resource programs, and evaluation procedures have been included in this revised edition. A major part of this revision is devoted to illustrations of specific learning objectives and prescriptive lessons for their accomplishment; the book is, therefore, a more complete resource guide to psychoeducational programming.

The rationale underlying this book can be summarized in my belief that specific human abilities and skills can be significantly developed and increased as a result of appropriate exercise, practice, and experience. This handbook will simulate professionals to select, design, and present appropriate learning experiences and opportunities to those who may profit from them.

There are several premises to the successful application of these resource programs or selected learning tasks. I have recognized these premises in the form of personal attitudes that must characterize the diagnostic-prescriptive teacher or specialist. Briefly stated, these are:

- a belief in education as a means to total human growth and self-actualization.
- a belief in the importance of developing psychomotor, cognitive, *and* affective abilities and skills.
- a belief in developmental growth stages and the critical importance of sensory-motor-perceptual abilities and their integration for symbolic learning.
- a belief in the early identification and analysis of learning and behavioral problems and the development of specific learning abilities and programs as a prevention of future or potential disabilities.
- a belief in providing environmental structure and opportunities for individualized prescriptive learning for all persons while encouraging continuous progress toward realistic goals and objectives.
- a belief in the fundamental importance of developing unique personal abilities and strengths, self-esteem, and self-direction as an essential component of all prescriptive learning programs.

The Remediation of Learning Disabilities begins with a list of operational definitions and illustrations of fifty-three basic learning abilities. These abilities have been grouped under six major developmental learning areas: gross motor development, sensory-motor integration, perceptual motor skills, language development, conceptual skills, and social skills. The fifty-three resource programs are then presented in numerical order for prescriptive use. Each resource program contains a definition and an educational rationale, followed by a number of beginning, middle, and advanced learning tasks and activities. A sample program worksheet, a number of related program references, suggested instructional materials, relevant evaluation and diagnostic aids, and various readings are also included. A prescriptive illustration including a priority teaching objective, pretest task, specific teaching procedure, and performance evaluation is given for each resource program.

Other correlated materials in the Valett Learning Disability Series are presented in the Appendix for reference use. Several forms useful in applying the handbook include the Individual Prescriptive Lesson Plan Outline, A Recommended Daily Class Schedule, and the Pupil Progress Report by Teacher. Also included are lists of

Prescriptive Remedial Activities Correlated with Psychological Subtests, and Commonly Used Diagnostic-Prescriptive Tests and Suppliers.

It should be recognized that all of these resource programs, illustrations, and forms are only beginning suggestions for professional use and application. They are intended as an initial source of ideas for possible selection as *part* of a learning program designed for the individual pupil. It is important to modify, supplement, and extend these resource programs and tasks in the attempt to meet the needs of each pupil. If wisely used, they should serve as a stimulus to creative prescriptive programming and innovative teaching or psychoeducational therapy.

The Remediation of Learning Disabilities may also be used in teacher training and professional development programs. It is commonly used as a laboratory and clinical manual for self-instruction. For example, the prospective teacher might select one of the priority learning objectives presented in the handbook and attempt to devise an alternative teaching procedure and postevaluation, including the formulation of new learning and teaching objectives.

For best use in the development of a sound diagnostic-prescriptive education program, the resource programs in this handbook should be implemented through the conjoint planning of teacher, administrator, and psychological or educational consultant.

Many acknowledgments are due to those who contributed to the development of this book. It has been gratifying to receive suggestions from teachers, psychologists, physicians, and specialists in schools, clinics, and hospitals who have been experimenting with the development of basic learning abilities. It is encouraging to know that the reference to basic learning skills, abilities, and disabilities is gaining support as opposed to the continuation of traditional medical-legal-psychological categories, classifications, and labels, which have been of little value in psychoeducational programming. To all those who are engaged in such educational reform and innovation, and who have supported my efforts in this regard, I am most appreciative.

The following persons have made specific contributions, which I have adopted or modified for incorporation in this revision, and to them I owe a special acknowledgment: Mark Allen, Marge Ambrose, Shirley Boucher, Arnold Buchheimer, James Clark, Pat Coleman, Betty Darke, Stella Dean, Aileen Elliott, Janice Emerzian, Alice Gallaher, Rita Hodgkins, Carmenia Juarena, Jody Jeschien, Janet Jorgensen, Elaine Juhasz, Cecelia Kammerer, Leon Kent, Harmenia Kourtjian, M. A. Kwint, Marian Lail, Jim Manriguez, Geraldine Milligan, Carolyn O'Rourke, Mearlene Page, Chlele Payne, Pat Rankin, Diana Robinson, Tom Rapchinski, Douglas Steuber, Ellen Schrimsher, Ruby Spackman, Jim Thomas, Luella Williams, and Carol Westeren.

A special appreciation is extended to my wife, Shirley B. Valett, a gifted teacher and educational therapist, without whose contributions and encouragement this work would not have been possible.

ROBERT E. VALETT

A PSYCHOEDUCATIONAL DEFINITION OF BASIC LEARNING ABILITIES

An operational definition (A) and illustration (B) of basic learning abilities for use in developing specific educational programs.

Gross Motor Development
The development and awareness of large muscle activity.

1/Rolling
A. The ability to roll one's body in a controlled manner.
B. From a supine position, with arms over head, pupil can roll from back to stomach. Pupil can do sequential rolling to right and left, can roll down hill or incline.

2/Sitting
A. The ability to sit erect in normal position without support or constant reminding.
B. Pupil can demonstrate proper poise in sitting at desk with feet on floor, back straight, and head and arms in correct position for work at hand.

3/Crawling
A. The ability to crawl on hands and knees in a smooth and coordinated way.
B. With eyes fixated on target, pupil first crawls in homolateral fashion. Pupil progresses to cross-pattern crawling program.

4/Walking
A. The ability to walk erect in a coordinated fashion without support.
B. With head up and shoulders back, pupil walks specified path and walking line. Can walk backward and sideways without difficulty.

5/Running
A. The ability to run a track or obstacle course without a change of pace.
B. Pupil runs a straight track of easy distance without difficulty. Can change direction through a simple obstacle course without stopping or significantly changing pace.

6/Throwing
A. The ability to throw a ball with a reasonable degree of accuracy.
B. Pupil throws a ball to another person so that it may be caught. Can throw ball accurately into box or basket.

7/Jumping
A. The ability to jump simple obstacles without falling.
B. Pupil can jump from chair to floor without difficulty. Can jump from jumping board without falling. Can jump over knee-high obstacles.

8/Skipping
A. The ability to skip in normal play.
B. Pupil can skip, alternating feet, around circle of players. Can skip rope forward both by hopping and alternate-foot skipping.

9/Dancing
A. The ability to move one's body in coordinated response to music.
B. In young children, free movement and eurythmic expression. Progression to more formal dance steps with older pupils.

10/Self-identification
A. The ability to identify one's self.
B. Pupil can identify self by name, respond to name when called, identify self in pictures and mirrors.

11/Body Localization
A. The ability to locate parts of one's body.
B. Pupil can locate eyes, hands, mouth, hair, nose, feet, eyebrows, fingernails, shoulders, elbows, knees, back, neck, chin, forehead, wrist, arms, legs, toes.

12/Body Abstraction	A. The ability to transfer and generalize self-concepts and body localizations.
	B. Pupil can identify others by names and pictures. Can locate body parts on others, generalize to pictures, complete body picture puzzles.
13/Muscular Strength	A. The ability to use one's muscles to perform physical tasks.
	B. Pupil can touch floor by bending from standing position; can sit up and touch toes from supine position; can raise legs off floor for a few seconds from supine position; can do one push-up; can chin self from bar.
14/General Physical Health	A. The ability to understand and apply principles of health and hygiene and to evidence good general health.
	B. Pupil has good personal health and hygiene habits—no chronic absences for health reasons, no unusual accidents or health history, no significant physical disabilities interfering with learning.

Sensory-Motor Integration
The psychophysical integration of fine and gross motor activities.

15/Balance and Rhythm	A. The ability to maintain gross and fine motor balance and to move rhythmically.
	B. Pupil is able to balance on balance board or rail. Can move rhythmically in playing jacks and in bouncing on trampoline or spring.
16/Body-spatial Organization	A. The ability to move one's body in an integrated way around and through objects in the spatial environment.
	B. Pupil can run maze on playground or in classroom without bumping. Can move easily through tunnels and use playground monkey bars. Can imitate body positions in space.
17/Reaction-Speed Dexterity	A. The ability to respond efficiently to general directions or assignments.
	B. Pupil can attend to the teacher sufficiently to comprehend total directions. Can proceed to organize self and respond adequately to complete the given assignment within a normal time expectancy.
18/Tactile Discrimination	A. The ability to identify and match objects by touching and feeling.
	B. With hidden toys and materials, pupil can match objects with both left and right hands, name or classify materials or substances, differentiate weights, discriminate temperatures.
19/Directionality	A. The ability to know right from left, up from down, forward from backward, and directional orientation.
	B. Pupil can write and follow picture story or reading material from left to right, discriminate right and left body parts and those of other people, locate directions in room and school.
20/Laterality	A. The ability to integrate one's sensory-motor contact with the environment through establishment of homolateral hand, eye, and foot dominance.
	B. Pupil has consistent right- or left-sided approach in use of eyes, hands, and feet in tasks such as kicking ball, cutting paper, sighting with telescope.
21/Time Orientation	A. The ability to judge lapses in time and to be aware of time concepts.
	B. Pupil is prompt in attending class, completing timed assignments, and following directions. Pupil is aware of day, month, year, time of day, and seasons.

Perceptual-Motor Skills
The functional utilization of primary auditory, visual, and visual-motor skills.

22/Auditory Acuity
A. The ability to receive and differentiate auditory stimuli.
B. Pupil responds functionally to watch tick, hidden sound toys, and general normal conversational directions. Pupil has no significant decibel loss.

23/Auditory Decoding
A. The ability to understand sounds or spoken words.
B. Pupil can follow simple verbal instructions, can indicate by gesture or words the meaning or purpose of auditory stimuli such as animal sounds, nouns, or verbs.

24/Auditory-vocal Association
A. The ability to respond verbally in a meaningful way to auditory stimuli.
B. Pupil can associate with verbal opposites, sentence completion or analogous verbal responses.

25/Auditory Memory
A. The ability to retain and recall general auditory information.
B. Pupil can act out (charades) Santa Claus, simple plots of common nursery rhymes ("Jack and Jill"), can verbally relate yesterday's experiences, meals, television, and story plots.

26/Auditory Sequencing
A. The ability to recall in correct sequence and detail prior auditory information.
B. Pupil can imitate specific sound patterns, follow exactly complex series of directions, repeat digit and letter series.

27/Visual Acuity
A. The ability to see and to differentiate meaningfully and accurately objects in one's visual field.
B. Pupil sees without noticeable fatigue, holds material at appropriate working distance, has no significant loss of acuity on Snellen or Illiterate E chart.

28/Visual Coordination and Pursuit
A. The ability to follow and track objects and symbols with coordinated eye movements.
B. With head steady, pupil can move eyes to fixate on stable objects in varied places, pursue moving objects such as finger positions, follow picture and word stories left to right without jerky movements.

29/Visual-Form Discrimination
A. The ability to visually differentiate the forms and symbols in one's environment.
B. Pupil can match identical pictures and symbols such as abstract designs, letters, numbers, and words.

30/Visual Figure- Ground Differentiation
A. The ability to perceive objects in foreground and background and to separate them meaningfully.
B. Pupil can differentiate picture of self and friends from group picture, differentiate objects in "front" and "back" part of pictures and mock-ups, differentiate his name from among others on paper or chalkboard, perceive simple forms and words imbedded in others.

31/Visual Memory
A. The ability to recall accurately prior visual experiences.
B. Pupil can recall from visual cues where he stopped in book, can match or verbally recall objects removed or changed in the environment, can match briefly exposed symbols.

32/Visual-Motor Memory
A. The ability to reproduce motorwise prior visual experiences.
B. Pupil can draw designs and symbols following brief exposure, can reproduce letters, numbers, simple words on demand, can portray prior objects or events through gestures or drawings, can reproduce varied patterns and identify hidden materials.

33/Visual-Motor Fine Muscle Coordination	A. The ability to coordinate fine muscles such as those required in eye-hand tasks.
	B. Pupil can write legibly, trace, and imitate precise body movements without difficulty, can cut, manipulate, and judge fine physical responses without gross errors.
34/Visual-Motor Spatial-Form Manipulation	A. The ability to move in space and to manipulate three-dimensional materials.
	B. Pupil can build block houses and designs, draw three-dimensional pictures, complete shop and craft projects, integrate form and space puzzles.
35/Visual-Motor Speed of Learning	A. The ability to learn visual-motor skills from repetitive experience.
	B. Pupil can respond with increasing speed to rote learning tasks such as copying digit or letter sequences, spelling, specific arithmetic processes, and gross motor skills such as jumping over a rope.
36/Visual-Motor Integration	A. The ability to integrate total visual-motor skills in complex problem solving.
	B. Pupil can play complex team sports, swim, draw accurate pictures including people, may play musical instrument, write extended letters, move freely about neighborhood and community.

Language Development
The current functional stage of total psycholinguistic development.

37/Vocabulary	A. The ability to understand words.
	B. Pupil has a basic receptive vocabulary in accord with chronological age and educational opportunity.
38/Fluency and Encoding	A. The ability to express oneself verbally.
	B. Pupil can communicate verbally, has average fluency of speech without undue hesitation or stuttering, uses coherent sentence structure.
39/Articulation	A. The ability to articulate words clearly without notable pronunciation or articulatory problems.
	B. Pupil uses words with correct pronunciation of initial, medial, and final sounds.
40/Word Attack Skills	A. The ability to analyze words phonetically.
	B. Pupil can make proper phonetic associations, break down words phonetically, recognize component words.
41/Reading Comprehension	A. The ability to understand what one has read.
	B. Pupil can recall story and paraphrase plot, can explain or relate meaningfulness of what has been read.
42/Writing	A. The ability to express oneself through written language.
	B. Pupil can write simple sentences and communicate ideas through paragraph, letter, story, or essay.
43/Spelling	A. The ability to spell in both oral and written form.
	B. Pupil spells within general age expectancy.

Conceptual Skills
The functional level of concept attainment and general reasoning ability.

| 44/Number Concepts | A. The ability to understand and use the concepts of quantity, sets, number, numeral, shape, size, position, and measurement. |

B. Pupil can arrange objects into sets, can count the number in each set, and recognize the numeral that represents that number.

45/Arithmetic Processes

A. The ability to add, subtract, multiply, and divide whole numbers, fractions, and decimal fractions.

B. Pupil can demonstrate knowledge of basic mathematical operations within relation to his level of understanding of mathematical concepts.

46/Arithmetic Reasoning

A. The ability to apply mathematical concepts to problem solving in personal and social situations.

B. Pupil can purchase goods and account for funds, can demonstrate knowledge of coinage and exchange, can calculate time differentials, and can understand weights and measures.

47/General Information

A. The ability to acquire and utilize general information from education and experience.

B. Pupil is aware of major local and national current events, knows local geography, has concept of city, state, and nation.

48/Classification

A. The ability to recognize class identities and to use them in establishing logical relationships.

B. Pupil can sort objects by classification, recognize subclasses, verbalize common elements in class identity.

49/Comprehension

A. The ability to use judgment and reasoning in common sense situations.

B. Pupil responds to factual reasoning when situation is explained to him, can recognize alternatives in situations and can judge actions accordingly, can identify logical reason for given actions.

Social Skills
The skills involved in social problem solving.

50/Social Acceptance

A. The ability to get along with one's peers.

B. Pupil can relate meaningfully to others and is accepted in both one-to-one and group situations.

51/Anticipatory Response

A. The ability to anticipate the probable outcome of a social situation by logical inference.

B. Pupil can predict the consequences of his own behavior and that of others in given situations.

52/Value Judgments

A. The ability to recognize and respond to moral and ethical issues.

B. Pupil has a sense of right and wrong, controls own actions, demonstrates proper behavior.

53/Social Maturity

A. The ability to assume personal and social responsibility.

B. Pupil is socially mature and independent, demonstrates appropriate citizenship, and assumes social responsibilities.

Gross Motor Development

1/Rolling

DEFINITION: The ability to roll one's body in a controlled manner.

ILLUSTRATION: From a supine position, with arms over head, pupil can roll from back to stomach. Pupil can do sequential rollings to right and left, can roll down hill or incline.

EDUCATIONAL RATIONALE: Rolling—either parts of one's body or the entire body itself in accord with specific instructions—furthers neurophysiological control and development. Physically immature and poorly coordinated children should be given increasingly difficult rolling tasks and taught fundamental body control skills.

SUGGESTED PROGRAM IDEAS

1. Beginning

"Today we are going to begin some rolling exercises that you will find are lots of fun":

a. "Lie down on the blanket [quilt, mat, etc.], with your feet together and your hands at your sides. Look at the ceiling, Now relax quietly and imagine you see a fly flying in a circle. Keep your head and body still, but follow the fly with your eyes, rolling them in a circle like this [demonstrate], going first to the right and then to the left."

b. "Put your arms straight out at your sides with the palms down. Now roll them over on their backs. Now put your hands on their backs at your sides and roll them over on their palms." Repeat routine several times.

c. "Lie on your back with hands over your head and feet together. Roll over slowly to the right. Roll back two times to the left. Now hold a ball in your hands over your head and roll as I tell you."

d. "Lie on this trampoline and roll first to the right as far as you can go and then to the left. Describe your feelings."

2. Middle

a. "Put one hand over your head and the other by your side. Roll right four times, roll left two times." Exchange hands and repeat; hold ball in hand and repeat.

b. "Place your hands by your sides and your feet together. Now roll to the right three times, roll back to the left three times. Now cross your arms over your chest and roll."

c. Outside on grass: "Clasp your hands over your head and roll right. Now roll left. Now roll in the same way down this grassy incline as far as you can go. Now try to roll back up as far as you can."

d. "Lie on the edge of this blanket and slowly roll yourself up in it with your head sticking out; now unroll yourself."

3. Advanced

a. Have one child lie down on edge of blanket with hands clasped over head. Then have several pupils grasp edge of blanket and roll child out. Repeat rolling child out and down grassy incline.

b. Teach simple somersaults—forward, then backward. Have pupils hold utility ball and do somersaults. Show pupils how to squat and clasp knees and roll to right and left. Have two pupils grasp one another and roll together following teacher's directions.

c. Have three children hold hula hoops in a line while other children somersault through them.

d. For older children, teach directional rolling in the water, rolling and somersaults on the trampoline, and rolling in circles to music while holding ankles.

e. Place hula hoop on the ground, lie down with hands on hoop, and roll in circle around it.

REFERENCES

Andrews, Gladys. *Creative Rhythmic Movement for Children.* Englewood Cliffs, N.J.: Prentice-Hall 1954.

O'Donnell, Patrick A. *Motor and Haptic Learning.* San Rafael, Calif.: Dimensions Publishing, 1969.

Related Programs
* Getman, G. N.; Kane, E. R.; Halgren, M. R.; and McKee, G. W. *Physiology of Readiness: An Action Program for the Development of Perception for Children.* Minneapolis: Programs to Accelerate School Success., 1964.
* Hackett, Layne C., and Jensen, Robert G. *A Guide to Movement Exploration.* Palo Alto, Calif.: Peek Publications, 1967.
* Adaptive physical education and community recreational programs (YMCA, etc.)

Instructional Materials
* Rest and exercise mats, Constructive Playthings, 1040 E. 85th Street, Kansas City, Mo.
* Heavy quilt for covering floor in classroom
* Old clothes or gym clothes—depending on extent of program
* Outline of exercises for parent use and follow-through
* Utility balls
* Blanket or canvas sheet
* Tennis balls for hand grasping while rolling
* Spot trainers and incline mats, Port-a-Pit, P.O. Box C, Temple City, Calif.
* Barrel Roll, J. A. Preston Corp., 71 Fifth Avenue, New York, N.Y.

Further Evaluation
* Pediatric examination for young children
* Subjectively devised exercises dependent on age and disability of the child
* Lincoln-Oseretsky Motor Development Scale (for related tasks)

PRESCRIPTIVE ILLUSTRATION

Priority Teaching Objective: Paul, thirteen years old, minimal cerebral dysfunction. Using the athletic mat, Paul will be able to make three successive somersaults from a running position, ending upright on his feet at the end of the mat.

Pretest Tasks: Paul could make only one somersault before losing body control and going off the side of the mat. His poor control was the subject of much teasing by his classmates.

Specific Teaching Procedures: "Paul, today we are going to begin work on somersaults. When we have finished, you will be able to start from the black line, run to the mat, do three somersaults without going off the mat, and then end up on your feet."

"Watch me. I will do them slowly to show you what I mean. Watch where I put my hands and how I hold my legs together. I will also put my head down right in the middle of the mat [teacher demonstrates]."

"Now to begin with, we will start here at the end of the mat. I will take a position and you copy me. First I get down on my hands and knees like this—now you do it. Good!"

"Next we place our heads like this. Then we push up with our feet and go over. Notice where our hands are when we complete the roll."

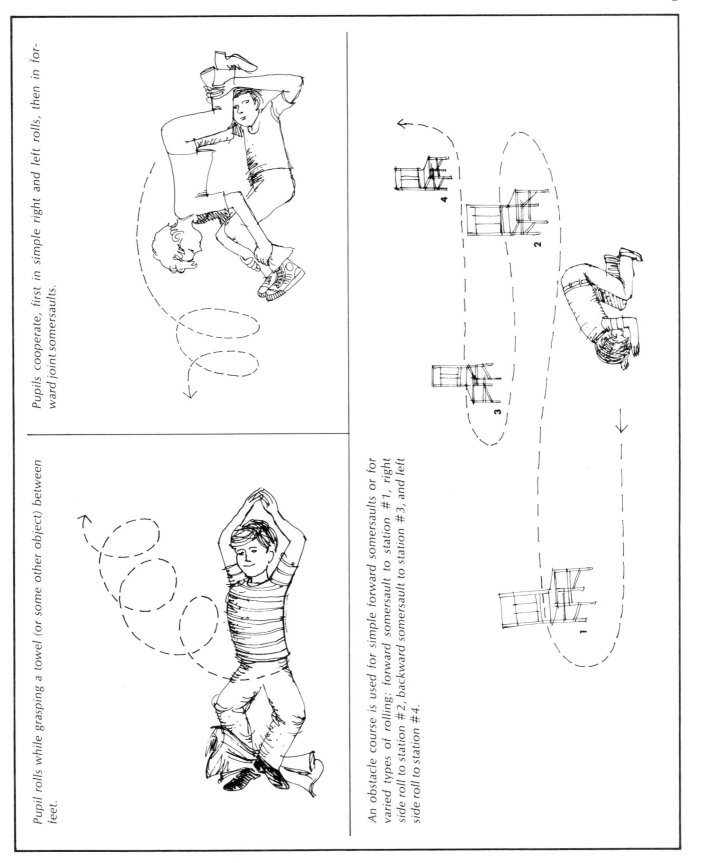

Pupils cooperate, first in simple right and left rolls, then in forward joint somersaults.

Pupil rolls while grasping a towel (or some other object) between feet.

An obstacle course is used for simple forward somersaults or for varied types of rolling: forward somersault to station #1, right side roll to station #2, backward somersault to station #3, and left side roll to station #4.

All programs should be modified or extended to meet the needs of individual pupils.

"Now you try it—fine! For the next few tries I am going to position your body and help you make the roll until you get the feel of it. Now do one at a time slowly until we get your hands and feet in the right place. That's the idea!"

Performance Evaluation: At the completion of the first 45-minute lesson, Paul was able to make two successful rolls. It was difficult for him to position himself after each roll.

Analysis and Comments: Although hesitant at first, Paul was well motivated through continued support and praise for his efforts. Because of his general poor coordination, he needs practice in running and approaching the mat and in correct body placement. The task was a good beginning lesson but needs much follow-up.

For Self-instruction: Devise a teaching procedure and performance evaluation method for this pupil: Tricia, ten years old, orthopedically handicapped. Tricia will be able to make two consecutive roll-overs to her right in the three-foot-deep side of the therapy pool. This will require that she submerge her face in the water as she rolls.

Gross Motor Development

2/Sitting

DEFINITION: *The ability to sit erect in normal position without support or constant reminding.*

ILLUSTRATION: *Pupil can demonstrate proper position sitting at desk with feet on floor, back straight, and head and arms in correct position for work at hand.*

EDUCATIONAL RATIONALE: *To work and learn effectively, children must be taught how to relax and to maintain proper sitting for reading, writing, and participation in varied activities. The relationship of poise and body control to fatigue and poor performance should be demonstrated and corrected where required.*

SUGGESTED PROGRAM IDEAS

1. Beginning Relaxation and Control
   a. "Today we are going to learn how to relax while sitting at our desks. Now sit up, place your head in your arms on your desk, and listen to this pretty music. As you sit there you can feel how good it is to rest—let your legs and arms relax, let your back and shoulders relax, let your head and neck relax. Close your eyes and relax your entire body." Extend and repeat relaxation suggestions.
   b. "Now we are going to sit in the correct posture for reading. Sit straight with your back against the chair, hold your head up, place both arms on the desk, and open the book to a story that you wish to read. Let's see if you can sit like this until you finish the story."
   c. "This time we are going to sit on the floor Indian-style with our legs crossed and arms folded. Let's sit like this as we relax and listen to music."
   d. "We are now going to sit on different things and count to ten to see if we can sit properly in various places." Sit on different-sized boxes, rocking chair, armchair, benches without backs.
   e. For physically handicapped, use supportive sitting equipment.

2. Middle Stage
   a. Demonstrate correct sitting and writing angle for both left- and right-handed children. Have children draw pictures and copy simple board work demonstrating proper position.
   b. Discuss proper sitting and poise at the dinner table. Practice around reading table or school lunch table. Demonstrate proper sitting behavior in front and back automobile seats. Discuss sitting manners in theaters and public gatherings.
   c. Discuss the importance of balance and poise; demonstrate by having pupil sit at desk and balance book (empty basket, etc.) on top of head as long as possible.
   d. Have pupil sit on revolving stool, with legs and arms extended, and balance as teacher slowly moves child in a circle.

3. Advanced Stage
   a. Have pupil sit on sawhorse and balance book on head. Use small stepladder for sitting on top and balancing book. Use balance beam between chairs, etc., to practice sitting balance.
   b. Have pupil sit and balance on seesaw, playground slide, bicycle, and different-sized fences. Use typewriter chair adjusted to pupil and give practice in correct posture with primary typewriter.

c. Extend program to include balance and control in sitting on the back and shoulders of another person. Use skateboard for sitting balance. Teach sitting balance on feet of another person who is lying on his back.

d. Have pupils rate and evaluate each other's posture during regular desk work periods.

REFERENCES

Hackett, Layne C., and Jensen, Robert G. *A Guide to Movement Exploration.* Palo Alto, Calif.: Peek Publications, 1967.

Related Programs

- *Adventures in Resting,* Vol. H2 (record), Educational Record Sales, 157 Chambers Street, New York, N.Y.
- *Music for Relaxation* (record), Educational Record Sales
- Young, Helen L. *A Manual-Workbook of Physical Education for Elementary Teachers.* New York: Macmillan, 1963.
- *How Do You Sit?* (posture teaching aids), National Dairy Council, 111 N. Canal Street, Chicago, Ill.

Instructional Materials

- Varied chairs and tables
- Stools
- Stepladder
- Floor mat
- Sawhorse
- Books and empty basket for balancing
- For physically handicapped: wheelchairs, sitting-riding toys, multipurpose mobile chair-table combination, kindergarten chair with straps, footboard and skis, bulldozer, giant rocker, floor sitter, push scooter, J. A. Preston Corp., 71 Fifth Avenue, New York, N. Y.

Further Evaluation

- Parent judgment and evaluation of home behavior
- Teacher judgment of general classroom poise
- Specific evaluation tasks as decided by the examiner
- Lincoln-Oseretsky Motor Development Scale (for related tasks)

PRESCRIPTIVE ILLUSTRATION

Priority Teaching Objective: Ralph, nine years old, educable mentally retarded. Ralph will be able to sit correctly, without being reminded, during the time he writes his name, address, birthday, days of the week, and months of the year.

Pretest Tasks: The teacher reminded Ralph to sit up straight while doing his assignments. The teacher then gave Ralph a check every time she saw him in the correct posture. The checking continued while Ralph wrote his name, address, birthday, days of the week, and the months of the year. Ralph took 25 minutes for this assignment and received three checks.

Specific Teaching Procedures: "Ralph, I want you to remember to have good posture. While you are writing your name, address, birthday, days of the week, and months of the year, Arthur will sit beside you and give you a plus check mark every time he sees you sitting in the correct way."

"Now, Ralph, watch me as I show you the correct way to sit at your work. Here is a picture of a boy sitting correctly, which I will leave on your desk to remind you of correct posture. OK, now tell me, Ralph, what we are going to do."

The pupil sits erect while balancing a book and a block on top of his head. The task should be timed for incentive purposes.

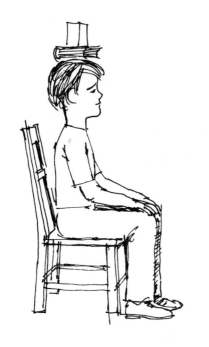

The pupil sits Indian-style on a box and balances a book.

The pupil is required to identify the sitting and writing position he should use.

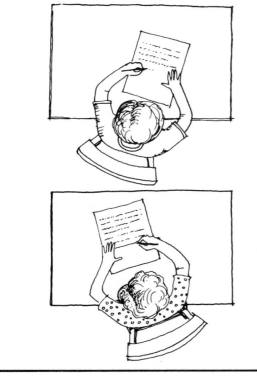

This advanced sitting-balancing exercise can be extended to include turning, spinning, and related skills.

All programs should be modified or extended to meet the needs of individual pupils.

Pupil: "I'm going to sit right and write. Why does Arthur get to use the red pencil?"

"Arthur will give you good check marks as you do your work. Make Arthur work hard giving you checks. OK, now let's see you sit in the correct way while you begin your work."

Performance Evaluation: "Good, Ralph, you earned seventeen checks in twenty minutes and your written work is very good."

Pupil: "I can't always remember to sit right."

Analysis and Comments: The task was very appropriate, and pupil attitude and motivation were good. Ralph enjoyed the attention and the check marks. Ralph's receiving checks motivated the entire class to sit correctly. He wants to try again and remember to "sit right." I believe Ralph will benefit from continuing this exercise. The same technique can be used through different assignments at different times of the day.

For Self-instruction: Devise a teaching procedure and performance evaluation method for this pupil: Susan, eleven years old, neurologically handicapped. Susan will be able to sit erect in the reading circle, holding her book and participating in the lesson with poise, for ten minutes.

Gross Motor Development

3/Crawling

DEFINITION: The ability to crawl on hands and knees in a smooth and coordinated way.

ILLUSTRATION: With eyes fixated on target, pupil first crawls in homolateral fashion. Pupil progresses to cross-pattern crawling program.

EDUCATIONAL RATIONALE: Crawling is a developmental skill, beginning with creeping and extending to complex target-oriented programs furthering neurophysiological integration. Children should be provided with ample opportunity to crawl and should be taught specific body coordination skills through varied crawling activities.

SUGGESTED PROGRAM IDEAS

1. Beginning Stages
    a. Demonstrate creeping by having pupil lie on floor, placing his hands under his chest. Then, by moving elbows and hips, have him creep forward with stomach touching floor. To music of *Creepy, Crawly Caterpillar*, have him creep forward and backward.
    b. Show how to crawl in homolateral pattern moving arm and leg on each side together. Have pupil crawl forward to a goal (chair, book, thumbtack marker, etc.), then crawl backward.
    c. Teach cross-diagonal crawling, moving opposite arm and leg together toward target goal. Crawl backward in same pattern.
    d. Place varied toys on floor and have pupil crawl and retrieve them.

2. Middle Stages
    a. Alternating homolateral and cross-pattern movements, have pupil crawl to music and imitate animals: "fast like a horse, slow like a turtle." Pair appropriately-sized children for horseback races (rider on back).
    b. Play "chug-chug train," crawling and chug-chugging back and forth over air mattress. Crawl under chairs, over benches, through cardboard boxes, tunnels, etc.
    c. Lay out yarn or ribbon race course for timed crawling race. Have children crawl up and down grass hills. Hide small ball or toy in grass and have children crawl about to find it.
    d. Have pupils take turns being tunnels with other children crawling under them without touching.

3. Advanced Stages
    a. Cut out red patterns for right hand and knee and yellow patterns for left hand and knee; distribute patterns on floor and have pupil follow layout. Lay out obstacle course pattern on chalkboard (from door to desk by window, etc.); have pupils follow through.
    b. Use twelve-inch-wide board suspended between chairs for crawling forward and backward. Extend to crawling on walking rail and trampoline.
    c. Extend activities to team games and relays: potato race—crawling and pushing potato with nose toward target; spoon relay—hold small jackball in tablespoon between teeth and crawl to target without dropping ball. Develop advanced relays through obstacle courses.
    d. Arrange classroom desks and tables in the shape of a square and have the class crawl in and out, following a leader.

REFERENCES

Delacato, Carl. *Neurological Organization in the Classroom*. Chicago: Systems for Education, 1965.

Related Programs
- Hackett, Layne C., and Jensen, Robert G. *A Guide to Movement Exploration*. Palo Alto, Calif.: Peek Publications, 1967.
- Teacher-developed crawling programs
- *Primary Physical Fitness Activities,* Album 14 (record), Educational Record Sales, 157 Chambers Street, New York, N.Y.
- *Animal Rhythms* (record), Educational Record Sales
- *Creepy Crawly Caterpillar* (record), Educational Record Sales

Instructional Materials
- Tunnel of Fun (for crawling through), Constructive Playthings, 1040 E. 85th Street, Kansas City, Mo.
- Fun Drum Set (for crawling), Lakeshore Equipment Co., 1144 Montague Avenue, San Leandro, Calif.
- Scott, Louise B., and Thompson, J. J. "Choo-Choo Train Poem." *Talking Time.* Manchester, Mo.: Webster Publishing, 1966.
- Cardboard boxes, overturned chairs
- Cardboard or rubber cutout right and left hand and circles
- Colored yarn for laying out crawling trails
- Utility balls
- Board—ten feet long and twelve inches wide
- Crawligator, Creative Playthings, Princeton, N.J.
- Crawler, J. A. Preston Corp., 71 Fifth Avenue, New York, N.Y.
- Crawling Coordination Training Unit, Preston
- Crawling Tunnel, Preston
- Geometric Shapes Creating Block, Preston

Further Evaluation
- Subjectively arranged crawling tasks
- Lincoln-Oseretsky Motor Development Scale (for related tasks)

PRESCRIPTIVE ILLUSTRATION

Priority Teaching Objective: Mark, seven years old, educable mentally retarded. Upon completion of this lesson, Mark will be able to crawl a determined course through a hole in a box and following three or four curves laid out for the course.

Pretest Tasks: Mark was asked to crawl with the teacher across the floor toward a book, a ball, and a pencil while background music was played to provide rhythm. He was able to crawl in cross-pattern movement but not in homolateral fashion. Mark did not crawl straight toward the targets and tended to drag his right hand.

Specific Teaching Procedures: "Mark, in this lesson, I want you to crawl, carefully following the red tape around each curve to the box and then go through it."

"Watch me now. See how I crawl following the red tape line around this curve, and then this curve, and then I go through the box."

"Now, Mark, tell and show me what you are to do."

Pupil: "I am to crawl on the red line like this to the box and then go through the hole."

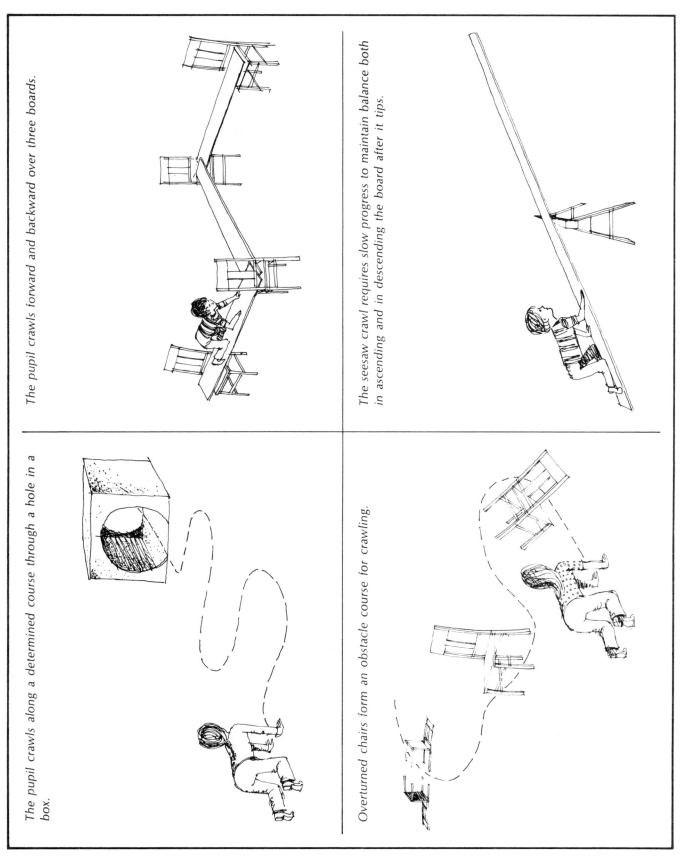

The pupil crawls forward and backward over three boards.

The seesaw crawl requires slow progress to maintain balance both in ascending and in descending the board after it tips.

The pupil crawls along a determined course through a hole in a box.

Overturned chairs form an obstacle course for crawling.

All programs should be modified or extended to meet the needs of individual pupils.

"That's right. Now for each curve that you correctly follow the red tape around, you will receive a candy. You will also receive one candy for going through the box. OK, now start here. Let's see if you can carefully follow the red tape line."

Performance Evaluation: "That's good! You earned four candies, Mark, and you only made one mistake. Do you remember what it was?"

Pupil: "I didn't follow the red line all the way. At the end I went straight through the box."

Analysis and Comments: The lesson was partially appropriate with Mark correctly crawling three of the four curves. His motivation was good as he carefully followed the curving line to the end. There he seemed to be more motivated to get through the hole in the box. He was able to correct his mistake and on posttests he was successful. Mark should continue crawling exercises on more difficult obstacle courses to develop cross-pattern crawling and smooth coordination. He should also help plan and lay out his own obstacle course so he can anticipate what he will be doing.

For Self-instruction: Devise a teaching procedure and performance evaluation method for this pupil: Shirley, eleven years old, educable mentally retarded. Upon completion of the lesson, Shirley will be able to crawl on hands and knees on a course under and around three tables. She will crawl with coordination and rhythm and without touching the tables.

Gross Motor Development

4/Walking

DEFINITION: The ability to walk erect in a coordinated fashion without support.
ILLUSTRATION: With head up and shoulders back, pupil walks specified path and walking line. Can walk backward and sideways without difficulty.
EDUCATIONAL RATIONALE: Walking is a neuromuscular act requiring balance and coordination. Children should be presented with opportunities to develop increasing skill in more difficult tasks.

SUGGESTED PROGRAM IDEAS

1. Beginning Activities
   Have pupil do the following:
   a. Barefoot walk: Walk barefoot through mud, water, sand, dirt, and over rocks, cement, floors, etc., and describe feelings involved.
   b. Forward walk: Walk straight or curved path to target-goal and back; teacher records time. Walk forward up and down steps.
   c. Walking sideways: First walk to right one step at a time. Next, cross left over right foot. Repeat, moving to the left.
   d. Variations: Walk and march to music and/or drum beat. Walk on tiptoe forward, backward, etc. Walk with arms out at sides, straight over head, etc. Walk over trampoline or air mattress.
   e. Line walk: Heel-to-toe walk on chalkline or tape.
   f. Command walk: Walk fast, walk with big steps, walk slow, etc.

2. Middle Stage Animal Walks
   Have pupil do the following:
   a. Rooster: Holding the head and chest high, strut forward with knees straight and hands at the side of the chest. Wiggle elbows as if flapping wings.
   b. Bear: Bend over from the waist and touch the floor with the hands, keeping the legs stiff. Move forward, walking the hands and plodding the feet, while keeping the head up.
   c. Elephant: Bend forward at the waist, allowing the arms to hang limp. Take big lumbering steps, swaying side to side, imitating an elephant and his trunk.
   d. Ostrich: Bending forward at the waist, grasp the ankles; keep the knees stiff while walking forward, stretching neck in and out.
   e. Duck: Do a deep knee bend. Place hands behind back with the outsides together and fingers extended as the tail of a duck; walk forward one foot at a time, but remain in the bent-knee position.
   f. Design walk: Walk a figure eight, a circle, a triangle, a square, a spiral, etc.

3. Advanced Stages
   a. Arm walk: Pupil lies flat on the floor and pushes up entire body with the arms, keeping the knees straight; walks forward with the arms while the feet drag behind.
   b. Chair-board walk: Arrange chairs, boxes, stools in varied patterns for walking and balancing. Walk up and down seesaw board.
   c. Walking beam: Use long two-by-four placed flat on the floor for forward, backward, and sideways walking in stocking feet and shoes. Raise walking beam between blocks for advanced skills, moving to walking on the two-inch side. Walking beam exercises: Heel-to-toe walk with eyes on target. Walk backward, heel-to-toe, with

arms crossed on chest. Ribbon walk across beam with arms outstretched, moving flowing ribbons up and down. Walk on tiptoes across beam. Walk across board bouncing rubber ball by side. Walk across board throwing beanbag from left to right hand. Walk across board balancing beanbag on head.

d. Walk about room with arms outstretched balancing erasers or beanbags on backs of hands.

e. Blindfold walks: Use all previous exercises—including walking beam—while blindfolded. Do blindfolded walking, using stilts.

REFERENCES

Getman, G. N.; Kane, E. R.; Halgren, M. R.; and McKee, G. W. *The Physiology of Readiness Programs*. Chicago: Lyons & Carnahan, 1966.

Related Programs

* Farina, Albert M.; Furth, Sol; and Smith, Joseph. *Growth Through Play*. Englewood Cliffs, N.J.: Prentice-Hall, 1959.
* Hackett, Layne C., and Jensen, Robert, G. *A Guide to Movement Exploration*. Palo Alto, Calif.; Peek Publications, 1967.
* *Marches* (record), Educational Record Sales, 157 Chambers Street, New York, N.Y.
* *The Rhythms Hour* (record), Educational Record Sales
* *World of Marches* (record), Educational Record Sales
* Walking-posture teaching aids, National Dairy Council, 111 N. Canal Street, Chicago, Ill.

Instructional Materials

* Wood Hi-Sticks (stilts), Creative Playthings, Princeton, N.J.
* Climbing equipment, Constructive Playthings, 1040 E. 85th Street, Kansas City, Mo.
* Balance Blocks and Boards, Constructive Playthings
* Stepping Stones—Numerals, Lakeshore Equipment Co., 1144 Montague Avenue, San Leandro, Calif.
* Record player
* Drum and beater
* Inclined Tapered Balance Beam, J. A. Preston Corp., 71 Fifth Avenue, New York, N.Y.
* Foot Placement Ladder, Preston

Further Evaluation

* Lincoln-Oseretsky Motor Development Scale: Test #1, walking backwards six feet; #21, winding thread while walking
* Subjectively developed walking tasks

PRESCRIPTIVE ILLUSTRATION

Priority Teaching Objective: Barbara, seven years old, developmentally immature. Upon completing this lesson Barbara will be able to walk forward and backward on the balance beam to five designated colored lines painted on the beam.

Pretest Tasks: On the four-inch side of a ten-foot balance beam, six inches off the floor, Barbara was able to follow only one direction—to walk forward to the green line—before she lost her balance and fell off the beam. Approximately 45 seconds elapsed before she lost her balance.

Specific Teaching Procedures: "Barbara, I want you to start walking from the end of this balance beam and walk forward to the green line painted there. Then you walk backward to the red line. After that you listen carefully and follow my directions by walking to the next line without falling off. Now tell me what you are to do."

Pupil: "I'm to start here and walk forward to the green line, then backwards to the red line, and then follow your directions."

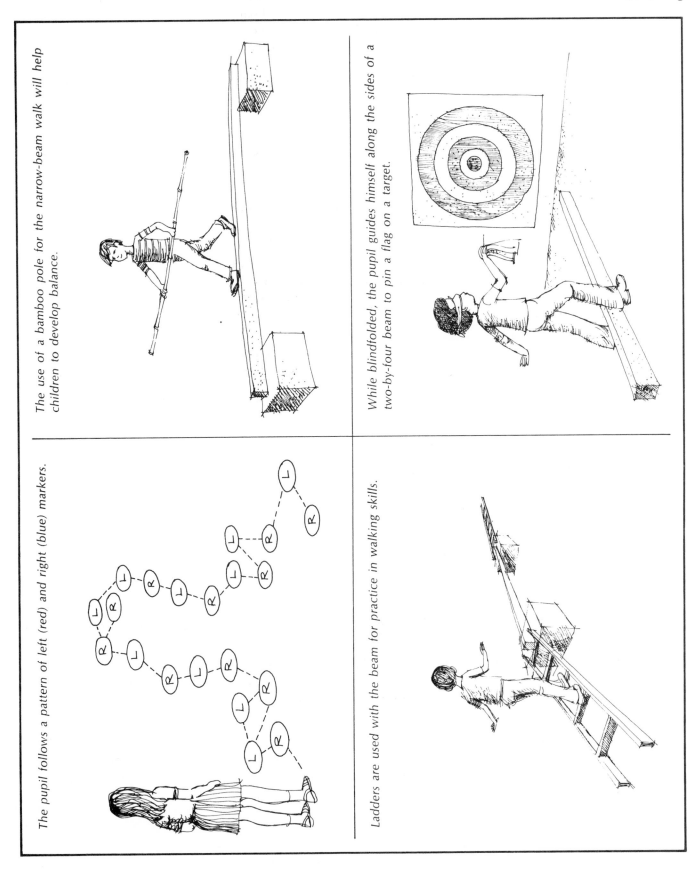

The use of a bamboo pole for the narrow-beam walk will help children to develop balance.

While blindfolded, the pupil guides himself along the sides of a two-by-four beam to pin a flag on a target.

The pupil follows a pattern of left (red) and right (blue) markers.

Ladders are used with the beam for practice in walking skills.

All programs should be modified or extended to meet the needs of individual pupils.

"Good, now go ahead. That's fine. Now walk forward again to the green line."
"Now backward halfway to the end of the black line."
"Now forward to the yellow line."
"Now go backward halfway between the green and the black line."
"Now walk forward to the orange line."

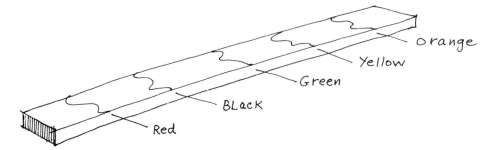

Performance Evaluation: "You did very well, Barbara, as you were able to follow five of my seven directions. Do you know which ones you missed?"

Pupil: "Yes, I fell off once and did not go just halfway between the green and black line."

Analysis and Comments: The lesson was only partially appropriate as it was too difficult for Barbara to follow as a beginning exercise. It should be revised with fewer directions. It would also be helpful for Barbara to repeat each direction as she walks on the beam.

For Self-instruction: Devise a teaching procedure and performance evaluation method for this pupil: Paul, nine years old, minimal cerebral dysfunction with clumsiness and shuffling gait. Paul will be able to remove his shoes and stockings, walk slowly on tiptoe until he must drop back on the whole foot, and gradually increase the pace to a running motion.

Gross Motor Development

5/Running

DEFINITION: The ability to run a track or obstacle course without a change of pace.

ILLUSTRATION: Pupil runs a straight track of easy distance without difficulty. Can change direction through a simple obstacle course without stopping or significantly changing pace.

EDUCATIONAL RATIONALE: The ability to run requires muscular strength, coordination, and endurance, and contributes to total psychomotor learning. Running skills and related activities should be taught as an integral part of the physical education program.

SUGGESTED PROGRAM IDEAS

1. Beginning Activities

   Have pupil do the following:

   a. Running in place: Assume relaxed stance. Begin slow run in place. Gradually increase pace to hard run, bringing knees high. Return to original slow pace.

   b. Timed run in place: Run in place while counting to 100. Run in place for one minute, two minutes, three minutes. Run to music.

   c. Aisle run: Run up and down aisles without falling, while being timed.

   d. Self race: Run around school, field, track, etc., keeping record of time and distance.

   e. Maze run: Teacher lays out maze or obstacle course in classroom or on field for timed running.

2. Middle Stage Activities

   a. Three-legged race: Tie left leg of one pupil to right leg of another. Have them run over a course and record time required. Have three-legged races, using different pairs each time.

   b. Bird run: Pupil stands on tiptoes and waves arms up and down. Have relay contest, running on tiptoe, flapping wings.

   c. Crab run: In a squatting position, pupil reaches backward with the arms and puts both hands flat on the floor behind him, then raises up until the head, neck and body are in a straight line. The head should be parallel with the floor. Pupil runs in this inverted position.

   d. Dog run: Pupil gallops by running forward with both hands on the floor and the knees slightly bent.

   e. Horse gallop: Runs like a galloping horse; while running, alternately slaps chest with left hand, right thigh with right hand to make a galloping noise.

3. Advanced Activities

   a. Sprinting: Teach sprint positions and organize class races covering 25, 50, or 75 yards.

   b. Field run: Lay out modified cross-country run (around school, across field, along fence, back around school to starting point, etc.).

   c. Piggy-back race: Children race one another while carrying rider on back.

   d. Football run: Mark out running area for sprinting and catching football while in stride.

   e. Endurance run: Begin with quarter-mile and gradually extend to half-mile, three-quarter, and mile run. Race pupil against his own time.

17

    f. Follow-the-leader run: Vary the pace and stance.

    g. Bounce run: Run while bouncing a ball.

    h. Relays: Teams run with footballs to goal and back.

    i. Tire run: Timed run through tires placed edge to edge.

REFERENCES

Clarke, H. Harrison, and Clarke, David H. *Developmental and Adapted Physical Education*. Englewood Cliffs, N.J.: Prentice-Hall, 1963.

Related Programs

- *Fundamental Steps and Rhythms* (record), Educational Record Sales, 157 Chambers Street, New York, N.Y.
- Track and field activities
- Adaptive physical education programs
- "Capture the Flag" and related field games

Instructional Materials

- Relay batons or flags
- Stopwatch
- Hula hoops
- Old automobile tires
- Tag games
- Materials for relay contests
- Jump Standard, J. A. Preston Corp., 71 Fifth Avenue, New York, N.Y.

Further Evaluation

- Toronto Physical Fitness Rating Scales: 300-yard run. Hayden, Frank J. *Physical Fitness for the Mentally Retarded*, Metropolitan Toronto Association for Retarded Children, 186 Beverly Street, Toronto 2B, Ontario, Canada
- Specific tasks developed for each pupil with limited or poor running ability

PRESCRIPTIVE ILLUSTRATION

Priority Teaching Objective: Harry, fifteen years old, educable mentally retarded. Harry is in training for track events at the special Olympics for the retarded. Upon completion of this lesson he will be able to run through a rubber tire obstacle course, without falling, under one minute as timed (see course below):

Pretest Tasks: Although one of the better runners in his class, Harry had difficulty coordinating his arm and leg movements. When he first tried the tire obstacle course he was able to run only to the third tire before he misjudged, stepped on the side and fell down.

Specific Teaching Procedures: "Harry, we are going to begin work on your running. We will practice running through this tire obstacle course. When you have mastered it, you

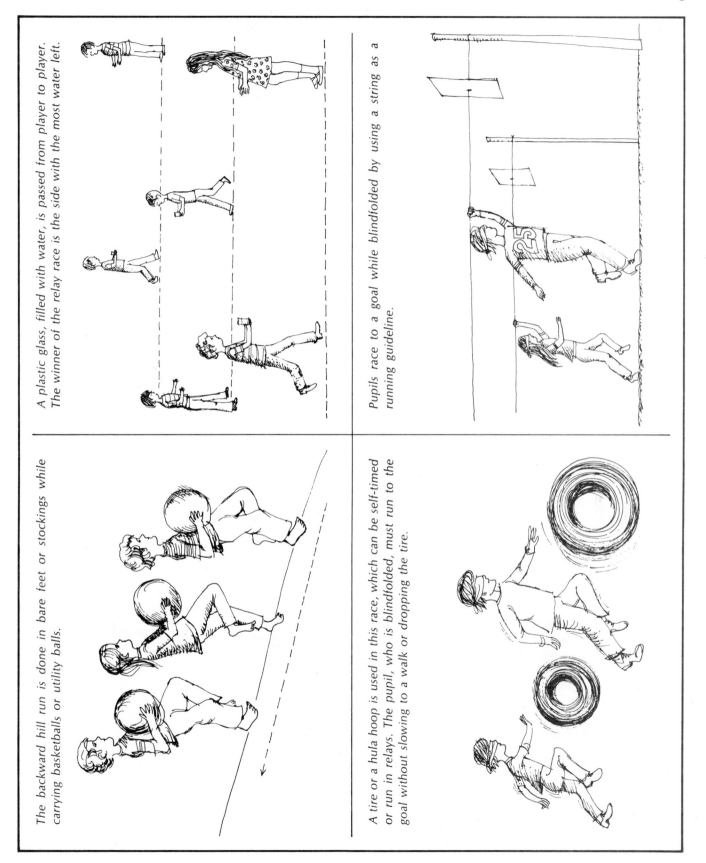

A plastic glass, filled with water, is passed from player to player. The winner of the relay race is the side with the most water left.

Pupils race to a goal while blindfolded by using a string as a running guideline.

The backward hill run is done in bare feet or stockings while carrying basketballs or utility balls.

A tire or a hula hoop is used in this race, which can be self-timed or run in relays. The pupil, who is blindfolded, must run to the goal without slowing to a walk or dropping the tire.

All programs should be modified or extended to meet the needs of individual pupils.

should be able to run through it in less than one minute without stepping on a tire or falling down."

"To begin with, we will run in and out of one tire like this [teacher demonstrates]. Now you do it. See, we step in with one foot then out with the other. You try it."

"That's right. Now we will use two tires spread apart like this."

"This time we have lined up three tires, each a bit off center. See, your right foot goes in this one, then immediately your left foot goes over here, and then back to your right foot. Now practice that several times."

"Now you can see that some of the tires are off center, some in a straight line, and some at an angle. There are eleven tires all together. Run slowly and take your time going through them. We will speed up later."

Performance Evaluation: "That was pretty good for the first lesson, Harry. You did it in just less than one minute, but you made some mistakes. Do you know what they were?"

Pupil: "Yes, I stepped on three tires and fell down once, but I'll do better tomorrow!"

Analysis and Comments: Harry was highly motivated, and the task was an appropriate but somewhat demanding one. It was a new experience for him. He needs most practice in running through a straight-line course where he tends to get off balance.

For Self-instruction: Devise a teaching procedure and performance evaluation method for this pupil: Rosa, twelve years old, a slow-learning, awkward girl. Rosa is not often accepted in running games because she is so slow and awkward. Upon completion of this lesson Rosa will be able to run between baskets on the basketball court while dribbling the ball and without stopping to rest.

Gross Motor Development

6/Throwing

DEFINITION: The ability to throw a ball with a reasonable degree of accuracy.

ILLUSTRATION: Pupil throws a ball to another person so that it may be caught. Can throw ball accurately into box or basket.

EDUCATIONAL RATIONALE: Children should be taught to throw various types of balls with a fair degree of accuracy. Boys should be provided specific remedial instructions if their throwing skills are notably impaired.

SUGGESTED PROGRAM IDEAS

1. Beginning Skills
   a. Texture ball throw: Using an infant sponge or texture ball, child begins with underhand toss to friend standing close by. Gradually extend distance as accuracy improves. Move to overhand throw.
   b. Texture ball basketball: Use shoe box with bottom removed. Tape to wall for indoor basketball.
   c. Texture ball tag: Play dodge ball, dividing class into two teams. Last child standing wins, as does child able to hit the most players.
   d. Ring toss games: Play indoor quoits, horseshoes, etc., requiring different throwing skills.
   e. Beanbag toss: Practice throwing, using large holes as target. Use beanbags for pitching games to see who can come closest to a line or floor marker. Run, toss bags in air and catch.
   f. Paper throw: Pupil crumbles paper into paper balls and "shoots" them into wastepaper basket placed in corner.
   g. Checkerboard toss: Throw buttons or washers so they land in squares.

2. Middle Stage Skills
   a. Softball throw: Begin with underhand toss, then overhand throw. Try distance throws.
   b. Tennis ball throw: This is more difficult as the ball tends to bounce and must therefore be "cupped" in the hands.
   c. Milk carton toss: Use plastic milk bottle or cartons stacked in pyramid. Knock down with softball and tennis ball.
   d. Rock throws: Select golf-ball-sized rocks. Hold contests in hitting telephone poles, knocking down tin cans on a bench, and distance throws.
   e. Bucket throw: Place either a bucket or wastebasket at appropriate distance for throwing utility ball, softball, and hardball. Place bucket on floor and then on raised boxes and chairs.
   f. Empty box throw: Remove bottom from cardboard box and place it on side on chair, ladder, or ledge. Pupil throws softball through box without hitting box or disturbing its placement.
   g. Target bounce: Throw a basketball to a person so it bounces only once in the middle. Run and bounce ball back and forth.

3. Advanced Skills
   Have pupils do the following:
   a. Hardball throw: Throw to one another at close range to guarantee accuracy; gradu-

ally extend distance as speed and confidence develop. Practice distance throws. Use baseball gloves.

b. Tennis ball toss-back: Throw tennis ball high against brick or cement wall and catch it before it bounces.

c. Pitch back: Use pitch-back net for close-in throwing and catching of hardball.

d. Javelin throw: Use bamboo poles or small javelins for different muscle exercise.

e. Football throw: Practice straight throws, running throws, throwing into boxes.

f. One-legged throws: Stand on one leg and throw various balls at target.

g. Thow-and-catch puff ball game. Use the top half of a gallon bleach container to catch ball.

h. Two pupils run toward target while throwing and catching a beanbag between them.

i. Dart boards: Play dart board games from varied distances.

REFERENCES

Schwartz, Alvin. *A Parent's Guide to Children's Play and Recreation*. New York: Collier Books, 1963.

Related Programs

- Judy Clown Beanbag Set, The Judy Company, Minneapolis, Minn.
- Quoit set
- Rubber horseshoe set, Constructive Playthings, 1040 E. 85th Street, Kansas City, Mo.
- Baseball and softball games
- Basketball and water polo
- *Rope Jumping and Ball Handling* (record), Bowman Records, 622 Rodier Drive, Glendale, Calif.

Instructional Materials

- Ring toss sets
- Pitch-back sets from Sears, Roebuck or sports stores
- Plastic milk bottles or milk cartons
- Tin cans
- Softball, hardball, tennis ball, basketball, utility ball
- Baskets and boxes
- Texture ball, Creative Playthings, Princeton, N.J.
- Javelin for throwing
- Sponges
- Old tires and hula hoops
- Takraw (rattan catching game) from Macy's

Further Evaluation

- Lincoln-Oseretsky Motor Development Scale: Test #22, throwing a ball
- Throwing tasks developed for the individual child
- Parent evaluation of child's throwing skills

PRESCRIPTIVE ILLUSTRATION

Priority Teaching Objective: Darrin, six years old, orthopedically handicapped, with poor coordination. Upon completion of this lesson Darrin will be able to throw a rubber ball to the teacher eight out of ten underhand and overhand shots, fairly accurately and with acceptable posture.

Pretest Tasks: Darrin was given a ball and asked to throw it to me from where he was standing five times underhand as demonstrated, and then five times overhand, so that I could catch it where I was standing, the distance varying from six feet to fifteen feet. Of the five underhand throws, I could catch only two as they tended to be overthrown. Of

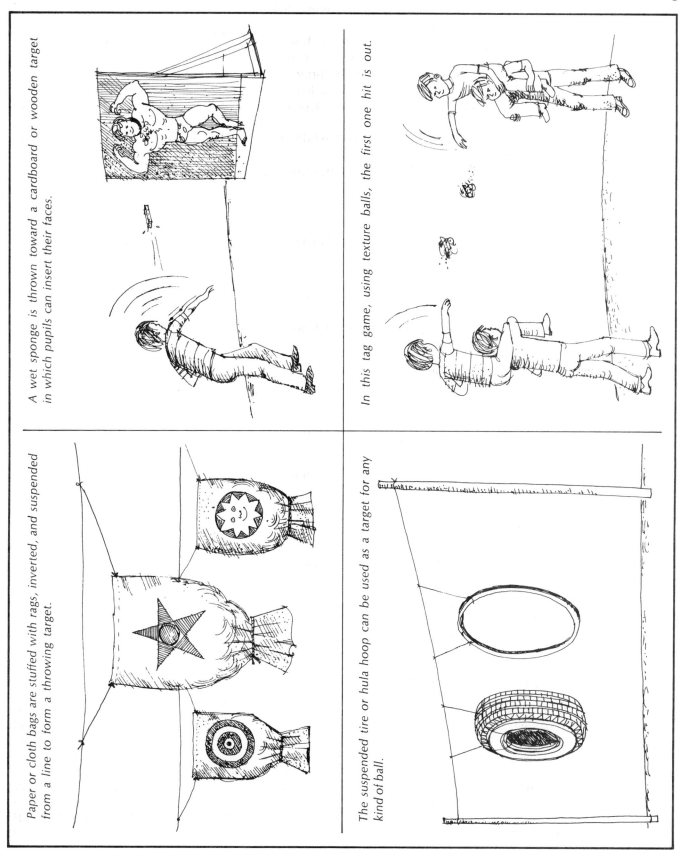

A wet sponge is thrown toward a cardboard or wooden target in which pupils can insert their faces.

In this tag game, using texture balls, the first one hit is out.

Paper or cloth bags are stuffed with rags, inverted, and suspended from a line to form a throwing target.

The suspended tire or hula hoop can be used as a target for any kind of ball.

All programs should be modified or extended to meet the needs of individual pupils.

the five overhand throws, I could catch only three because they tended to be under-thrown and to one side.

Specific Teaching Procedures: "Darrin, in this exercise, I would like you to stand behind the string and throw the ball to me ten times underhand so that I can catch it; then ten times overhand. You can count to keep track, OK?"

"I will show you how first, so watch me. See, I am standing behind the string, and I am throwing the ball to you underhand, without going over the line. Now I am throwing the ball to you overhand, raising my arm way up to throw, but not moving my body very much, just my arm. You try it now and tell me what you are to do."

Pupil: "I stand behind the line and raise my arm like this with my feet apart and throw the ball to you. I'll try to get my arm up high."

"That's right, Darrin, get your arm high and spread your feet like this. Let me help you. Now take your time and throw the ball right to me as many times as you can. We'll have a break and little treat later on, OK?"

Performance Evaluation: "Very good, Darrin, you threw eight good underhands to me and six good overhands. You missed only a few. Do you know why you missed those?"

Pupil: "Yes, I threw the ball too far or too short, and I stepped over the line once. I think I can do better if I try again."

Analysis and Comments: The task was partially appropriate with fourteen correct responses out of twenty tries. Darrin enjoyed playing with the ball and tried very hard to do what was demonstrated and asked of him. He is a lively child and likes praise. He was willing to try and improved on repeated exercises even though he began to tire quickly. Although a broken collarbone has healed, his strength and ability are still limited. He did well on the posture and time limitations put to him, and I feel he will improve quickly. He needs extended practice in varied throwing positions and activities.

For Self-instruction: Devise a teaching procedure and performance evaluation method for this pupil: Mari, eight years old, an awkward, regular second-grade child. Mari will be able to throw crumpled three-inch newspaper balls in an underhand position and hit a clown-face target ten feet away.

Gross Motor Development

7/Jumping

DEFINITION: The ability to jump simple obstacles without falling.

ILLUSTRATION: Pupil can jump from chair to floor without difficulty; can jump from jumping board without falling; can jump over knee-high obstacles.

EDUCATIONAL RATIONALE: Children should be taught to coordinate themselves as required in simple jumping tasks. Physical education programs should include personalized instruction in jumping skills and activities.

SUGGESTED PROGRAM IDEAS

1. Beginning Activities
   a. Jumping together: Face child and hold hands. Jump together while counting to ten.
   b. Jumping line: Pupil jumps backward and forward over line (crack, tape, etc.) for a given number of times.
   c. One-foot jump: Pupil jumps back and forth over line four times on right foot, then left foot, and repeats.
   d. Chair jump: Children hold chair while pupil jumps from seat of chair to a line drawn or indicated on the floor.
   e. Standing jump: Jump forward for distance from standing position.
   f. Hopscotch: Lay out course, teach rules, and test pupil on proficiency; keep record.
   g. Rhythm jump: Jump to varied musical records and poems.

2. Middle Stage Activities
   Have pupil do the following:
   a. Snake jump: Crouch in squat position with hands on floor. Jump up toward person with hands outstretched like body of a snake.
   b. Kangaroo jump: Stand with feet together. Bend the elbows out from the body. Let the hands dangle limply. Do a deep knee bend and jump forward. Repeat three times. Repeat with rubber utility ball held between knees.
   c. Rabbit jump: Squat low on heels. Place the hands palms down, fingers pointing behind him. In this position, move the hands forward and bring the feet forward between the hands with a little jump. Repeat, imitating a rabbit.
   d. Mattress jump: Use an air mattress three-quarters filled. Jump forward and backward without falling.
   e. Jack-be-nimble: Place unlighted candle in holder on floor. Jump over forward and backward without knocking down candle. Chant "Jack-be-nimble" nursery rhyme.
   f. Simple rope jump: Jump forward and backward to count of ten, lifting both feet at once.
   g. Box jump: Arrange several cardboard boxes in a row and adjacent to one another. Pupil jumps from box to box with feet together without overturning boxes.
   h. Potato sack race: Teams jump in sacks toward goal.

3. Advanced Activities
   a. Tire jump: Jump in and out of tires. Jump from tire to tire. Frog jump to tires.
   b. Rope jump: Pupil alternates one foot forward and one foot backward, holding own rope; runs in and jumps while others turn rope; jumps for time and speed records.
   c. Jumping board: Pupil stands on board and jumps for distance; runs, springs, and jumps.

d. Jumping shoes: These are commercially available with heavy-duty springs for hardy use.
e. Running broad jump: Mark take-off line and measure distance. Keep individual records for improving performance.
f. High jump: Use regular high jump poles and bars.
g. Hurdles: Begin with low hurdles. Introduce high hurdles and races.
h. Circular rope jump: Jump over folded rope swung under feet in circular motion by another pupil.
i. Bamboo pole jump: Jump between poles held by two people and rhythmically clapped together.

REFERENCES

Daniels, Arthur S., and Davies, Evelyn A. *Adaptive Physical Education*. New York: Harper and Row, 1965.

Mosston, Muska. *Developmental Movement*. New York: Merrill, 1965.

Related Programs
- Track and field events
- Trampoline training programs
- Adapted calisthenics and physical education programs
- *Rope Jumping and Ball Handling* (record), Bowmar Records, 622 Rodier Drive, Glendale, Calif.

Instructional Materials
- Hopscotch, Constructive Playthings, 1040 E. 85th Street, Kansas City, Mo.
- Spring-O-Lene Wood Jumping Trampoline, Creative Playthings, Princeton, N.J.
- Jumping Board (for use between sawhorses or large blocks), California Correctional Industries, 1400 S Street, Sacramento, Calif.
- Jump rope
- High jump poles and posts
- Bamboo poles
- Boxes and assorted chairs
- Stopwatch
- Trampa (floor trampoline), Trampa Manufacturing Co., 1710 Bell Avenue, Houston, Texas
- Pre-School Trampoline, J. A. Preston Corp., 71 Fifth Avenue, New York, N.Y.

Further Evaluation
- Lincoln-Oseretsky Motor Development Scale: Tests #19, jump and turn about; #30, jump and touch heels; #33, jumping and clapping
- Adapted jumping tasks and tests suited for the individual pupil
- Hopscotch performance record

PRESCRIPTIVE ILLUSTRATION

Priority Teaching Objective: Kathy, nine years old, trainable mentally retarded. Upon completion of this lesson Kathy will be able to jump a rope, using both feet together, on a jumping board one foot from the ground, for at least ten seconds.

Pretest Tasks: Kathy was asked to jump rope using both feet for ten seconds. She was then asked to bounce on a jumping board for ten seconds. Kathy accomplished the task with obvious difficulty in balance and coordination.

Specific Teaching Procedures: "Kathy, today I am going to give you a lesson with the jump rope. Here is a rope. Now watch me. I want you to jump on both feet like this."
"Ok—do you understand?"
Pupil: "Yeah."
"OK—go! That's a good start."

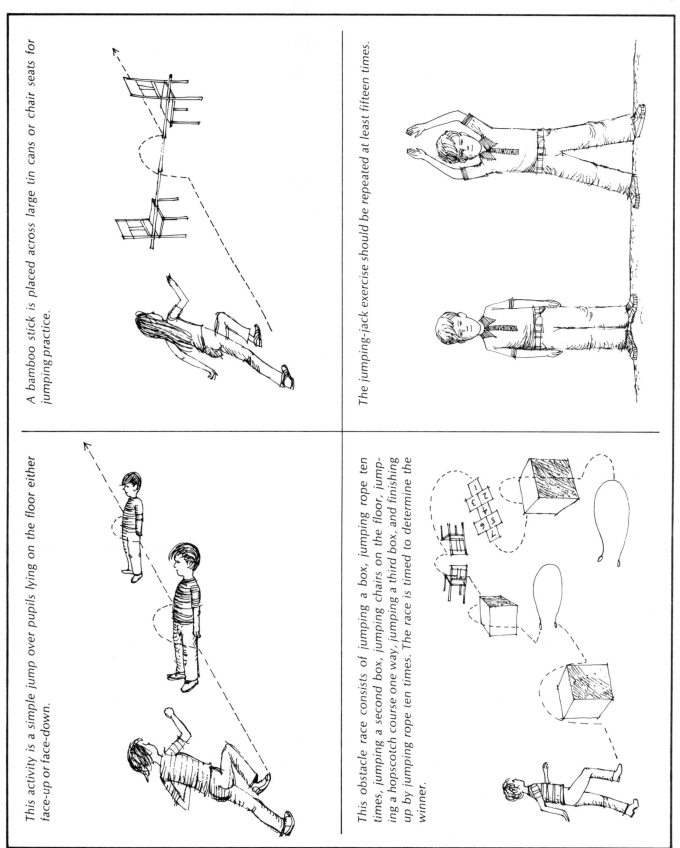

A bamboo stick is placed across large tin cans or chair seats for jumping practice.

The jumping-jack exercise should be repeated at least fifteen times.

This activity is a simple jump over pupils lying on the floor either face-up or face-down.

This obstacle race consists of jumping a box, jumping rope ten times, jumping a second box, jumping chairs on the floor, jumping a hopscotch course one way, jumping a third box, and finishing up by jumping rope ten times. The race is timed to determine the winner.

All programs should be modified or extended to meet the needs of individual pupils.

"Now I want you to jump on both feet on the bounce board while I count to twenty like this. I will hold your hands for the first time as you learn to balance."

"OK, Kathy, now when I say go, you jump on the board by yourself while I count to ten. Go!"

"Very good, Kathy. Now we will do something different. This time stand on the board and take the rope, and when I say go, jump the rope on both feet while I count to ten."

Performance Evaluation: "That was good, Kathy. You were able to jump to the count of eight before you lost your balance. Did you like that?"

Pupil: "Yeah—do it again!"

Analysis and Comments: This was an appropriate combined jumping task for Kathy. She met the challenge without hesitation, was very enthusiastic, and began to gain body control and some coordination. These exercises will be continued, with Kathy doing the counting.

For Self-instruction: Devise a teaching procedure and performance evaluation method for this pupil: George, six years old, developmental kindergarten. George will be able to make three successful jumps over a rope held by two people and swung back and forth ten inches off the floor.

Gross Motor Development

8/Skipping

> *DEFINITION:* The ability to skip in normal play.
>
> *ILLUSTRATION:* Pupil can skip, alternating feet, around circle of players. Can skip rope forward both by hopping and by alternate-foot skipping.
>
> *EDUCATIONAL RATIONALE:* For many children, skipping is a difficult task of coordination and timing that requires strength and endurance. Children should be taught to skip by direct imitation and guidance and through involvement in games and activities.

SUGGESTED PROGRAM IDEAS

1. Beginning Activities
    a. First skip: For young children with limited ability, start by having them stand erect and jump forward on the right foot and then bring the left foot up to the right. Child imitates in skipping around the room.
    b. Alternate skip: Child imitates teacher in consecutively alternating right and left foot in skipping around the room. For children having difficulty, the teacher should hold the child's hand, skipping together with him until the movement has been learned.
    c. Goal skip: Have child skip to table and skip back with a book or other designated object.
    d. Circle skip: Skip in small circle, large circle, figure eight.
    e. Line skip: Skip on line or crack in sidewalk, chalk line, or ribbon line laid out on grass. Repeat activity and record time required for each pupil.
    f. Hill skip: Child skips barefoot up and down grass or dirt hill, cement area, etc.

2. Middle Stage Games
    Have pupil do the following:
    a. Circle games: "Ring Around the Rosie," "The Farmer in the Dell," "London Bridge."
    b. Frog: Do a deep knee bend with hands on hips. Kick one leg to the side and return. Kick the other leg to the side and return. Skip forward, kicking one leg out at a time.
    c. Crane: Stand erect with one leg off the floor and arms out straight at sides. Slowly skip about room keeping arms out.
    d. Giraffe: Stand erect with hands held together straight up over the head to represent giraffe's neck and head. Skip slowly forward swaying arms slightly during movement.
    e. Piggy-back skip: Skip while holding a smaller child on back.
    f. Rope skip games: Skip rope forward and backward to chants and music.
    g. Follow-the-leader skip: Select pupils with different skipping styles as leaders.

3. Advanced Activities
    a. Backward skip: Children skip backward on predetermined course.
    b. Skip-and-carry race: Children skip race while carrying a book in each hand.
    c. Mule team: Using ribbon or rope, children pair off in teams of eight and skip race to goal and back while holding rope and staying in place.
    d. Bounce skip: Bouncing utility ball or basketball, children skip to goal and return.
    e. Blindfolded skip: A blindfolded pupil is led by ribbon or rope as he skips along predetermined path.
    f. Skip ball tag: Using texture ball, children play skip tag. Child is out when hit by texture ball.
    g. Free improvised skipping to record, "Skip to my Lou" or other music.

REFERENCES

Hackett, Layne C., and Jensen, Robert G. *A Guide to Movement Exploration.* Palo Alto, Calif.: Peek Publications, 1967.

Related Programs
- *Skip Rope Games* (record), Educational Record Sales, 157 Chambers Street, New York, N.Y.
- *Rhythmic Songs for Fun and Exercise* (Grades 2–3, record), Educational Record Sales
- *Hop, Skip and Sing,* Palfrey's Educational Supply Co., 7715 E. Garvey Boulevard, Rosemead, Calif.
- Track and field activities
- Jumping activities and games

Instructional Materials
- Jump rope
- Ribbons for relays and guiding games
- Blindfolds
- Record player or tape player
- Utility ball
- Texture ball, Creative Playthings, Princeton, N.J.

Further Evaluation
- Lincoln-Oseretsky Motor Development Scale: Test #7, jumping over a rope
- Youth Fitness Test, NEA, American Association for Health, Physical Education and Recreation, 1201 Sixteenth Street NW., Washington, D.C.
- Individually devised skipping activities

PRESCRIPTIVE ILLUSTRATION

Priority Teaching Objective: Adam, seven years old, educable mentally retarded. At the conclusion of the lesson, Adam will be able to skip, alternating feet, for at least five consecutive skips, counting aloud each time the lead foot hits the ground.

Pretest Tasks: Adam was asked to skip in a circle around the teacher, but he got his feet all mixed up.

Specific Teaching Procedures: "Adam, I want you to step out on one foot, then hop on the same foot while you keep your other foot off the ground. Then change feet and step-hop on the other foot. Now, watch very carefully. This is the way you do it. [Teacher demonstrates]."

"Now what are you going to do, Adam?"

Pupil: "I'm going to step on one foot and then hop, and then step on the other foot and hop."

"Good, now every time you step-hop correctly, you will get one red-hot candy, and when you skip by yourself, you will get two red-hots for every skip. I will hold your hand to begin with, and we will skip together. Ready? Step-hop, step-hop, step-hop . . ."

Performance Evaluation: "Very good, Adam. You earned six red-hots for step-hopping and ten for skipping, and you only made two mistakes. Do you remember what they were?"

Pupil: "I think I hopped two times on one foot and forgot to change feet once."

Analysis and Comments: The task was judged to be inappropriate as it was obviously too easy for Adam. In a posttest, Adam skipped five steps back to his beginning point and then skipped to his room. Adam did not need to have skipping broken down into its component movements. Adam would benefit more from exercises involving skipping to drum beats and music and in skipping games such as Farmer in the Dell, Drop the Handkerchief, and the Flying Dutchman.

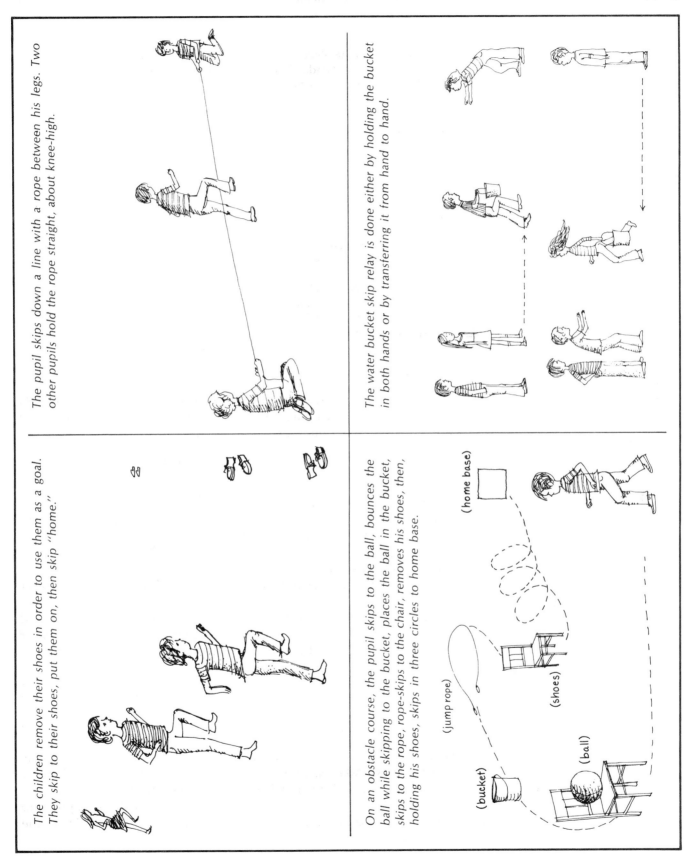

The pupil skips down a line with a rope between his legs. Two other pupils hold the rope straight, about knee-high.

The water bucket skip relay is done either by holding the bucket in both hands or by transferring it from hand to hand.

The children remove their shoes in order to use them as a goal. They skip to their shoes, put them on, then skip "home."

On an obstacle course, the pupil skips to the ball, bounces the ball while skipping to the bucket, places the ball in the bucket, skips to the rope, rope-skips to the chair, removes his shoes, then, holding his shoes, skips in three circles to home base.

(home base)

(jump rope)

(shoes)

(bucket)

(ball)

All programs should be modified or extended to meet the needs of individual pupils.

For Self-instruction: Devise a teaching procedure and performance evaluation method for this pupil: Darrel, five years old, a slow kindergarten child. The objective is for Darrel to be able to skip in normal play. Specifically, he should be able to skip twenty-five yards to a goal and back with 80 percent accuracy.

Gross Motor Development

9/Dancing

DEFINITION: The ability to move one's body in coordinated response to music.

ILLUSTRATION: In young children, free movement and eurythmic expression. Progression to more formal dance steps with older pupils.

EDUCATIONAL RATIONALE: Children need to be taught the enjoyment of free movement and emotional response to music and rhythm. Dancing and related skills should be a fundamental part of all physical education and remedial eurythmic programs.

SUGGESTED PROGRAM IDEAS

1. Beginning Activities
   a. Basic rhythm: Children sit and clap hands to drum beat. Sit, clap, and stamp feet to drum beat. Stand, clap, and march to beat. Have children use rhythm band instruments to learn to imitate the beat. Encourage free eurythmic expression to class rhythm band music.
   b. Action songs: Introduce records of children's action songs ("Row, Row, Row Your Boat," etc.) to teach movement responses to music.
   c. Free movement: Using music such as *The Nutcracker Suite*, teach pupils to move about freely with arms over head, waving arms at sides and in front of body, tiptoeing, doing bending movements, etc.
   d. Patterned movement: Using music such as "Volga Boatman," teach pupils to bend bodies, sway, and "pull ropes," push or carry heavy loads, etc.
   e. Fundamental steps: Use the Ruth Evans Childhood Rhythm Series 1–3 to introduce meters, steps, swinging, and movement.
   f. Circle steps: Pupils join hands in circle and follow directions of teacher to music.
2. Middle Stage Activities
   a. Bees: Using *Flight of the Bumblebee*, pupils run up and down, circling in and out like bees following a leader.
   b. Storm: Using *The Sorcerer's Apprentice* or similar music, children run with outstretched arms like the wind, tiptoe and run fast like the rain, crouch and jump for thunder and lightning, etc.
   c. Animals and people: Using *Peter and the Wolf* or similar music, children imitate wolf, bird, duck, hunters, etc.
   d. Indians: Use *RCA Indian Album* or similar record to provide different rhythms for Indian dances.
   e. Introductory circle dances: Ruth Evans Series 4—polka, gallop, circle formation, and change partners. Series 6—simple social dances.
   f. Bunny hop: Group "hop and kick" holding hips of person in front—make variations of hop.
   g. Use small parachute to teach eurythmic movements.
3. Advanced Activities
   a. Individual dance steps: Use records such as *Dances of Hawaii, Calypso for Children.* Do modern dances to contemporary tunes.
   b. Group dances: Simple folk and square dances such as Ruth Evans Series 8—folk dance patterns.

33

c. Waltz steps: Free movement, spins, twirling, etc., and formal waltz pattern with partner (Strauss waltzes, etc.).

d. Partner music: Introduce simple two-step, etc., using variety of music.

e. Self-expression: Free movement to "mood music" to express an emotion.

f. Peer instruction: Pupils teach a dance or step to other pupils.

REFERENCES

Bauer, Lois M., and Reed, Barbara A. *Dance and Play Activities for the Elementary Grades.* New York: Chatwell House, 1960.

Related Programs

* *Classroom Rhythms from the Land of Make-Believe* (record), Educational Record Sales, 157 Chambers Street, New York, N.Y.
* *Simplified Folk Dance Favorites* (record), Educational Record Sales
* *Square Dance Fair, Promenade and Do-Si-Do* (easy square dance records), Educational Record Sales
* *Ruth Evans Childhood Rhythm Records,* Palfrey's Educational Supply Co., 7715 E. Garvey Boulevard, Rosemead, Calif.

Instructional Materials

* Introductory Rhythm Band Set, Creative Playthings, Princeton, N.J.
* Popular Folk Games and Dances, Rhythmic Play Games and Dances, Palfrey's Educational Supply Co.
* Record player, tape recorder, classroom piano
* Richards, Mary Helen. *Threshold to Music.* Belmont, Calif.: Fearon Publishers, 1966, 1967.
* *Nutcracker Suite, Sorcerer's Apprentice, Action Songs and Rounds, Adventures in Rhythms, Boston Pops Picnic, Calypso for Children, Dances of Hawaii, Music of Johann Strauss* (records), Educational Records Sales
* *Indian Album for Elementary Grades,* RCA Victor Series, Educational Record Sales
* Parachute, J. A. Preston Corp., 71 Fifth Avenue, New York, N.Y.

Further Evaluation

* Beginning dance activities should be evaluated relative to the degree of participation and eurythmic expression on the part of the pupil.
* Formal dance steps for middle- and upper-grade children can be evaluated according to the amount of instruction provided and the accuracy of performance of specific steps.

PRESCRIPTIVE ILLUSTRATION

Priority Teaching Objective: Timmy, five years old, developmental kindergarten. Timmy will be able to do a simple Indian dance with coordinated hand, body, and foot movements, and to follow vocal dance commands.

Pretest Tasks: Timmy was requested to dance around the room to the beat of an early childhood Indian dance record. Although Timmy was listening to the music, he was unable to coordinate his movements but just walked around the room to the music.

Specific Teaching Procedures: "Timmy, I want you to watch me and listen as I dance to the beat of this tom-tom. See how each time I hit the drum I also take a step and lift my foot high."

"Now as I beat the drum and dance, you dance with me. Remember to lift your foot in time to the beat of the drum—that's good."

"Fine. Now this time James will beat the drum while I hold your hand and we dance together. That's the way to do it!"

"Now this time I want you to hold the tom-tom and to beat it and dance at the same time. Try it now and tell me what you are doing."

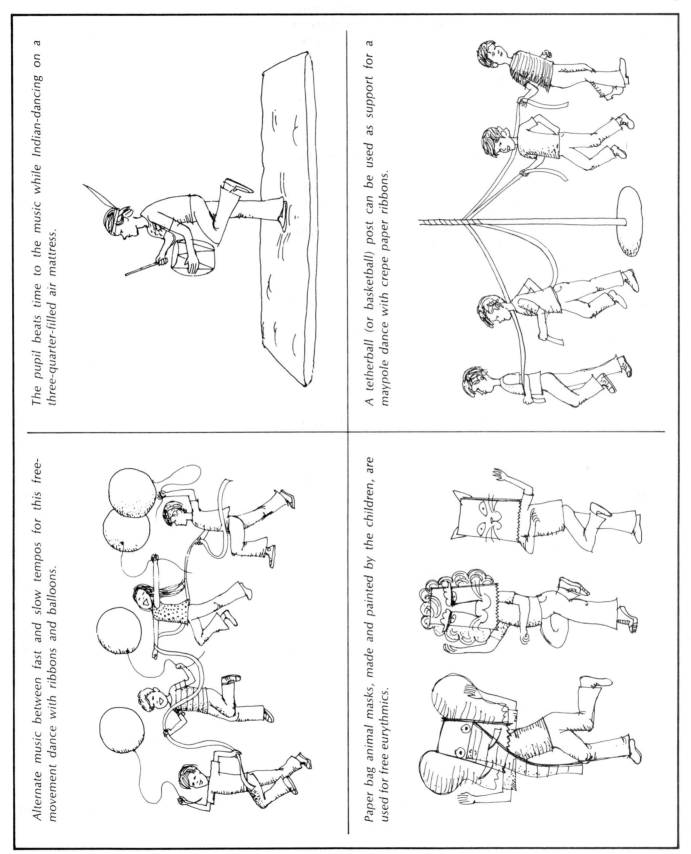

The pupil beats time to the music while Indian-dancing on a three-quarter-filled air mattress.

A tetherball (or basketball) post can be used as support for a maypole dance with crepe paper ribbons.

Alternate music between fast and slow tempos for this free-movement dance with ribbons and balloons.

Paper bag animal masks, made and painted by the children, are used for free eurythmics.

All programs should be modified or extended to meet the needs of individual pupils.

Pupil: "I'm to beat the drum and dance at the same time."

"That's right. You are doing a good job."

"Now listen to the drum beat on this record. You beat your tom-tom along with the record, and we will dance together around the room."

"Fine. Now we will join the other children and all dance to the record."

Performance Evaluation: With a different Indian-dance record, Timmy was able to dance around the room with the other children. He was obviously responding to the beat of the music with control and rhythm. However, when the beat changed, he was unable to adapt to the new rhythm without great difficulty.

Analysis and Comments: The task and sequential steps were good beginning activities for Timmy. His immediate gain in self-confidence was very important. The same activities should be extended until he has mastered the simple beat and change in rhythm.

For Self-instruction: Devise a teaching procedure and performance evaluation method for this pupil: Susan, ten years old, educable mentally retarded. At the conclusion of this lesson, Susan will be able to respond spontaneously and eurythmically to the "Blue Danube" waltz group dance, in which the children move in and out while holding a small parachute over their heads (see illustration).

Gross Motor Development

10/Self-identification

DEFINITION: The ability to identify one's self.

ILLUSTRATION: Pupil can identify self by name, respond to name when called, identify self in pictures and mirrors.

EDUCATIONAL RATIONALE: Primary to all conceptual learning is the awareness of self as a separate identity. The young preschool child must be taught to differentiate himself from other objects in the environment and to respond to his name.

SUGGESTED PROGRAM IDEAS

1. Beginning Activities
   Although most young children go through this stage without much difficulty, many autistic and severely mentally retarded pupils may require extensive training and conditioning to insure proper response.
   a. Full-length mirror: Child is placed in front of mirror with instructions, "See [name]." He is then taught to feel himself all over while watching in mirror and saying his name. He is then turned in several directions, taught to look and say "That is [name]," "I am [name]," etc.
   b. Photographic identification: A color slide picture of the child is first projected for identification. A recent color photo is presented next, followed by black and white pictures of the child engaged in varied activities. Pupils tell something about themselves (favorite foods, etc.) when pictures are shown.
   c. Respond to name: The child is taught to respond to his name and to follow simple directions: "Billy, raise your hand." Pupil is next taught to respond with his name when presented with self in mirror or pictures.
   d. Simon Says game: "Simon says everybody stand up," "Mary clap your hands," etc.

2. Simple Generalizing Activities
   a. Group identification: Mix pupil's photograph with pictures cut from magazine and require identification. Next, mix picture with photographs of other children and require identification. Present family photographs and require pupil to identify his picture and each member of his family.
   b. Developmental photographs: Use earlier photographs and teach pupil to arrange in their correct growth sequences, and discuss.
   c. Silhouettes: With projector, help pupil make profile silhouette of self; cut out and color. Identify self by name from other silhouettes. Let other children assemble silhouette puzzles.
   d. Name game: Play game of giving simple directions preceded by naming each pupil. Condition pupil to listen and to respond only to his name.
   e. Recorder games: Use the tape recorder, having different parents, teachers, and children talk. Pupil responds by identifying his own voice or following directions when his name is called.
   f. Funny stories: Teacher tapes silly things about children. Pupils listen and raise hands when name is mentioned.
   g. Video tape replay: Pupil watches self on TV replay and describes what he is doing.

3. Advanced Activities

    a. Mirror photography: Using Polaroid camera, pupil is taught to assume different positions in full-length mirror, take photograph, and then view picture and describe it into a tape recorder.

    b. Cut-up pictures: Using old photographs, pupil can identify self by name from partial pictures, i.e., missing head, picture cut lengthwise.

    c. Hand mirror: Pupil can use a hand mirror to identify and describe himself although only part of his body is visible. Tape-record description and play back.

    d. Written name: Child is taught to identify his name in both cursive and manuscript and to write it correctly. Pupil finds name from name tags on board. Pupil traces name written on mirror while seeing self.

    e. Draw picture: Pupil can draw and describe picture of himself even though it may not be a recognizable picture to the teacher.

    f. This is Your Life: Teacher tapes "life history" of child and plays it to class. Child must listen and identify self.

REFERENCES

Hiner, Gladys, W. "A Valentine Unit Suggests a Unit on Self-Awareness." *Exceptional Children* 30 (1964):317–319.

Related Programs

- *Basic Songs for Exceptional Children*, Vol. 1 (record), Educational Record Sales, 157 Chambers Street, New York, N.Y.
- *I'm Dressing Myself* (record), Educational Record Sales
- Individually developed programs involving physical contact, stimulation, and response between parents and the child
- Photography programs, including 16 mm home and school movies
- Bradfield, Joan and Roger. *Who Are You?* Racine, Wis.: Whitman Publishing, 1966.
- *Self-Image* (record), Bowmar Records, 622 Rodier Drive, Glendale, Calif.
- Flexi-Dexi Family Unit, Mafex Associates, Inc., Box 519, Johnstown, Pa.

Instructional Materials

- Full-length dressing mirrors
- Photographic pictures and slides of pupils
- Hand mirror
- Magnifying glass
- Black art paper
- White mounting board paper
- Tape recorder
- Opaque projector
- Scrapbook and paste

Further Evaluation

- A reliable indication of self-identification is whether the child will respond to his name and photograph presented by different people over a period of time.

PRESCRIPTIVE ILLUSTRATION

Priority Teaching Objective: Lois, six years old, transitional first grade. While viewing a series of 35 mm slides (provided by her parents), Lois will be able to find herself in the pictures and to describe her activity and feelings at the time the pictures were taken.

Pretest Tasks: When Lois was shown the class picture, she had great difficulty in finding herself. She failed to identify her last name among others on the chalkboard. She was also unable to tell anything about herself or her home or family life.

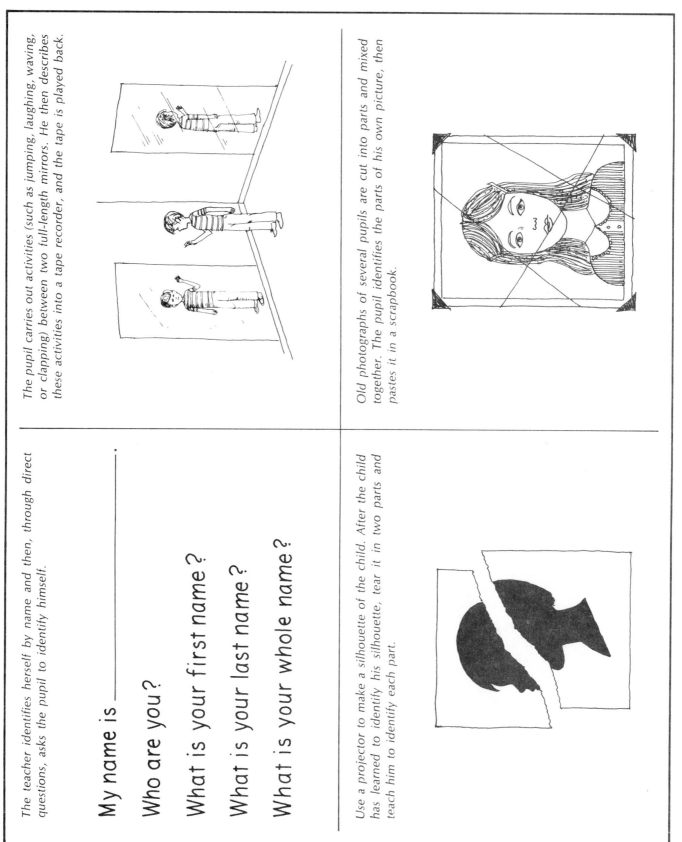

The pupil carries out activities (such as jumping, laughing, waving, or clapping) between two full-length mirrors. He then describes these activities into a tape recorder, and the tape is played back.

Old photographs of several pupils are cut into parts and mixed together. The pupil identifies the parts of his own picture, then pastes it in a scrapbook.

The teacher identifies herself by name and then, through direct questions, asks the pupil to identify himself.

My name is ⎯⎯⎯⎯⎯⎯⎯.

Who are you?

What is your first name?

What is your last name?

What is your whole name?

Use a projector to make a silhouette of the child. After the child has learned to identify his silhouette, tear it in two parts and teach him to identify each part.

All programs should be modified or extended to meet the needs of individual pupils.

Specific Teaching Procedures: "Lois, I'm going to show you several colored slides that your parents have loaned to our class. You are in some of the pictures. Please look carefully at each picture, then point to yourself if you are there, and also describe to the class what you and the other people are doing."

"Now let's try this first slide. It looks like some kind of party! Are you there?"

Pupil: "That was my birthday party. There I am [pointing]. That is my baby brother, Larry."

"Good. Now tell me what you are to do when I show you the next few pictures."

Pupil: "I will find my pictures and tell what I am doing."

"Fine. Now let's look at these pictures [pictures are of Lois and her first birthday cake, Lois with several young children at a family picnic, Lois at a Christmas party, Lois with her parents on a camping trip, Lois with her first grade class]."

Performance Evaluation: The task was only partially appropriate in that it required too much attention and verbal response from Lois in front of her class. She was able to locate and describe herself in three of the five slides.

Analysis and Comments: Lois should have been prepared through individual sessions with the teacher. She lacked motivation and was shy in front of the class. She had great difficulty in searching for herself in the class picture.

For Self-instruction: Devise a teaching procedure and performance evaluation method for this pupil: Michael, nine years old, autistic. Michael fails to reply when asked "What is your name?" Instead he repeats the exact question for the teacher. The objective is that when Michael is asked for his name, he will be able to respond, "My name is Michael [or the equivalent]."

Gross Motor Development

11/Body Localization

DEFINITION: The ability to locate parts of one's own body.
ILLUSTRATION: Pupil can locate eyes, hands, mouth, hair, nose, feet, eyebrows, fingernails, shoulders, elbows, knees, back, neck, chin, forehead, wrists, arms, legs, toes, etc.
EDUCATIONAL RATIONALE: Before a child can develop an adequate self-concept, he needs to be able to locate himself in space. Children should be taught to find and point out body parts and to describe them by name and function.

SUGGESTED PROGRAM IDEAS

1. Beginning Activities
   a. Basic part location: Point to your eye, nose, mouth, foot, hand, hair, legs. "What is this?" Examiner touches pupil's arm, etc., and demands oral reply. All parts missed should be taught and reinforced with practice.
   b. Counting parts: Pupil touches his body parts spontaneously while naming them and counting (toes—1, head—2, teeth—3, etc.).
   c. Other body parts: Teach location and names for eyebrows, fingernails, shoulders, elbows, knees, back, forehead, wrist, etc. Have pupil locate and name parts on self and on teacher. Use simple human-figure puzzles for reinforcement.
   d. Simon Says: "Shake your head; put your hands on your feet; grasp your right ear with your left hand; touch your knees with your elbows," etc.
   e. Calisthenic games:
   "Stand up and stretch for the sky with your arms up."
   "Stretch your neck like a turtle."
   "Kick your feet like a donkey."
   "Stretch your entire body—arms and legs. Now relax and be limp all over like a bowl of jelly."
   "Roll your eyeballs in circles. Blink. Shake your eyebrows!"
   "Walk with stiff legs like a wooden soldier."
   "Open your mouth like a lion."
2. Middle Stage Activities
   a. Hide and touch: Place a child under an old sheet. Child then holds up body part (foot, elbow, head, leg, etc.) to be described by other pupil and then named.
   b. Mirror identification: Child views self in mirror, points out, and names own body parts.
   c. Photographic identification: Child points out and labels body parts in photograph of self. Photographs can also be mounted in scrapbook, traced, cut up and labeled, etc.
   d. Hokey-pokey: Sing and play circle game: "Put your left foot in and pull your left out; put your left foot in and you shake it all about," etc.
   e. Body tracing: Children lie down on large sheets of kraft paper while others trace their body outline. Parts are then labeled, colored or painted, cut out for murals, etc.
3. Advanced Activities
   a. Subtle body awareness: Teach relaxation techniques and awareness of heartbeat, weight of clothes, breathing, scalp, etc. Play "Angels in the Snow," with pupil being taught to coordinate body parts.

b. Body details: Using magnifying glass, have pupil study details of knees, hair, fingerprints, toes. Use tape recorder to record impressions. Use microscope to view blood, hair, dried skin, etc.

c. Internal organs: Locate internal organs and functions.

d. Functional description: Use tape recorder to record answers to "What do our ears do?" "What makes us think?" "What is a heart?" etc. Obtain written descriptions of functions of body parts.

e. Composite picture: Assemble composite face and body from various magazine pictures and paste them together in a poster.

REFERENCES

McAninch, Myrene. "Body Image as Related to Perceptual-Cognitive Motor Disabilities." *Learning Disorders*, Vol. 2, edited by Jerome Hellmuth, pp. 139–169. Seattle: Special Child Publications, 1966.

Related Programs

- *Basic Concepts through Dance for Exceptional Children* (body image), Educational Activities, Inc., P.O. Box 392, Freeport, N.Y.
- Psychoeducational Resource Program No. 10: Self-identification
- Psychoeducational Resource Program No. 12: Body Abstraction.
- *Basic Songs for Exceptional Children*, Vol. 1 (concept records), Educational Record Sales, 157 Chambers Street, New York, N.Y.
- *Developmental Body Articulation*, Vol. 3 (concept records), Educational Record Sales
- Human Body Parts Flannel Aid, Milton Bradley Co., Springfield, Mass.
- Weighted wrist cuffs, J. A. Preston Corp., 71 Fifth Avenue, New York, N.Y.
- Weighted ankle cuffs, J. A. Preston Corp.
- Body Concept Spirit Masters 1 and 2, Developmental Learning Materials, 3505 N. Ashland, Chicago, Ill.
- Body Concept Template, Developmental Learning Materials

Instructional Materials

- Boy and Girl, The Judy Company, Minneapolis, Minn.
- Full-length dressing mirror
- Detailed models of body parts (The Beating Heart, The Seeing Eye, The Human Brain), Palfrey's Educational Supply Co., 7715 E. Garvey Boulevard, Rosemead, Calif.
- Stethoscope, Creative Playthings, Princeton, N.J.
- Record player and tape recorder

Further Evaluation

- Subjectively selected tests of body part identification
- Valett Developmental Survey of Basic Learning Abilities: conceptual development

PRESCRIPTIVE ILLUSTRATION

Priority Teaching Objective: Juanita, eight years old, educable mentally retarded. Juanita will be able to identify selected parts of her body by correctly pointing to twenty of twenty-two parts specified in the pretest.

Pretest Tasks: Juanita was asked to point out each of the following parts of her body:

Ear*	Shoulder	Eyebrow*	Thigh	Elbow	Fingernail*
Knee*	Finger*	Calf	Leg*	Neck	Eyes*
Stomach*	Ankle	Nose*	Wrist	Hand*	Chest
Waist	Thumb*	Hips	Teeth*		

She was able to correctly identify twelve of the above twenty-two body parts as marked (*).

The pupil uses a stethoscope in various positions while listening to the song, "What's Inside of Me" from Basic Songs for Exceptional Children.

Vocabulary words are to be defined orally and then written out for spelling practice and future reference.

ankle	nostril	navel
spine	toes	shoulder
throat	wrist	jaw

The pupil completes the face. This exercise teaches facial awareness and can be supplemented in many ways, such as by using cutout facial parts from magazine pictures.

The pupil is required to draw lines from the word to the proper body part.

elbow
teeth
waist
hand
neck
knee
heel
nose

All programs should be modified or extended to meet the needs of individual pupils.

Specific Teaching Procedures: "Juanita, I'm going to turn on this projector, and I want you to look at the white paper and tell me what you see."

Pupil: "That's me!"

"Good. Now we're going to play a game. It will be my turn first and I'll tell you a name of a part of your body. Then it will be your turn, and I want you to point to it. If you don't know where it is, just say, 'I pass,' and it will be my turn. I'll show it to you and it will be your turn again. Then you'll show it to me. After we have both had turns, you can take a yellow dot and stick it on the same part of the picture. When the game is over, you can take the picture down and count the yellow dots. Then we will put a check on your card for each dot. Do you understand how to play this game?"

Pupil: "Uh-huh."

"OK, show me your ear. That's right. Here is a yellow dot; go ahead and put it on the ear in the picture [process continued with other body parts]."

Performance Evaluation: "That's excellent, Juanita. Now count the number of dots on the paper [projector turned off]." I helped her keep place as she counted.

"That's a lot of dots. Now you can take the purple pen and make thirty checks on your card."

Analysis and Comments: Juanita missed only four of the pretest words when given later as a posttest. The task was appropriate and took about twenty minutes to complete. This was the first time I worked with her and she seemed tense at first. She needs continued work on the more difficult body parts and their names.

For Self-instruction: Devise a teaching procedure and performance evaluation method for this pupil: Kenneth, ten years old, hard of hearing with educational handicaps. Kenneth will lie on butcher paper while a classmate traces his body outline. He will then be able to draw in the details of his body parts including his ears.

Gross Motor Development

12/Body Abstraction

DEFINITION: The ability to transfer and generalize self-concepts and body localizations.

ILLUSTRATION: Pupil can identify others by names and pictures. Can locate body parts on others, generalize to pictures, complete body picture puzzles.

EDUCATIONAL RATIONALE: Children should be provided with varied experiences whereby they may gain psychophysical awareness and control of themselves. Educational programs should allow the child to consider himself relative to given situations and should contribute to the development of a sound self-concept.

SUGGESTED PROGRAM IDEAS

1. Beginning Activities
   a. Full awareness of others: Pupil is fully aware of other children and adults. Can locate their body parts. Can call them by name and appropriately interact with them.
   b. Doll play: Child can locate doll parts and dress doll. Teacher interacts with child during doll play to encourage abstraction of reality situations.
   c. Puzzle assembly. Child can quickly assemble Judy boy and girl puzzles. With practice, can assemble large body puzzles while blindfolded. Taking pictures of people from magazines, pupil can cut up and reassemble them.
   d. Sex identification: Identifies his own sex verbally and makes appropriate identification with boy or girl dolls, pictures, and puzzles.
   e. Family abstraction: Can identify teacher and family members in pictures.

2. Middle Stage Activities
   a. Group picture: Using chalkboard or art paper, children jointly construct picture of a man, beginning with discussion of the head. Second child describes another body part and adds it to the picture, etc.
   b. Body positions: Teach pupil to copy positions from pictures and silhouettes, or directly from position assumed by the teacher or another student. Children can also dance or skip to music until music is stopped when they assume position taken by the leader.
   c. Holiday cards: Children make pictures, representing humans engaged in various activities, for Valentine's Day, parents' birthdays, Halloween, etc.
   d. Draw self: Picture is completed appropriately for developmental level. Have child describe self and picture into tape recorder and play back.
   e. Draw body parts: Teach pupil to draw separately: nose, eyes, hair, mouth, arms, elbow, fingers, leg, foot, etc. Assemble various parts drawn by different children into a composite picture and paste together.
   f. Make clay models of self and family.
   g. Make hand and foot prints in clay and compare with those of other children.
   h. Describe body parts from head down, etc.

3. Advanced Activities
   a. Assemble physiological models: Have pupil assemble body parts in pastic models and describe functions. Play "Twenty Questions" to identify parts and functions— "Do you bite?" etc.
   b. Copy body parts: Present pupil with colored pictures of heart, lungs, brain, etc., for tracing and copying. Use *The Human Body Book* or similar resources.

45

    c. Body concept: Teach age, height, weight, race, size, etc. Tape pupil's description of himself for feedback discussions. Have child discuss personal characteristics including interests, feelings, strengths, etc.

    d. Self-concept development: Extend previous activities to include discussion of: "The person I am," "What I want to be," "My heroes." For older children use writing and speech projects on "The person I hope to become."

    e. Measure body parts (including face) in a mirror and draw pictures of parts to scale.

    f. Clothes matching: "Socks go on _____," "Gloves go on_____," "Hats go on _____."

    g. Positions: Pupils imitate body positions of leader.

    h. Body reconstruction: Cut photograph of face or body down midline; glue one-half on art paper. Pupil completes opposite side by drawing in missing parts.

    i. Mirror games: Move the opposite part of your body from mine—if I lift my right hand, you lift your left hand, etc."

    j. Writing: Have child write about differences in his own family members and how they appear.

    k. Charades: Act out what pupil wants to be or do when he grows up.

REFERENCES

Bodwin, R. F., and Bruck, M. "The Adaptation and Validation of the Draw-a-Person Test as a Measurement of Self-Concept." *Journal of Clinical Psychology* 16 (1960):427–429.

Related Programs

- White and Black Family Figures, The Judy Company, Minneapolis, Minn.
- Munsen, Francis, and Stanek, Muriel. *You and Your Family.* The Experiential Development Program. Chicago: Benefic Press, 1965.
- Psychoeducational Resource Programs No. 10, Self-identification, and No. 11, Body Localization.
- *The Human Body Book,* Palfrey's Educational Supply Co., 7715 E. Garvey Boulevard, Rosemead, Calif.
- *The Development of Body Awareness and Position in Space* (record), Educational Activities, Inc., Freeport, N.Y.
- The Kirshner Body Alphabet, Mafex Associates, 111 Barron Avenue, Johnstown, Pa.
- Position in Space Posters, Developmental Learning Materials, 3505 N. Ashland Avenue, Chicago, Ill.

Instructional Materials

- Boy, and Girl, The Judy Company
- Visible Man, and Visible Woman, Palfrey's Educational Supply Co.
- Judy's Friends Story Set, The Judy Company
- The Human Body Kit, Palfrey's Educational Supply Co.
- Children's picture-story books
- Doll house and materials

Further Evaluation

- Goodenough Draw-a-Person Test
- Goodenough-Harris Draw-a-Person
- Q-sorts of self and ideal concepts

PRESCRIPTIVE ILLUSTRATION

Priority Teaching Objective: Eric, fourteen years old, behaviorally disturbed. Eric will be able to describe his feelings about himself, how he thinks others see him, and what he would like to become someday.

Pretest Tasks: When asked to describe the kind of person he feels himself to be and how other people see him, Eric replied in a curt, negative tone of voice that he was "OK."

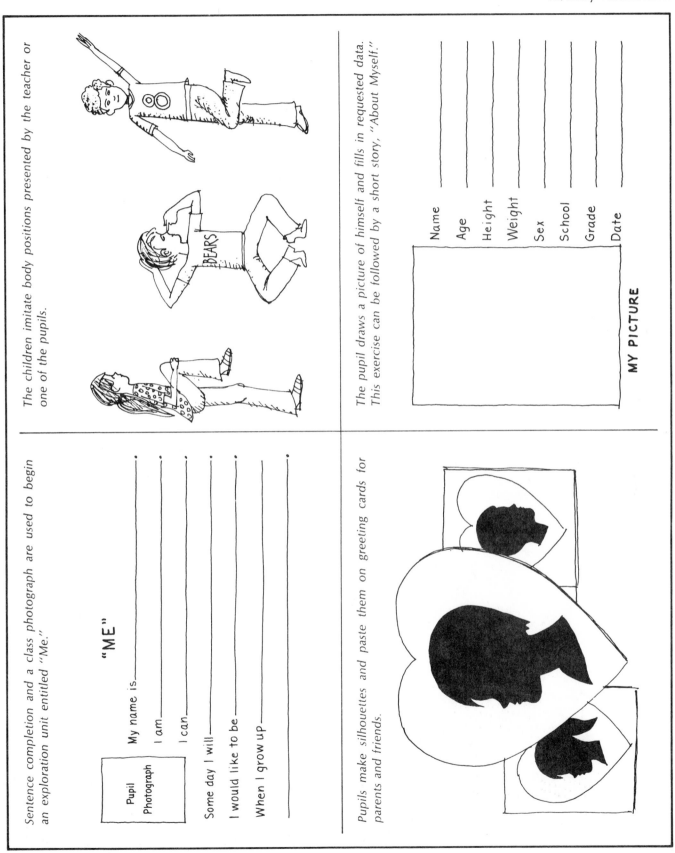

The children imitate body positions presented by the teacher or one of the pupils.

The pupil draws a picture of himself and fills in requested data. This exercise can be followed by a short story, "About Myself."

Name _____

Age _____

Height _____

Weight _____

Sex _____

School _____

Grade _____

Date _____

MY PICTURE

Sentence completion and a class photograph are used to begin an exploration unit entitled "Me."

"ME"

Pupil Photograph

My name is _____

I am _____

I can _____

Some day I will _____

I would like to be _____

When I grow up _____

Pupils make silhouettes and paste them on greeting cards for parents and friends.

All programs should be modified or extended to meet the needs of individual pupils.

Specific Teaching Procedures: "Eric, today I want you to think a little bit about how other people feel about you. You know, the kind of person they think you are and what they want you to do and be. Let's try it this way. I will tell you the names of several people. You complete the sentence I start and then add whatever you wish. Got the idea?"

Pupil: "Yeah."

"OK, think of Susan L. and complete this sentence: Susan feels I am _____."

"Now let's do these: My father thinks that I am _____. Most of my teachers feel that I_____. My friends feel that I _____. Usually, my mother feels that I _____. Most other people think that I am _____."

Performance Evaluation: "Good, Eric. You completed all of them with real feeling. You seem to have strong feelings about other people and how they seem to see you. Do you want to tell me more about any of them?"

Eric talked about his friends' perception of himself for ten minutes.

Analysis and Comments: Almost all of Eric's associations were hostile and negative. He obviously has a poor self-concept and feels that other people reject him because of physical oddities. The school psychologist will be consulted as to what might be done to help him in class.

For Self-instruction: Devise a teaching procedure and performance evaluation method for this pupil: Ruth, eleven years old, emotionally disturbed. At the completion of this lesson Ruth will be able to state accurately her height, weight, shoe size, waist measurement, and thigh measurement.

Gross Motor Development

13/Muscular Strength

DEFINITION: The ability to use one's muscles to perform physical tasks.

ILLUSTRATION: Pupil can touch floor by bending from standing position; can sit up and touch toes from supine position; can raise legs off floor for a few seconds from supine position; can do one push-up; can chin self from bar.

EDUCATIONAL RATIONALE: Muscular strength is best developed through a systematic physical fitness program adapted to individual growth patterns. Exercises and games involving all major body muscles should be included in the program.

SUGGESTED PROGRAM IDEAS

1. Beginning Activities
   Have pupil do the following:
   a. Crouch and jump: Crouch low and jump high. Crouch and jump several times.
   b. Pole hang: Hang with two arms from a pole while being timed.
   c. Foot push: With hands in air, partners sit, place feet against feet, and push.
   d. Hand push: Partners face one another and push against hands while trying to remain in stable position.
   e. Arm circles: With arms straight out, begin with small circles; gradually get larger. Make both forward and backward movements.
   f. Torso: With arms over head and feet spread, bend from waist and move torso about in wide circles.
   g. Standing run: Run about in small circles or run in place.
   h. Bicycle: With back on floor pupil raises legs and "pedals" as in riding a bicycle.

2. Middle Stage Activities
   Have pupil do the following:
   a. Stair climb: Run up and down stairs and climb monkey bars.
   b. Knee bends: Place hands out at sides and feet together. Bend knees and straighten until tired or balance is lost.
   c. Medicine ball throw: Toss medicine ball back and forth until tired.
   d. Leg circles: Sit on chair and hold chair seat. Place legs apart straight out and move each in circles. Change size and direction of circles.
   e. Floor touch: Stand erect with feet together and hands over head. Bend at waist and touch floor with fingers. Repeat until tired.
   f. Run: Run 100-yard dash as fast as possible.
   g. Swimming: Teach children to swim. Have them work to increase number of laps completed at one time.
   h. Jumping jacks: Do jumping jacks while counting.

3. Advanced Activities
   Have pupil do the following:
   a. Leg lift: Lie on back with hands behind head and feet together. Lift feet as far as possible. Slowly drop to within one inch of floor without touching. Repeat.
   b. Trunk-ups: Lie on stomach with feet together and hands behind head. Lift trunk and head up from floor while being timed.
   c. Sit-ups: Lie on stomach with feet together and hands behind head. With another pupil holding feet, sit up. Repeat until tired.

d. Push-ups: Lie on stomach, hold head up, and look straight ahead. Push up with arms and repeat.

e. Chin-ups: Hang from bar by hands and pull up to chin self.

f. Weights: Use simple, light, bar weights (about five pounds) for exercising biceps until tired.

g. Distance run: Run until tired.

h. Stair run: Run up and down stairs until tired.

REFERENCES

Barsch, Ray H. "Muscular Strength." *Achieving Perceptual-Motor Efficiency.* Seattle: Special Child Publication, 1967.

Ewing, Neil. *Games, Stunts, and Exercises: A Physical Education Handbook for Elementary School Teachers.* Palo Alto, Calif.: Fearon Publishers, 1964.

Related Programs

- Physical Fitness for the Younger Set (K-2 record), Educational Record Sales, 157 Chambers Street, New York, N.Y.
- *Exercise is Kid Stuff* (record), Educational Record Sales
- *78 Rhythms for Physical Fitness* (record), Educational Record Sales
- *Modern Dynamic Physical Fitness Activities for Primary Grades* (album), Educational Activities, Inc., P.O. Box 392, Freeport, N.Y.
- *Fun and Fitness* (record), Bowmar Records, 622 Rodier Drive, Glendale, Calif.
- Exer-Genie Program, American Physical Fitness of Northern California, 20 Harold Avenue, San Jose, Calif.

Instructional Materials

- Rest and exercise mats, Constructive Playthings, 1040 E. 85th Street, Kansas City, Mo.
- Climbing bars
- Record player
- Stopwatch
- Suspension bars
- Light weights
- Running areas and track if available
- Personal physical fitness record books for maintaining progress reports
- Texture ball, Creative Playthings, Princeton, N.J.
- Digitator Junior, J. A. Preston Corp., 71 Fifth Avenue, New York, N.Y.
- Wrist-ankle weights, Sears, Roebuck and Co.
- Lind Climber, J. A. Preston Corp.

Further Evaluation

- Kraus, Hans. "Kraus-Weber Tests for Minimum Muscular Fitness." *Therapeutic Exercises,* 2nd ed., pp. 125—126. Sprinfield, Ill.: Charles C. Thomas, 1963.
- Physical Fitness Rating Scales for Retarded Children, Metropolitan Toronto Association for Retarded Children, 186 Beverly Street, Toronto 23, Toronto, Canada.

PRESCRIPTIVE ILLUSTRATION

Priority Teaching Objective: Lynn, thirteen years old, educable mentally retarded. Lynn will be able to complete five good sit-ups from the knee-bent position with the teacher holding her feet as indicated below:

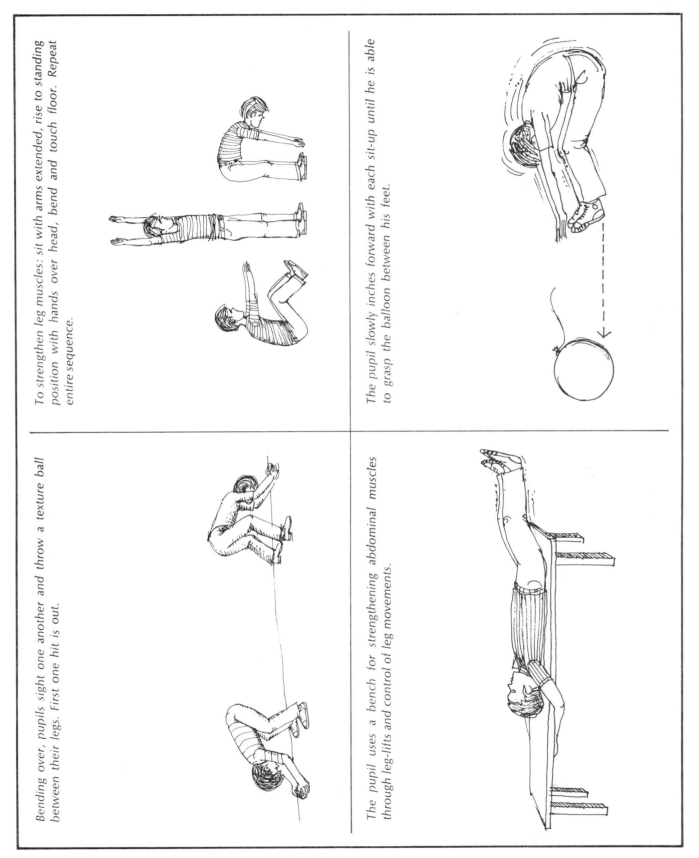

To strengthen leg muscles: sit with arms extended, rise to standing position with hands over head, bend and touch floor. Repeat entire sequence.

The pupil slowly inches forward with each sit-up until he is able to grasp the balloon between his feet.

Bending over, pupils sight one another and throw a texture ball between their legs. First one hit is out.

The pupil uses a bench for strengthening abdominal muscles through leg-lifts and control of leg movements.

All programs should be modified or extended to meet the needs of individual pupils.

Pretest Tasks: With the teacher holding her feet Lynn was able to complete only one good sit-up although she attempted two of them.

Specific Teaching Procedures: "Lynn, today we are going to begin lessons on doing sit-ups. When we are done, you should be able to do five sit-ups like this. You hold my feet down and notice how my knees are bent and my hands are behind my head. Now, I pull myself up until my elbows touch my knees like this."

"Now, tell me what we are going to try to accomplish."

Pupil: "I'm going to put my hands behind my head, bend my knees, and pull myself up so my elbows touch my knees."

"Good. Now to start with, I am going to have Joan hold your feet, and I will get behind your back and assist you as you pull yourself up. Now try it."

"That's good. You did it six times with my help. Now let's try it again, and I will not help you as much as before."

"Now we will practice this every day until you can begin to do them on your own."

Performance Evaluation: On the first attempt, Lynn did six assisted sit-ups. On the second attempt, she did ten more. The following day, she repeated the exercises and then did three with mild assistance. On the fourth practice day, she was able to do five unassisted bent-knee sit-ups, although the fifth was quite difficult for her.

Analysis and Comments: The task seemed quite appropriate for Lynn. She was able to progress gradually with assistance. As she is a flabby girl, she will need continued modification of this exercise for some time.

For Self-instruction: Devise a teaching procedure and performance evaluation method for this pupil: Alan, eleven years old, a slow learner. Upon completion of his climbing lessons, Alan will be able to climb to the top of a fifteen-foot suspended rope with muscular control.

14/General Physical Health

DEFINITION: *The ability to understand and apply principles of health and hygiene and to evidence good general health.*

ILLUSTRATION: *Pupil has good personal health and hygiene habits—no chronic school absences for health reasons, no unusual accidents or health history, no significant physical disabilities interfering with learning.*

EDUCATIONAL RATIONALE: *The child must be taught proper health habits that may affect his entire efficiency in learning. Educational consideration must be given to significant health, nutrition, and physical limitations.*

SUGGESTED PROGRAM IDEAS

1. Personal Cleanliness
   a. Washing-bathing: Teach importance of washing before meals, bathing, scrubbing fingernails, washing hair, care of feet, etc.
   b. Brushing teeth: Demonstrate proper brushing technique. Give out sample toothpaste. Develop poster contests on care of teeth.
   c. Care of colds: Discuss common cold and effects of sneezing, use of handkerchief, proper dress, etc.
   d. Personal grooming: Use filmstrip *Keeping Neat and Clean.* Explain how to brush clothes, shine shoes, and care for general appearance.
   e. Room cleanliness: Assign responsibilities for keeping school room clean and orderly. Have pupil discuss what he does and should do at home to maintain cleanliness in his room.

2. Proper Foods
   a. General nutrition: Use *Basic Songs for Exceptional Children,* Vol. 2, and develop follow-up projects on nutrition. Study value of vitamins.
   b. Breakfast: Have children bring in pictures and empty food containers to illustrate proper breakfast.
   c. Balanced meals: Discuss and illustrate importance of basic food groups. Have pupils plan menus including all food groups. If possible, help children to plan and prepare a class luncheon.
   d. Candy: Discuss proper use of candy, care of teeth after eating candy, etc.
   e. Calories: Cut out and label foods by calorie values.

3. Safety and Preventive Care
   a. Safety rules: Explain bicycle and pedestrian rules, traffic signs, drugs, tobacco danger signs, eye care, etc.
   b. Automobile safety: Discuss how to enter and leave an automobile, riding manners, automobile signs and warnings, etc.
   c. Sharp instruments: Illustrate proper care and use of knives, scissors, and hatchets.
   d. First aid: Teach elementary first aid for care of minor cuts and accidents. Explain what to do until help arrives. Make first aid kit.
   e. Community helpers: Assemble puzzles, view filmstrips, visit and discuss roles of nurses, physicians, firemen, librarians, etc.
   f. Antipollution club: Make posters, plan and carry out antipollution program in school.
   g. Smoking: Make picture charts on the risks and hazards of smoking.

    h. Drugs: Make picture charts on the dangers of drug use, including alcohol, marijuana, etc.

4. Rest and Relaxation

    a. Bedtime: Discuss proper bedtime routine, importance of sleep and rest, hours of sleep required, etc.

    b. Daytime relaxation: Teach simple relaxation technique of resting at desk, lying on floor or grass, deep breathing, etc.

    c. Nervous habits: Discuss normal fears and anxieties and how to feel better by talking with parents, teachers, and friends. Consider nail biting, tics, nervous habits, and ways to alleviate them.

    d. Exercise: Develop scrapbooks on favorite games and play activities and discuss the importance of poise, exercise, and physical fitness.

REFERENCES

de la Cruz, Felix, and La Veck, Gerald D. "The Pediatricians' View of Learning Disorders." *Learning Disorders*, Vol. 1, edited by Jerome Hellmuth. Seattle: Special Child Publications, 1965.

Related Programs

- *Basic Songs for Exceptional Children,* Vol. 2 (health, personal hygiene, nutrition), Educational Record Sales, 157 Chambers Sreet, New York, N.Y.
- *Health and Safety Through Music* (record), Educational Record Sales
- Hudson, Margaret W., and Weaver, Ann A. *Plans for Living: Your Guide to Health and Safety,* 2nd ed. Belmont, Calif.: Fearon Publishers, 1973.
- *Health and Safety* (workbook, grades 1–3) Continental Press, Elizabethtown, Pa.
- School Health Education Packet, Individual Health and Family Life, 3M Company, St. Paul, Minn.

Instructional Materials

- *Health Habits, Keeping Neat and Clean, Proper Food, Health Helpers* (filmstrips), Educational Record Sales, 157 Chambers Street, New York, N.Y.
- *Health Can Be Fun* (records), Educational Record Sales
- *Our Safety Book* (health activities), Palfrey's Educational Supply Co., 7715 E. Garvey Boulevard, Rosemead, Calif.
- Judy Puzzles: Doctor, Nurse, Dentist, The Judy Company, Minneapolis, Minn.
- *Health Workbooks* (grades 1–4), Palfrey's Educational Supply Co.
- First aid kit
- American Red Cross First Aid Manual
- Magazines for cutting out pictures of basic foods
- Tape recorder
- Toothpaste samples and kits from various companies
- Food Study Prints, Instructo Corp., Paoli, Pa.
- *Keeping Clean and Healthy* (posters), Instructo Corp.

Further Evaluation

- Physical and pediatric examinations
- Dental examination
- Subjective evaluation of pupil's health and safety habits by teacher
- Nurse's health and safety record check

PRESCRIPTIVE ILLUSTRATION

Priority Teaching Objective: Ann, eight years old, educable mentally retarded. As standard procedure, the members of the class brush their teeth as soon as they have finished their lunch. The day we started using the toothbrushes, I discovered that Ann had never used a toothbrush before and had no idea of what to do with it.

Ann will be able to brush her upper teeth in a downward motion. She will be able to brush her bottom teeth in an upward motion placing the tip and sides of the bristles close to the gum line before making each stroke.

The pupil considers, lists, and describes the contents of a simple first aid kit.

Band-aids

MY FIRST AID KIT

These exercises introduce simple relaxation techniques.

The pupil is required to draw and describe several safety signs.

The pupil plans a meal, then cuts out and pastes magazine pictures of the foods selected.

1. Milk
2.
3.
4.
5.
6.
7.

All programs should be modified or extended to meet the needs of individual pupils.

Pretest Tasks: When Ann finished her lunch, I asked her to bring her toothbrush so she could brush her teeth. I put some toothpaste on her brush and said she could go to the sink to brush. She began to squirm about, contorting her arms and body, and very shyly mumbled, "What do I do?"

Specific Teaching Procedures: "Ann, this is a toothbrush. It is to keep our teeth and mouth clean, and we need to know how to use it."

"Here is a model of your teeth. Watch how I brush these teeth. See how I brush down on the upper teeth. Now I brush upward on the bottom teeth."

"Now, watch how I brush my own teeth the same way."

"Here, Ann. You take your toothbrush and show me what you are to do, using the model first. Do you understand?"

Pupil: "I brush down on my top teeth and up on my bottom ones."

"I will help you a bit by saying 'brush down, brush down,' and then 'brush up, brush up.' OK, go ahead and brush your teeth."

Performance Evaluation: The lesson was fairly appropriate, although Ann followed the correct strokes only part of the time. She brushed for about six minutes experimenting with different strokes.

Analysis and Comments. At first Ann was shy and somewhat embarrassed, but she was eager to continue once she started. When her gums began to bleed, she became a bit frightened until I explained the reason to her. Since several of her front teeth are missing, brushing was a bit awkward for her. A dental checkup for her is a must.

For Self-instruction: Devise a teaching procedure and performance evaluation method for this student: Elizabeth, seventeen years old, trainable mentally retarded. For three consecutive days, Elizabeth will participate with two classmates in planning the hot lunch and will then assist in preparing and serving the meal.

Sensory-Motor Integration

15/Balance and Rhythm

DEFINITION: The ability to maintain gross and fine motor balance and to move rythmically.

ILLUSTRATION: Pupil is able to balance on balance board or rail; can move rythmically in playing jacks and in bouncing on trampoline or spring.

EDUCATIONAL RATIONALE: The maintenance of body balance and the perception and expression of rhythmic patterns are fundamental to readiness for more advanced perceptual-motor experiences. An integrated balance and rhythm program should be an essential part of physical education and formal readiness training.

SUGGESTED PROGRAM IDEAS

1. Beginning Activities
   a. Tiptoes: Pupil stands on tiptoes and runs forward and backward. Stands on toes while counting aloud to ten.
   b. One foot stand: With arms out to side, pupil stands on one foot and counts to five. Stands on other foot and gradually extends times.
   c. Metronome: Set metronome slow and teach walking to rhythmic beat. Gradually increase beat.
   d. Simple balance games: Play Topple Tower, Tip-it, etc. Stack blocks and checkers. Make playing card houses.
   e. Records: Use varied rhythm records and teach children to move to beat of the music. Tap with pencils and fingers to music.
   f. Ball bounce: Use basketball or utility ball and teach slow bouncing in one place. Bounce ball to music. Close eyes and bounce ball.
   g. Rhythm band: Use drum and rhythm band instruments to teach simple steady beat (tap-tap-tap-tap). Gradually introduce varied beats (Tap-**tap**! Tap-**tap**! Tap-**tap**!).

2. Middle Stage Activities
   Have pupil do the following:
   a. Jacks: Play jacks to steady rhythm record.
   b. Balance relays: Have relays, balancing books on head and moving to beat of music.
   c. Running bounce: Bounce ball to and from goal. Bounce with alternate hands to music.
   d. Balance beam: Walk two-by-four balance beam to varied drum beats and music.
   e. Jump board: Jump on board or trampoline to music.
   f. Balance board: Balance board first on wide fulcrum while counting to ten. Gradually decrease size of fulcrum and count to twenty.
   g. Bongo drums: Teacher explains simple beats and alternating rhythms. Gradually teach how to keep time to musical records.
   h. Roller skating: Teach basic balance and develop rhythmic skating to music.
   i. Balloon balance: Walk and balance balloons on palms of hands.
   j. Broom balance: Balance broom handle upright on hand.

3. Advanced Activities
   a. High rail balance: Place walking rail three to four feet high above grass. Child moves back and forth while beating time to drum.

57

b. Basketball: Teach basketball and play by time limitations.

c. Contemporary dances: Teach rhythm to current dances.

d. Snare drum: Teach rhythm to snare drum. Gradually introduce other drums and extend complexity of the beat.

e. Morse code: Teach basic elements of the code together with rhythm. Decipher simple messages.

f. Reverse binoculars: Pupil holds binoculars to eyes in reverse positions and focuses on line or walking board while walking along.

g. Unicycle: Teach use of simple unicycle and aid the child in beginning balance activities.

h. Tennis: Teach balance and rhythm in hitting tennis balls. Play regular tennis games.

i. Hula hoop: Keep hoop going to rhythm of music.

j. Ping-pong bounce: Hit ping-pong ball against wall in steady rhythm.

k. Swimming: Teach rhythmic swimming strokes and water movements.

REFERENCES

Rice, Arthur H. "Rhythmic Training and Body Balancing Prepare Child for Formal Learning." *The Nation's Schools,* February 1962, pp. 1–11.

Related Programs

- *Classroom Rhythms: First Experiences, Animal Rhythms, Interpretive Rhythms* (records), Educational Record Sales, 157 Chambers Street, New York, N.Y.
- *Creative Music for Exceptional Children* (record), Educational Record Sales
- *Basic Concepts Through Dance* (record), Educational Record Sales
- *Phoebe James Creative Rhythms* (record), Educational Record Sales
- *Exploring Perceptual-Motor Needs of Primary-Level Children* (record), Educational Activities, Inc., P.O. Box 392, Freeport, Long Island, N.Y.
- *Agility and Dynamic Balance—Using Mats and Balance Beams* (activity records), Educational Activities, Inc.
- Robins, Ferris and Jennet. *Educational Rhythmics for Mentally Handicapped Children.* Zurich, Switzerland: RA-Verlag, 1962.

Instructional Materials

- Unicycle
- Balance Boards, Constructive Playthings, 1040 E. 85th Street, Kansas City, Mo.
- Jumping Board, California Correctional Industries, 1400 S Street, Sacramento, Calif.
- Climbing Rope, Rope Ladder, Punching Bag Set, Lakeshore Equipment Co., 1144 Montague Avenue, San Leandro, Calif.
- Tip-it, Ideal Toy Co., 200 Fifth Avenue, New York, N.Y.
- Utility balls, basketballs, footballs
- Skateboards
- Standard Bongo-Board (grooved board on roller), F. A. O. Schwarz, 745 Fifth Avenue, New York, N.Y.
- Pogo stick, Constructive Playthings
- Mighty Tyke Trampoline, Leflar Enterprises, 6840 S.W. Macadam Avenue, Portland, Ore.
- Trampa Skills Coordinator, Trampa Manufacturing Co., 1710 Bell Avenue, Houston, Texas
- Vestibular Board, J. A. Preston Corp., 71 Fifth Avenue, New York, N.Y.

Further Evaluation

- Lincoln-Oseretsky Motor Development Scale: Test #2, crouching on tiptoe; #3 and #32, standing on one foot; #9, standing heel to toe; #15, balancing a rod crosswise, #28 and #34, balancing on tiptoe; #36, balancing a rod vertically

PRESCRIPTIVE ILLUSTRATION

Priority Teaching Objective: Bobby, eleven years old, educationally handicapped. Upon completion of this lesson Bobby will be able to maintain his balance, on the balance beam or on tiptoes, while bouncing a ball to the rhythm of drums.

Shown here are a variety of balance-board activities: balancing a book while shifting weight on the four-inch side of a two-by-four; balancing utility balls while shifting weight on the two-inch-side; and balancing a bamboo pole on a triangular fulcrum.

Walking the board, the pupil keeps time to a drumbeat while holding a glass of water in each hand and balancing a boiled egg held in a spoon between his teeth.

The pupil jumps on a sponge rubber mat while keeping time to a metronome.

All programs should be modified or extended to meet the needs of individual pupils.

Pretest Tasks: Bobby attempted to stand on tiptoes and bounce a ball to the rhythm of drums for approximately one minute. He was wobbly, could not keep the beat, and did not stand very high on his toes.

Specific Teaching Procedures: "Bobby, I want you to do three things for me today. Watch me now as I do each of the three things that you will be doing in a few minutes. First, I want you to walk this line on the floor, standing on your tiptoes, to the rhythm of the drums and looking at me, like this . . ."

"Second, you are to bounce the ball to the rhythm of the drums as you walk around the room without stopping or touching anything."

"Last, I want you to walk forward on the balance beam while bouncing the ball beside you to the rhythm of the drums, like this . . . Now tell me what you are to do."

Pupil: "I walk this line on tiptoes, bounce the ball around the room, and walk the balance beam and bounce the ball."

Performance Evaluation: Bobby walked the line with good balance, although his rhythm was off on slow beats. He could not change his rhythm in bouncing the ball, and he lost control once. He walked the beam well but lost the ball on fast beats.

Analysis and Comments: The task was appropriate but demanding for Bobby. Over a minute time period, he got four out of nine possible points on my scoring system. He needs much practice varying bounces to different rhythms, using the metronome or records.

For Self-instruction: Devise a teaching procedure and performance evaluation method for this pupil: Sylvia, ten years old, educable mentally retarded. Sylvia will be able to remain standing when a moving object on which she is standing (the "Lovable Legs" boards) comes to a sudden stop—in at least six out of eight trials. Sylvia received roller skates for Christmas, but complained that she fell over whenever she tried to stop, slow down, or go around the corner. Because she is obese and refuses to participate in many athletic activities, I felt it was necessary to teach her the skills that would make her play more enjoyable.

16/Body-Spatial Organization

DEFINITION: The ability to move one's body in an integrated way around and through objects in the spatial environment.

ILLUSTRATION: Pupil can run maze on playground or in classroom without bumping; can move easily through tunnels and use playground monkey bars; can imitate body positions in space.

EDUCATIONAL RATIONALE: Body awareness and control of movement in space should be taught through imitative and exploratory exercises. Provision should be made for special playground activities together with programs designed for use within the regular classroom.

SUGGESTED PROGRAM IDEAS

1. Beginning Activities
   a. Finger plays: Introduce elementary finger plays and poems. Teach advanced body position poems using *Finger Fun* or similar books.
   b. Spontaneous body organization: Children take turns calling out names of animals (monkey, elephant, lion, snake, etc.) and other pupils imitate animal positions.
   c. Climbing: Teacher gives directions: "Climb *on* the table. Climb *around* the chair. Climb *under* the table. Climb *in* the box. Climb *over* the chair. Climb *through* Billy's legs. Climb the ladder," etc.
   d. Record activities: Assume body position as directed in record, *Developing Body-Space Perception Motor Skills,* and similar recordings.
   e. Maze walk: Pupil walks through simple classroom chair maze without bumping.
   f. Freeze tag: Pupils play tag and freeze body position when touched.

2. Middle Stage Activities
   a. Twister game: First, pupil plays game by self to develop body control. Next, he plays with two or three others in competition.
   b. Climbing patterns: Using Climbing Crate or Monkey Bars, have pupils imitate teacher's climbing patterns. Play Follow-the-Leader.
   c. Simon Says: With a pupil-leader, play game with class following leader. "Simon says stand on your right leg like this, crawl like a dog, play tennis, climb a mountain, wash a window," etc.
   d. Running maze: Lay out chair maze in room and have pupils run it for time records without bumping. Gradually reduce size of maze to require better body control.
   e. Body position exercises: Follow exercises from Frostig and Kephart programs.
   f. Rocket ship: Pupils crouch down, count to "blast-off," jump up and run around other pupils placed as planets in space.
   g. Charades: Act out favorite story using objects and body positions.

3. Advanced Activities
   a. Maze bounce: Pupils run complex classroom maze while bouncing a ball, without disturbing floor arrangement.
   b. Chinese jump rope: Two pupils spread large plastic band between their feet. Player jumps in and out, crosses feet, moves band with feet, etc.
   c. Obstacle course: Lay out outdoor obstacle course involving varied body movements and control of position in space.
   d. Paddle tennis: Teach regular paddle tennis and eye-hand-body control and position.

61

e. Mirror image: Pupil first imitates teacher's body movement, watching the *back* of the instructor. Teacher then turns and faces pupil who imitates body movements with correct right and left orientation. Use full-length mirror for pupil to see himself while assuming mirror positions so that he may make comparisons with teacher's model.

f. Sports: Teach body positions required in tennis and skiing and provide for participation.

g. Alphabet positions: Leader calls out letters of the alphabet and pupils attempt to create letters with body positions.

REFERENCES

Barsch, Ray H. "Spatial Awareness." *Achieving Perceptual Motor Efficiency.* Seattle: Special Child Publications, 1967.

Dunsing, Jack D., and Kephart, Newell C. "Motor Generalizations in Space and Time." *Learning Disorders,* Vol. 1, edited by Jerome Hellmuth, pp. 77–121. Seattle: Special Child Publications, 1965.

Related Programs

* *Developing Body-Space Perception Motor Skills* (record), Educational Record Sales, 157 Chambers Street, New York, N.Y.
* *Nursery Rhymes for Dramatic Play* (record), Educational Record Sales
* Painter, Genevieve. "The Effect of a Rhythmic and Sensory Motor Activity Program on Perceptual-Motor Spatial Abilities of Kindergarten Children." *Exceptional Children,* October, 1966, pp. 113–116.
* Frostig, Marianne, and Horne, David. "Relationship of the Body to Other Objects" and "Duplicating Various Body Positions." *The Frostig Program for the Development of Visual Perception: Teacher's Guide.* Chicago: Follett Publishing, 1964.
* Wagner, Guy, et al. *Educational Games and Activities.* Darien, Conn.: Teachers Publishing, 1966.
* Goldstein, Herbert, and Levitt, Edith. *A Reading Readiness Workbook in Spatial Discrimination.* Parkinson Program for Special Children. Chicago: Follett Publishing, 1965.

Instructional Materials

* Twister Game, Milton Bradley Toy Company
* Record player
* Rest Pads, California Correctional Industries, 1400 S Street, Sacramento, Calif.
* Crawl-through Barrel Horse, California Correctional Industries
* *Finger Play Poems for Children, Finger Fun,* Palfrey's Educational Supply Co., 7715 E. Garvey Boulevard, Rosemead, Calif.
* Body Board, Lyndon Craft Educational Equipment, P.O. Box 12, Rosemead, Calif.
* Complete Lind Climber Unit with Beam, Lind Climber Co., 807 Reba Place, Evanston, Ill.
* Rocking chair

Further Evaluation

* Purdue Perceptual-Motor Survey
* Lincoln-Oseretsky Motor Development Scale: Test #4, touching nose; #5, touching fingertips; #6, tapping rhythmically with feet and fingers; #8, finger movement

PRESCRIPTIVE ILLUSTRATION

Priority Teaching Objective: Joyce, eight years old, minimal cerebral dysfunction. When presented pictures of body positions in space, Joyce will be able to imitate four of the five positions correctly.

Pretest Tasks: When Joyce was presented the first two body position pictures and asked to imitate them, she put her hands over her head and walked around the room.

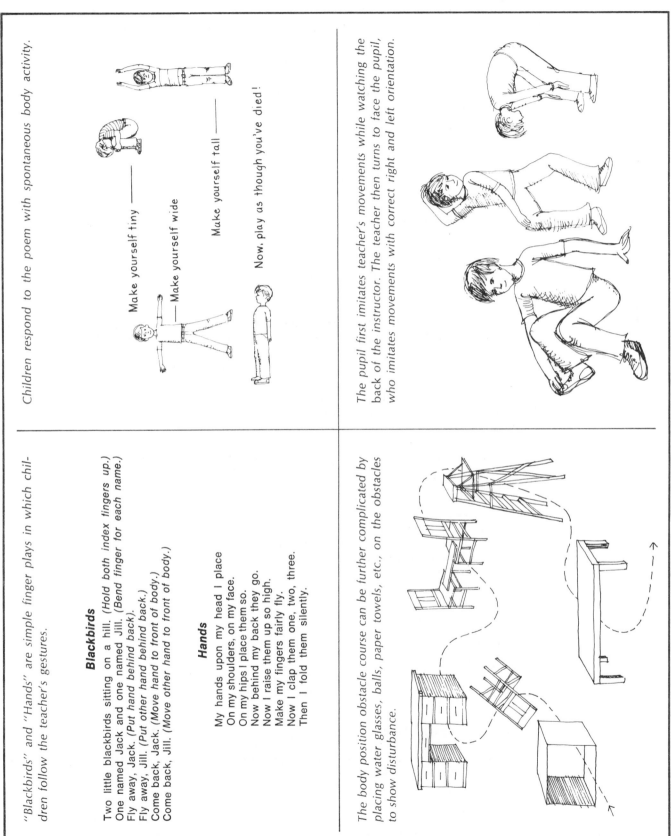

Children respond to the poem with spontaneous body activity.

Make yourself tiny

Make yourself wide

Make yourself tall

Now, play as though you've died!

The pupil first imitates teacher's movements while watching the back of the instructor. The teacher then turns to face the pupil, who imitates movements with correct right and left orientation.

"Blackbirds" and "Hands" are simple finger plays in which children follow the teacher's gestures.

Blackbirds

Two little blackbirds sitting on a hill. *(Hold both index fingers up.)*
One named Jack and one named Jill. *(Bend finger for each name.)*
Fly away, Jack. *(Put hand behind back).*
Fly away, Jill. *(Put other hand behind back.)*
Come back, Jack. *(Move hand to front of body.)*
Come back, Jill. *(Move other hand to front of body.)*

Hands

My hands upon my head I place
On my shoulders, on my face.
On my hips I place them so.
Now behind my back they go.
Now I raise them up so high.
Make my fingers fairly fly.
Now I clap them one, two, three.
Then I fold them silently.

The body position obstacle course can be further complicated by placing water glasses, balls, paper towels, etc., on the obstacles to show disturbance.

Specific Teaching Procedures: "Joyce, look at me! See how I am standing like this picture with my feet together and my arms over my head."

"Now watch the picture as I put your legs together like that girl's. Now I am putting your arms over your head like hers. That's right!"

"Look at yourself in this mirror now. See how your legs and arms are together like the picture. That was good, and here is a corn chip for you to eat because you did that just right."

"Now look at this picture. See how the girl's feet are spread apart, and her arms go straight out from her shoulders? Watch how I do it. See me in the mirror!"

"There, now, I have moved your feet apart. Put your arms out and look in the mirror. Fine. Here is another corn chip to eat."

"You know what to do now, don't you? You stand like the girl in the picture."

Pupil: "Mmmm, mmmm—stand like the girl in the picture."

"Here are some other pictures for us to imitate."

Performance Evaluation: The initial lesson took about twenty-five minutes and Joyce did make an attempt to imitate the body positions as long as she was reinforced with corn chips. For the first three positions, she had to be assisted arranging her body parts in space. The fourth picture was demonstrated by the teacher and quickly imitated. The fifth picture was imitated directly by Joyce with no errors.

Analysis and Comments: The task was appropriate and quite demanding for Joyce. It will be continued on a reduced reinforcement schedule.

For Self-instruction: Devise a teaching procedure and performance evaluation method for this student: Manuel, thirteen years old, minimal cerebral dysfunction. Upon completion of this training program, Manuel will be able to follow the leader in using the Lind Climber. He will be able to duplicate the leader's body positions without gross error.

Sensory-Motor Integration

17/Reaction-Speed Dexterity

DEFINITION: The ability to attend and respond efficiently to general directions or assignments.

ILLUSTRATION: Pupil can attend to the teacher sufficiently to comprehend total directions; can proceed to organize self and respond adequately to complete the given assignment within a normal time expectancy; can demonstrate attention to task, concentration, and order.

EDUCATIONAL RATIONALE: Remedial activities should be planned so that they may be clearly understood and successfully accomplished within a given period of time. Children should be guided through problem-solving procedures, including listening and analytical skills, and good study habits.

SUGGESTED PROGRAM IDEAS

1. Beginning Activities
   a. Simple directions: Give simple directions to the individual pupil, e.g., "Bring me that book," "Sharpen these pencils," and reward for prompt and accurate responses.
   b. Sound patterns: "Listen carefully to this drum beat, because when I finish, I want you do it right after me."
   c. Story poems: Use finger and story poems which require pupils to pay attention and respond immediately.
   d. Puzzle race: Keep individual pupil time records for completing various puzzles. Reward (candy, etc.) for significant improvement in performance. Sort nuts and bolts by sizes and record time required.
   e. Animal care assignment: Assign pupil to feed animals and clean cages. Outline steps involved and supervise to successful accomplishment.
   f. Dressing: Time individual performance in getting sweaters, coats, shoes, boots, etc., on and off. Reward improvement.
   g. Copy work: Assign simple copy work assignment from chalkboard and record time. Reward significant improvement in accuracy and time of completion.
   h. Follow the leader games: "Run," "Jump," "Touch the floor," "pinch your nose," etc.
   i. Fire drill: Practice improving time in fire drill exercises.
2. Middle Stage Activities
   a. Jacks: Play jacks, time performance, and record improvement.
   b. Echo game races: Using teams, have first child run to next and relay message. Continue down the line. Winner is team that successfully competes given instructions in least time.
   c. Poems: Teach simple nursery poems in step-by-step sequence and use tape recorder upon accomplishment.
   d. Study office: For easily distracted children, use individual 3' × 3' × 5' study booths with individual teacher aid, listening post, or tape recorder.
   e. Pegboard programs: Use Judy Pegboards for timed manipulation and completion of designs.
   f. Construction projects: Assign and time individual construction projects using Tinker Toys, models, etc.
   g. Play attention games: Scissors-Rock-Paper, Red Light–Green Light, Pick-up-Sticks, etc.; ping-pong, treasure hunts (timed), card games like Slap Jack.

65

3. Advanced Activities
   a. Craft and shop projects: Teach objectives, pattern, procedure of project; record beginning and completion times and dates.
   b. Cooking: Teach efficient timed cooking projects (fudge, cookies, etc.).
   c. Drama: Assign parts for simple classroom play and teach appropriate timed responses.
   d. Study habits: Teach procedures of determining objectives, planning, surveying, reading, analyzing, applying, evaluating.
   e. Individual projects: Develop and assign individual study projects in applied and academic subjects. Guide and supervise pupil to insure successful completion of project in required time.
   f. Self letters: Pupil writes short letter to himself each day explaining what he did yesterday and what he plans to do today.
   g. Object assembly: Time assembly of assorted nuts and bolts, washers, simple models, puzzles, etc.
   h. Thread film projectors and recorders.

REFERENCES

Cohen, Rosalyn S., and La Vetes, Ruth. "Clinical Principles of Curriculum Selection." *Educational Therapy*, Vol. 1, edited by Jerome Hellmuth, pp. 139–154. Seattle: Special Child Publications, 1966.

Related Programs

- *Kindergarten-Primary Art Activities, Golden Do-It Book, Creative Crafts, Craft Ideas for Girls*, Palfrey's Educational Supply Co., 7715 E. Garvey Boulevard, Rosemead, Calif.
- Sutphin, Florence E. *Listening: A Perceptual Testing-Training Handbook for First Grade Teachers*, pp. 84–85. Winter Haven, Fla.: Winter Haven Lions Research, 1964.
- Model-building and craft programs of all kinds from toy stores
- *What to Do for Primary Plays* (costumes and scenery projects), Lakeshore Equipment Co., 1144 Montague Avenue, San Leandro, Calif.
- *TAC—Training of Attention and Concentration Program*, Dept. SC, Educational Research Association, Inc., P.O. Box 6604, Philadelphia, Pa.
- *Impulse Control and Relaxation Training* (activity records), Educational Activities, Inc., Freeport, Long Island, N.Y.
- *Following Directions and Sequence* (workbook 4-94), Milliken Publishing Co., 611 Olive Street, St. Louis, Mo.

Instructional Materials

- Senior Mixed–Shape-Finding Set, Teaching Aids, 159 W. Kinzie Street, Chicago, Ill.
- Peg Grading Board, Post and Tablet Fitting Board, Peg Levelling Board, Judy 100 Pegboard, Palfrey's Educational Supply Co.
- Listening post, record player, tape recorder
- Tinker Toys
- Model cars, boats, and airplanes for model building
- Stopwatch
- Assorted nuts and bolts for sorting tasks
- Assorted Judy Puzzles, The Judy Company, Minneapolis, Minn.
- Projectors and tape recorders for threading
- Origami (with instructions), Palfrey's Educational Supply Co.

Further Evaluation

- Lincoln-Oseretsky Motor Development Scale: Test #10, close and open hands alternately; #16, describing circles in the air; #12, catching a ball
- Wechsler Intelligence Scale for Children: coding subtests
- Subjective evaluation of speed and accuracy in completing assigned classroom tasks

This simple puzzle code can be placed on the board. Pupils should replace numbers on the puzzle with the specified designs.

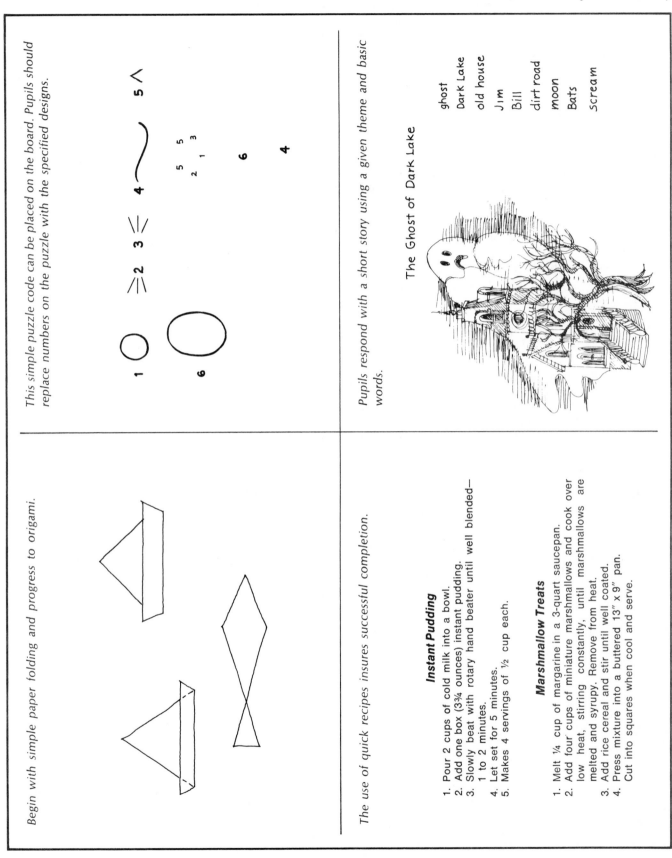

Pupils respond with a short story using a given theme and basic words.

The Ghost of Dark Lake

ghost
Dark Lake
old house
Jim
Bill
dirt road
moon
Bats
Scream

Begin with simple paper folding and progress to origami.

The use of quick recipes insures successful completion.

Instant Pudding

1. Pour 2 cups of cold milk into a bowl.
2. Add one box (3¾ ounces) instant pudding.
3. Slowly beat with rotary hand beater until well blended— 1 to 2 minutes.
4. Let set for 5 minutes.
5. Makes 4 servings of ½ cup each.

Marshmallow Treats

1. Melt ¼ cup of margarine in a 3-quart saucepan.
2. Add four cups of miniature marshmallows and cook over low heat, stirring constantly, until marshmallows are melted and syrupy. Remove from heat.
3. Add rice cereal and stir until well coated.
4. Press mixture into a buttered 13″ x 9″ pan. Cut into squares when cool and serve.

All programs should be modified or extended to meet the needs of individual pupils.

Priority Teaching Objective: John, thirteen years old, repeating regular sixth grade. John is easily distracted by outside stimuli as well as internal ones. It is difficult for him to follow a series of directions or attend to a task for any length of time. He seldom completes assignments and if he does, they are handed in late. John will be able to follow a series of oral directions and perform the physical task to completion, without distraction, for a given time of no less than one minute.

Pretest Tasks: John was given two oral directions requiring him to complete a perceptual block design and was unknowingly timed. He needed repetition of the directions and was distracted within forty seconds.

Specific Teaching Procedures: "John, we are going to do a number of things to help you improve your concentration. I want you to do each one as quickly and as well as you can. Here is a stopwatch. When you have completed each task, you can write down the time it took you. We will also keep this chart to see how well you are doing and how many errors you may have made."

"Now here is the first one. Look at this block design and then make one just like it on this blocked-off paper."

"Good! The next task is to finish this dot-to-dot picture as well as you can."

"Now arrange these geometric shapes in this pattern as quickly as you can."

Performance Evaluation: John was praised as he worked on his tasks. It quickly became important for him to "beat the clock." On a posttest of three oral directions, he proceeded without questions and distractions and beat his last record of three minutes and fifty seconds.

Analysis and Comments: Since the time element seemed to intrigue John, we will continue with it, slowly increasing the difficulty of the assignments and lengthening the time expectancy. We will also involve John in doing some of these tasks with several other children directly around him.

For Self-instruction: Devise a teaching procedure and performance evaluation method for this pupil: Laurie, eight years old, regular second grade. Laurie has a very short attention span, poor work habits, and great difficulty in starting her written work. Upon completion of these lessons, Laurie will be able to follow three-step written directions from the teacher as presented to her in letter form.

18/Tactile Discrimination

DEFINITION: The ability to identify and match objects by touching and feeling.
ILLUSTRATION: With hidden toys and materials, pupil can match objects with both left and right hands, name or classify materials or substances, differentiate weights, and discriminate temperatures.
EDUCATIONAL RATIONALE: Since tactile discrimination and sensory integration are primary to higher level perceptual and cognitive learning, all preschool, primary, and remedial education programs should provide systematic training in these areas.

SUGGESTED PROGRAM IDEAS

1. Basic Tactile Awareness
   a. Animal textures: Teach textures by playing with chickens, turtles, rats, dogs, cats, birds, snakes, etc. Feel differences between whiskers, nails, body, etc. Explore, feel, and discuss human hair, nails, skin, body parts.
   b. Wet materials: Explore texture of mud, wet sand, finger paint, moist clay, water, milk, syrup, etc.
   c. Dry elements: Explore texture of dry sand, dirt, pebbles, rocks, cement, brick, wood, cloth, rough and smooth paper, etc.
   d. Clothing textures: Explore and label differences in velvet, furs, satin, silk, wool, cotton, nylon, etc. Make books from different types of cloth.
   e. Food discrimination: Explore tactually the texture, size, and shape differences of apples, oranges, bananas, pears, potatoes, tomatoes, grapes, etc.
   f. Geometric form discrimination: Explore differences between wooden geometric forms.
   g. Symbol exploration: Feel differences between wooden letters and numerals.
   h. Pour water, sand, buttons, stones, mud, etc. from can to can, pail to pail, test tube to test tube, glass to glass, etc.
   i. Place ice cube on arms and body. Write how it feels.
   j. Place hot washcloths on hands and face. Write feelings.
   k. Use small muscle vibrator to stimulate arms and back. Describe feelings.
   l. Make clay objects and mud bricks or adobe.
   m. Splash water in sinks, pools, etc. for tactile awareness.
2. Tactile Matching and Discrimination
   a. Common objects: Teach tactual differences between common objects; e.g., spoon, knife, fork, glass, ball, shoe, nail, tack, coin, string, etc. Play hidden matching games with duplicate objects, using small tablecloth as cover.
   b. Gradations: Teach tactual gradations of fine to rough sandpaper, long and short sticks, light and heavy objects (wood blocks, marbles, fishing sinkers, etc.), big and little forms (squares, circles, triangles).
   c. Scissors activities: Use scissors for tactile-kinesthetic matching and duplication by cutting fringes, curves, straight lines, and forms from paper, cloth, cardboard, and leafy vegetables, such as cabbage leaves, potato peels, and fruit skins.
   d. Body localization: Teach child to duplicate teacher stimulation of pupil body areas such as touching points on head, face, soles of feet, hands and fingers held behind back, neck, etc., using blunt pencil or nail.

69

e. Blindfold games: Pupil is blindfolded and led to teacher's desk, etc. Must describe where he is by feeling surroundings.

3. Stereognosis

a. Finger designs: Teacher draws forms on child's palm while child's hand is behind back. Child then reproduces design on teacher's hand and on paper with pencil drawing.

b. Temperature differentiation: Teach child to feel differences in four bowls of water. Arrange in sequence from cold, cool, warm, hot.

c. Basic form patching: Present child a hidden geometric form or parquetry block in his right hand under the tablecloth. Have him find identical form under another cloth using his left hand. Repeat, reversing hands.

d. Form generalization: Teach child to match hidden forms which vary only by size, e.g., large and small blocks, triangles, wooden letters, numbers, etc.

e. Symbol matching and generalization: First present single wooden letter or numeral so it can be seen and felt with one hand. Then require pupil to find identical hidden symbol with other hand. Extend exercise, covertly presenting the symbol to one hand and requiring covert matching with other hand. With older pupils, teach the name of the symbol and require verbal identification together with hidden tactual matching.

f. Simultaneous reproduction: Pupil draws picture of hidden object (bottle, ball, etc.) which he is feeling with other hand.

g. Blindfold tasks: Put simple puzzles and objects together while blindfolded. Identify coins while blindfolded.

REFERENCES

Anderson, Robert P. "Physiologic Considerations in Learning: The Tactual Mode." *Learning Disorders,* Vol. 2, edited by Jerome Hellmuth, pp. 97–112. Seattle: Special Child Publications, 1966.

Montessori, Maria. "Sensory Education." *Dr. Montessori's Own Handbook,* pp. 65–123. New York: Schocken Books, 1965.

Related Programs
- Montessori Thermal Cylinders, and Touch Boards (teaching aids), A. Daigger & Co., 159 W. Kinzie Street, Chicago, Ill.
- Touch Alphabet-Object Boards, Touch Numbers Board, My Guide to Safety Tactile Materials, Touch Incorporated, Albany, N.Y.
- Programs developed to teach differentiation of tastes and smells
- Montessori program adaptations
- Tactile Letter Block Board, Childcraft Equipment Co., Inc., 155 E. 23rd Street, New York, N.Y.

Instructional Materials
- Texture Ball, Creative Playthings, Princeton, N.J.
- Kinesthetic Alphabet, R. H. Stone Products, Box 414, Detroit, Mich.
- Graded Cylinder Blocks with Knobs, Constructive Playthings, 1040 E. 85th Street, Kansas City, Mo.
- Touch ABC Lower-case Letters, Warrens' Educational Supplies, 980 San Bernardino Road, Covina, Calif.
- Box of assorted fabrics
- Large Geometric Solids, Small Geometric Solids (teaching aids), Daigger & Co.
- Wood Lower-case Letters, Wood Numerals, Constructive Playthings
- Sandbox
- Fingerpaint
- Clay and crock
- Scissors and cutting materials
- Cans and boxes of rocks, gravel, soils, etc.
- Sandpaper Touch Boards (teaching aids), Daigger & Co.

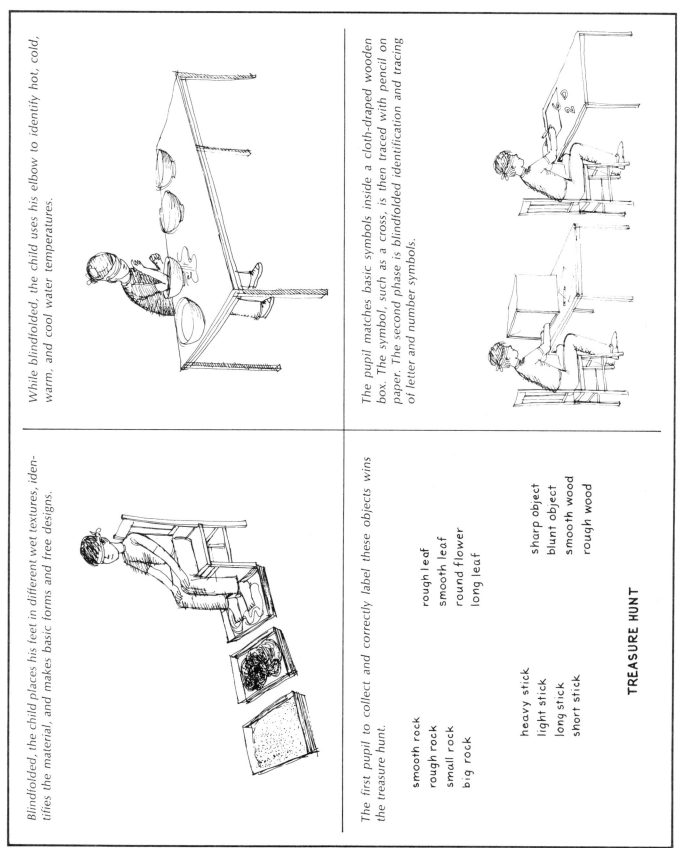

While blindfolded, the child uses his elbow to identify hot, cold, warm, and cool water temperatures.

The pupil matches basic symbols inside a cloth-draped wooden box. The symbol, such as a cross, is then traced with pencil on paper. The second phase is blindfolded identification and tracing of letter and number symbols.

Blindfolded, the child places his feet in different wet textures, identifies the material, and makes basic forms and free designs.

The first pupil to collect and correctly label these objects wins the treasure hunt.

smooth rock
rough rock
small rock
big rock

rough leaf
smooth leaf
round flower
long leaf

heavy stick
light stick
long stick
short stick

sharp object
blunt object
smooth wood
rough wood

TREASURE HUNT

All programs should be modified or extended to meet the needs of individual pupils.

- Letter Form Board, Houghton Mifflin Co., 110 Tremont Street, Boston, Mass.
- Feeley Meeley Game, Sears, Roebuck and Co.
- Massager, Sears, Roebuck and Co.

Further Evaluation
- Subjectively developed tactile tests of object recognition
- Ayres Southern California Kinesthesia and Tactile Perception Test
- Valett Developmental Survey of Basic Learning Abilities: tactile discrimination

PRESCRIPTIVE ILLUSTRATION

Priority Teaching Objective: Betty, seven years old, educationally handicapped. Betty will be able to identify the wooden letters A, B, G, Y, X, and T by touch, upon feeling them in a covered cloth bag.

Pretest Tasks: Betty was presented the letters A, B, G, Y, X, and T in a cloth bag. She was asked to reach in with her right hand and bring out one letter at a time as requested. She was able to identify only the letter T.

Specific Teaching Objectives: "Betty, look at each of these letters. Here are A, B, G, Y, X, and T. As I place each letter in your right hand, you name it for me. Let's start with this one [G]. What is it?"

Pupil: "The G."

"Good. Now here are the others. This time, as I give you each letter, I want you to feel it carefully with your right hand, rub your fingers around it, touch it all over, and then tell me what it is. Now take this one [X]. Feel it and tell me what it is."

Pupil: "It is the X and feels funny."

"Fine. Now as I give you each letter, feel it with your right hand, then your left hand, and then both hands together. Feel it carefully and tell me what it is. After you have told me what it is, I want you to drop the letter in this bag."

"Now you have three letters in the bag. Reach in and take one letter, feel it, and tell me what it is. Then show it to me."

"All of the letters are in the bag now. This time, reach in and tell me what the letter is and then show them all to me, one at a time."

Performance Evaluation: The task was an appropriate one for Betty. She seemed to respond immediately to touching the letter. She made no mistakes as the lesson progressed.

Analysis and Comments: Betty was highly motivated to learn these letters for the first time, as the alphabet usually "turns her off." She has some difficulty using her left hand. The same exercise will be continued with other alphabet letters.

For Self-instruction: Devise a teaching procedure and performance evaluation method for this pupil: Elaine, nine years old, regular third grade with reversal problems. Upon completion of these lessons, Elaine will be able to identify the following numbers and letters when they are "written" on her back with a small mechanical vibrator: 2, 3, 6, 9, b, d, p, q, u, n. After she has identified them orally, Elaine will be able to write the letters and numbers correctly.

Sensory-Motor Integration

19/Directionality

DEFINITION: The ability to know right from left, up from down, forward from backward, and directional orientation.

ILLUSTRATION: Pupil can write and follow picture story or reading material from left to right, discriminate right and left body parts and those of other people, locate directions in room and school.

EDUCATIONAL RATIONALE: Since many learning and problem-solving situations require directional orientation, it is important that these skills be specifically taught if necessary. Such instruction should begin with body orientation and proceed to object relationships and concrete applications.

SUGGESTED PROGRAM IDEAS

1. Body Orientation
   a. Hand and foot identification: Place red ribbon or bracelet on right hand and leg. "Simon says touch the floor with your right hand. Shake your left foot. Touch your right foot," etc.
   b. Other body parts: Teach right and left ears, fingers, toes, shoulders, ankles, knees, legs, arms, elbows, wrist, teeth, sides of body. Play body identification games such as Follow-the-Leader.
   c. Music and rhythm: Play marching music and give commands—"Stamp your left foot. Slap your right side," etc.
   d. Tracing: Trace and cut out right and left hands and feet. Color or paint, and place on bulletin board for constant reference.
   e. Whole body movement: Give directions—"Move over to the left of John. Sit in the chair to the right of my desk. Crawl under the first table to the left of the door," etc.
   f. Finger localization: Ditto off standard left and right hand designs. Give directions— "Color the left fingers green. Place a ring on the right first finger. Put an x on the left thumbnail. Place your left thumb on your right little finger," etc.
   g. Body imitation: Teach pupil to name what body part teacher or other pupil is moving and then to duplicate the movement ("left thumb," etc.).
2. Object Relations
   a. Paper marking: Teach marking and drawing on right, left, middle, top, and bottom parts of paper according to directions.
   b. Alternate commands: Instruct pupil to respond with the opposite direction—"Raise your right hand. Grasp your left shoulder," etc.
   c. Sorting games: Have children sort right and left gloves, shoes, paper hand and foot outlines, up and down objects (birds, submarines, etc.).
   d. Dressing: Have children put on right or left shoe, glove; untie and tie shoelaces; place things in pockets, etc.
   e. Up-down/above-below. Teach concepts and practice placing the book *up* on the shelf, putting the paper *down* in the basket, tossing the ball *above* the head, crawling *below* the table, etc.
   f. Map directions: Teach north, south, east, west. Locate and mark sides of the room. Generalize to school layout. Play games with children placing themselves according to map directions: "Billy, go north of Mary." Design and use "treasure hunt" maps.
   g. Jump to music: "Jump in—jump out—jump north—jump south," etc.

h. General objects: Teach right-left discrimination of animals, cars, buildings, trains, theaters, etc.

i. Drawing: Place x mark on the left side of board or paper for pupil to begin drawing.

3. Application and Generalization

a. Pledge of Allegiance: Stand on *right* side of the desk with *right* hand on the heart.

b. Picture identification: Show photographs and magazine pictures of persons and directional objects and have pupil identify. Use colored slides and films for directional discussion.

c. Chalkboard and paper orientation: Practice marking and doing exercises on right, left, top, bottom, middle, etc. Use marble boards.

d. Map projects: Locate directions, common buildings, and places on city and area maps. Draw map of school, classroom, and neighborhood.

e. Writing: Trace patterns and words with crayon, beginning at left side marker and proceeding to the right. Have children sign their names on paper in upper *left* corner to avoid reversals.

f. Sequential activities: Arrange sequence puzzles or cartoons from left to right on desk, floor, chalkboard trays, etc. Arrange wooden number series and word forms from left to right.

REFERENCES

Benton, Arthur L. *Right-Left Discrimination and Finger Localization*. New York: Hoeber, 1959.

Related Programs

- *Developing Body-Space Perception Motor Skills,* Album 2 (record), Educational Record Sales, 157 Chambers Street, New York, N.Y.
- Pattison, William D. "Which Way: A Guide to Direction." *Going Places*. Chicago: Rand McNally, 1968.
- *Marching Along* (record), Educational Record Sales
- Frostig, Marianne, and Horne, David. "Differentiating Left from Right." *The Frostig Program for the Development of Visual Perception: Teacher's Guide,* pp. 54–68. Chicago: Follett Publishing, 1964.
- Kephart, Newell C. *The Slow Learner in the Classroom,* pp. 46–69. Columbus, Ohio: Merrill Books, 1962.
- Zweig-Bruno Stereo-Tracing Exercise Pads (for proper directionality), Keystone View Company, Meadville, Pa.
- Berkeley, Ethel. *Big & Little, Up & Down: Early Concepts of Size and Direction*. New York: Young Scott Books, 1960.
- Directional-Locational Audio Flashcard Set, Electronics Futures, Inc., 57 Dodge Avenue, North Haven, Conn.
- *Try: Experiences for Young Children,* Task 1-2-3, Noble and Noble, Inc., 750 Third Avenue, New York, N.Y.
- Directional-spatial pattern board exercises, Teaching Resources, 100 Boylston Street, Boston, Mass.
- The Foolers Game: Reversals in Reading or Writing, Facilitation House, Box 611, Ottawa, Ill.
- Left-Right Discrimination Program, Facilitation House

Instructional Materials

- Judy See-Quees, Series 12, The Judy Company, Minneapolis, Minn.
- Mazes and directional puzzles
- Old jewelry bracelets for arms and legs
- Colored ribbons for activity programs
- Record player
- School-made map and layout, city, state, U.S.; world maps
- Felt pens and drawing paper
- Stencils and forms for directional tracing

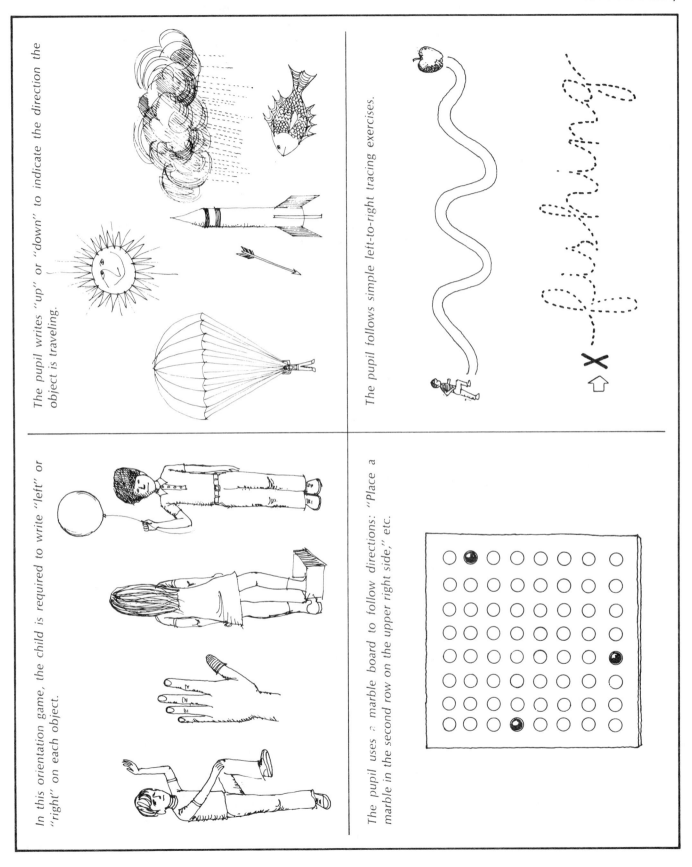

The pupil writes "up" or "down" to indicate the direction the object is traveling.

The pupil follows simple left-to-right tracing exercises.

In this orientation game, the child is required to write "left" or "right" on each object.

The pupil uses a marble board to follow directions: "Place a marble in the second row on the upper right side," etc.

All programs should be modified or extended to meet the needs of individual pupils.

- Wood Lower-case Letters, Wood Numerals, Constructive Playthings, 1040 E. 85th Street, Kansas City, Mo.
- Motor and Hand-Eye Coordination—Left to Right (transparency-duplicating book), Milliken Publishing Co., St. Louis, Mo.

Further Evaluation
- Money Roadmap Test of Direction Sense, Johns Hopkins Press, Baltimore, Md.
- Porteus Maze Tests
- Subjective appraisal of pupil response to directional commands, drawing, and writing activities

PRESCRIPTIVE ILLUSTRATION

Priority Teaching Objective: Raymond, ten years old, educationally handicapped. Upon completion of the lesson, Raymond will be able to follow tape-recorded directions requiring that he mark eight symbols on a directional training worksheet.

Pretest Tasks: Raymond was presented a simple worksheet with six symbols arranged on it. He was unable to mark any of the symbols correctly according to their location on the paper.

Specific Teaching Procedures: "Raymond, I want you to look at this worksheet. You see it has a lot of symbols on it in six different sections. You can see that the top and bottom and left sides of the pages are marked. Put your finger on the top of the page. Good! Now put your finger on the bottom of the page. Now point to the right side. Now point to the left side."

"This tape recorder contains directions for you to listen to and follow. Listen carefully and mark the symbol with this red felt pen as it directs you to do so."

(Sample direction: "Mark the circle in the left top box. Mark the letter *B* in the middle box on the bottom.")

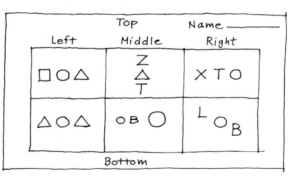

Performance Evaluation: Raymond was given training on several of the directional worksheets. On the posttest he was able to mark correctly seven of the eight symbols.

Analysis and Comments: The task was demanding and appropriate for Raymond. His motivation and attention increased noticeably with use of the tape recorder. The symbols should be increasingly more difficult and eventuate in practice exercises locating nonsense words and real words on worksheets of various sizes.

For Self-instruction: Devise a teaching procedure and performance evaluation method for this pupil: Dale, seven years old, educable mentally retarded. During music, I discovered that Dale was often confused about "right" and "left" body parts. Also, during the Pledge of Allegiance, he frequently used the left hand and asked if that was the right hand. I would like Dale to be able to place the right and left body parts (hands and feet) on the "pumpkin man" after the parts have been traced on paper (using his hands and feet for the shapes), identified, and cut out.

Sensory-Motor Integration

20/Laterality

DEFINITION: *The ability to integrate one's sensory-motor contact with the environment through establishment of homolateral hand, eye, and foot dominance.*
ILLUSTRATION: *Pupil has consistent right- or left-sided approach in use of eyes, hands, and feet in tasks such as kicking balls, cutting paper, sighting telescope, writing, etc.*
EDUCATIONAL RATIONALE: *Lateral consistency in body orientation to problem-solving situations reduces psychomotor conflict and furthers sensory-motor integration and learning. Where gross inconsistency and neurological immaturity exist, training programs should reinforce laterality and help to establish habitual modes of response.*

SUGGESTED PROGRAM IDEAS

1. Body Organization
   a. Visual orientation: Indicate visual target and teach turning, creeping, crawling, walking, and running to the target.
   b. Crawling: Teach cross-pattern crawling toward targets. Right hand and left knee (left hand and right knee) should touch floor simultaneously.
   c. Walking: Teach cross-pattern, target-oriented walking, with opposite hand and foot moving forward at the same time.
   d. Running: Teach cross-pattern, target-oriented running with head held up and easy breathing.
   e. Walking board balance beam: Teach coordinated movement toward visual target.
   f. Trampoline: Use trampoline or mattress to reinforce body control.
   g. Batting stance: Teach softball stance and practice on side of dominant hand and eye.
   h. Directionality: Teach conscious awareness of directions and body orientation.

2. Hand Dominance: Reinforce the naturally preferred and strongest hand.
   a. Squeezing: Squeeze clutch ball, sponges, clothespins, and handgrip springs; crumple paper.
   b. Cutting: Cut paper, cardboard, cloth. Then coordinate hand and eye with form cut-outs.
   c. Throwing: Begin with underhand toss for accuracy; extend to overhand softball throw into target.
   d. Drawing: Practice drawing and painting with dominant hand.
   e. Tracing: Hold objects with subdominant hand and trace with dominant. Trace forms and wooden letters blindfolded. Trace subdominant hand on chalkboard using dominant hand.
   f. Kinesthetic exercises: Use dominant hand to feel and identify objects, scribble on chalkboard, erase board, finger and hand paint, manipulate finger and hand puppets, wind mechanical toys, feel thread, string, and rope.
   g. Sewing: Use large needle and thread. Sew simple patterns coordinating dominant hand and eye.
   h. Writing: Teach proper writing position and practice with dominant hand. Write wearing bracelet or wrist band to reinforce dominance.
   i. Typewriting: Encourage finger typing with dominant hand.
   j. Puppets: Use hand puppets on dominant hand in a skit.

3. Foot Dominance: Reinforce the foot on the same side as the dominant hand.
   a. Kicking: Teach how to kick football and soccer ball. Play soccer.
   b. Hopping: Have hopping relays on dominant foot.
   c. Object sorting: Using dominant foot and toes, sort colored marbles, toys, crumpled paper, etc.
   d. Toe painting: Using finger paints, make pictures with dominant foot.
   e. Drawing: Use big crayons or felt pens for scribbling and drawing exercises with dominant foot.
   f. Guiding exercises: Using dominant foot, push wood block along taped or chalked course to target.

4. Eye Dominance: Reinforce the eye on the same side as the dominant hand.
   a. Sighting: Sight targets through cardboard and paper tubes, peep-holes in paper, telescope.
   b. Visual pursuit: Teach child to follow pencil or thumbtack target held by teacher and then by self while blocking subdominant eye.
   c. Occlusion: Use temporary eye patch or cardboard square held in front of subdominant eye to reinforce dominant eye during visual tracking or reading exercises.
   d. Games: Play darts, archery, target shooting, sighting with dominant eye.
   e. Mirror tracing: For nonreaders with obvious mixed laterality, use mirror tracing and training procedures to establish visual-motor orientation and integration.
   f. Reading: For readers with mixed laterality, use stereo training programs.

REFERENCES

Fernald, Grace M. "Theories of Causation of Reading Disability." *Remedial Techniques in Basic School Subjects*, pp. 157–178. New York: McGraw-Hill, 1943.

Goddes, William H. "The Needs of Teachers for Specialized Information on Handedness, Finger Localization, and Cerebral Dominance." *The Teacher of Brain-Injured Children*, edited by W. Cruickshank, pp. 207–221. Syracuse: Syracuse University Press, 1966.

Related Programs

- *Developing Body-Space Perception Motor Skills,* Album 2 (record), Educational Record Sales, 157 Chambers Street, New York, N.Y.
- Kephart, Newell C. *The Slow Learner in the Classroom.* Columbus, Ohio: Merrill Books, 1962.
- Stereo-reader Training: Combined Delacato (pads AA) and Leavell (pads BB) materials, Keystone View Company, Meadville, Pa.
- Barger Mirror Technique Mirror Reading Board and Manual, R. L. Borclay Manufacturing, P.O. Box 633, Great Neck, Long Island, N.Y.
- *Neurological Organization in the Classroom,* Systems for Education, Inc., 612 N. Michigan Avenue, Chicago, Ill.
- The Left-Right Discrimination Program, Facilitation House, Box 611, Ottawa, Ill.

Instructional Materials

- Mirror Tracing, LaFayette Instrument Co., N. 26th Street and 52 By-pass, LaFayette, Ind.
- School Play Mat, Lakeshore Equipment Co., 1144 Montague Avenue, San Leandro, Calif.
- Hand Dynamometers, LaFayette Instrument Co.
- Clutch ball, Creative Playthings, Princeton, N.J.
- Footballs, utility balls, jump rope
- Punching Bag Set, Lakeshore Equipment Co.
- Six-spring Hand Grip, Sears, Roebuck and Co.
- *The Treatment of Speech and Reading Problems* (teacher training film), Systems for Education, Inc., 612 N. Michigan Avenue, Chicago, Ill.
- Tantalizer Game, F. A. O. Schwarz, 745 Fifth Avenue, New York, N.Y.

Further Evaluation

- The Harris Tests of Lateral Dominance, Psychological Corporation, 304 E. 45th Street, New York, N.Y.
- Ophthalmological examination

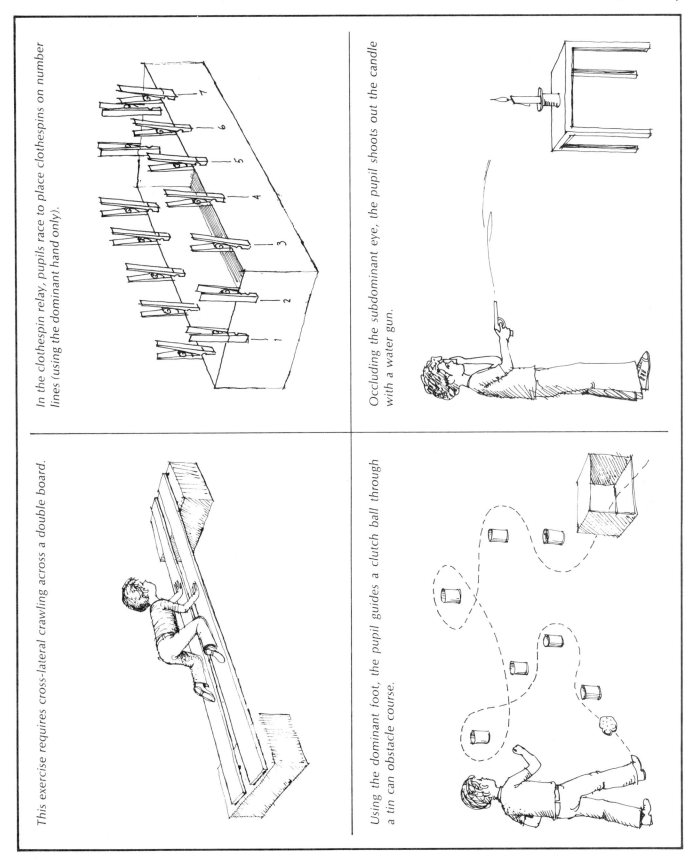

In the clothespin relay, pupils race to place clothespins on number lines (using the dominant hand only).

Occluding the subdominant eye, the pupil shoots out the candle with a water gun.

This exercise requires cross-lateral crawling across a double board.

Using the dominant foot, the pupil guides a clutch ball through a tin can obstacle course.

All programs should be modified or extended to meet the needs of individual pupils.

• Gesell, Arnold. *The First Five Years of Life,* pp. 91–101. New York: Harper and Brothers, 1940.
• Subjective tests of lateral performance

PRESCRIPTIVE ILLUSTRATION

Priority Teaching Objective: Teresa, six years old, neurologically handicapped. Teresa will be able to hold the five large plastic form templates (circle, square, triangle, rectangle, and cross) on drawing paper with her left hand and trace the forms with a large primary pencil in her right hand.

Pretest Tasks: Teresa uses both hands to draw, paint, and work. Dominance tests indicate a preference for right sidedness, which will be reinforced.

Specific Teaching Procedures: "Teresa, today we are going to begin to draw some forms. Here is a large plastic circle, this is a square, this is a triangle. This is called a rectangle, and this is a cross. See how I pick up this circle with my right hand and put it on the paper. I want you to do the same with your plastic circle. That's right, pick it up with your right hand."

"Now, we hold the circle with our left hand and then draw around it with our pencil in our right hand like this. Show me how you do it."

"Fine. Now let's do the same thing with the square. Point to my hand that I should use to pick it up with. Good! You are going to use your right hand."

"Go ahead, Teresa, pick up the other forms one at a time with your right hand, and then hold them with your left hand while you draw them."

"Those are nice looking forms. Now here is a box of crayons. Color in each of the forms. Pick a crayon and color the form using your right hand."

"Very nice. Now here is a pair of scissors. Cut out each of the colored forms using your right hand to hold the scissors."

Performance Evaluation: Teresa did quite well on the first task, although she switched to holding the triangle with her right hand and drawing with her left.

Analysis and Comments: The lesson seemed appropriate. She wanted to switch hands while using the crayon, and cutting the forms out on the lines was most difficult. Continued practice in all of these tasks will be planned.

For Self-instruction: Devise a teaching procedure and performance evaluation method for this pupil: Gordon, eleven years old, educationally handicapped. Following laterality training, Gordon will be able to bat consistently left-handed and throw a softball consistently left-handed.

21/Time Orientation

DEFINITION: The ability to judge lapses in time and to be aware of time concepts.
ILLUSTRATION: Pupil is prompt in attending class, completing timed assignments, and following directions. Pupil is aware of day, month, year, time of day, and seasons.
EDUCATIONAL RATIONALE: Body organization in time reflects sensory-motor integration in space and is prerequisite for advanced perceptual and conceptual skills. Children should be provided opportunities to explore and judge space-time relationships in order to develop synchrony of movement.

SUGGESTED PROGRAM IDEAS

1. Body Organization and Rhythm
   a. Finger touch: In rhythm with slow metronome, teacher calls out "nose," "mouth," "hair," "right eye," "left foot," etc. Pupil responds by touching body part with index finger while keeping the beat.
   b. Walking: "Walk slowly to the end of the room." "Walk fast to the end of the room." Following exercises, ask how much time was required. In same way teach movement to given time allocations.
   c. Running broad jump: Lay out course and jumping line. Teach pupils to run and judge body movements in time and distance in order not to cross the line or board before jumping.
   d. Serial movements: In time to metronome, place pegs in Judy Pegboard. Vary time and size of pegboards.
   e. Dance rhythms: Teach marching to rhythms for young pupils and dancing to the beat for older children.
   f. Bouncing: Bounce balls to metronome. Bounce to music. Play jacks.
   g. Jumping: Jump rope to metronome, music, counting, and rhymes.
   h. Hitting and games: Teach pupil to bat ball suspended from string. Practice tetherball, basketball, tennis, softball.

2. Visual time Orientation
   a. Morning-evening: Use magazine pictures, photographs, slides, etc., to teach morning, noon, evening, A.M., P.M., etc.
   b. Seasons: Use pictures, holidays, growing periods, sports, vacations, position of the earth, etc., to teach seasons.
   c. Timer activities: Use ten- and twenty-second marble timers and have child count seconds involved; with this frame of reference, have him judge time required to write his name, sharpen a pencil, tie his shoes, etc. Extend activties to include use of stopwatch and self-timing.
   d. Clock activities: Teach principle of hourglass, water clock, candle clock, and sundial. Show pupils internal workings of clocks and watches and let them manipulate the parts. Teach seconds, minutes, and hours.
   e. Calendar activities: Review seasonal activities. Teach months, holidays, weeks, days in the year, and earth-sun space relationships for each month. Have children make calendars.
   f. Age progression: Use pictures to teach age differentials of young and old; apply to humans, animals, vegetables and trees, clothes, etc.

3. Conceptualization

    a. Games: Use "Tell Time Quizmo," clock stamps, and games for practice.

    b. Drawing-painting: Have pupils make pictures representing different seasons, time of day, and periods or events in their lives.

    c. Story telling: Use tape recorder to record pupils' stories of "When I was Little," "Last Summer," "When I Grow Up," etc.

    d. Personal time orientation: Have pupil judge and measure time required to get to school, walk to the office, write his spelling lesson, complete projects; time left in football or basketball quarters.

    e. Personal history: Explain time line beginning with pupil's family (from the birth of his father and other family members to the present and projected into the future). Write letters to friends sequencing events in time.

    f. General time line: Teach formal time line in history. Discuss the recording of time as B.C. and A.D. On the same line, locate the history of man, discovery of America, statehood, birth of the pupil. Speculate on future events relative to the past. Make time line for birth of classmates.

REFERENCES

Bateman, Barbara B. *Temporal Learning.* Dimensions in Early Learning Series. San Rafael, Calif.: Dimensions Publishing, 1968.

Dusing, Jack R., and Kephart, Newell C. "Motor Generalization in Space and Time." *Learning Disorders*, Vol. 1, edited by Jerome Hellmuth, pp. 77–121. Seattle: Special Child Publications, 1965.

Related Programs

- *All About the Seasons* (record), Educational Record Sales, 157 Chambers Street, New York, N.Y.
- *Telling Time—Facts and Fun* (record), Educational Record Sales
- *Calendar Series* (filmstrips), Educational Record Sales
- *Let's Look at Children: A Guide to Understanding and Fostering Intellectual Development in Young Children* (concepts of space and time), Educational Testing Service, Princeton, N.J.
- Wiley, Bertha M. *Time and Telling Time.* Belmont, Calif.: Fearon Publishers, 1967.

Instructional Materials

- Talking Clock, Mattel, Inc., 5150 W. Rosecrans, Hawthorne, Calif.
- See-through Alarm Clock, Constructive Playthings, 1040 E. 85th Street, Kansas City, Mo.
- Time Learner, Constructive Playthings
- Judy Clock, The Judy Company, 310 N. Second Street, Minneapolis, Minn.
- Judy Hundred Pegboard, The Judy Company
- Judy Calendar, The Judy Company
- Tell Time Quizmo, Constructive Playthings
- Ten-second Timer, Twenty-second Timer, Constructive Playthings
- Stopwatch
- Wind-up clock
- Metronome
- Records for dancing and marching
- Old kitchen clocks and wrist watches

Further Evaluation

- Actual time-of-completion records for body organization tasks and classroom assignments
- Teacher-devised pencil and paper tests covering time concepts

PRESCRIPTIVE ILLUSTRATION

Priority Teaching Objective: Orin, six years old, educable mentally retarded. When shown six different picture sequences of people and animals, Orin will be able to mark the "youngest" or "oldest" on each of the sequences.

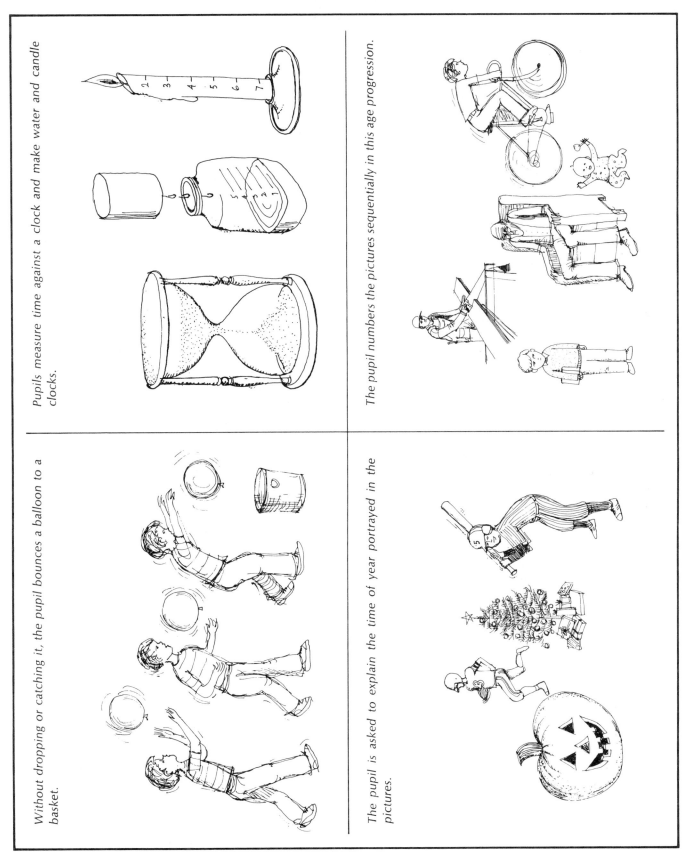

Pupils measure time against a clock and make water and candle clocks.

The pupil numbers the pictures sequentially in this age progression.

Without dropping or catching it, the pupil bounces a balloon to a basket.

The pupil is asked to explain the time of year portrayed in the pictures.

Pretest Tasks: When shown pictures of animals and people, Orin did not have any concept of "youngest" or "oldest."

Specific Teaching Procedures: "Orin, look at this picture. See, there are three different persons there. One of them is a young girl, another is an elderly grandmother, and one is a very young baby. The grandmother is the oldest and the baby is the youngest. Put your finger on the grandmother. Good! We would call her the _____."
   Pupil: "Oldest."
   "That's right. Now put a pencil mark on the oldest. Now mark the youngest."
   "Now, here is a picture of some chickens. Mark the one you think is the youngest."

   "Here are some other pictures: [Two young kittens, old cat. Three older dogs, one puppy. Old man, old woman, young girl. Kitten, old man, old woman.] Now mark each one that I tell you to."

Performance Evaluation: "That was really good, Orin; you marked the youngest or oldest correctly on five of the pictures. Do you know which one you missed?"
   Pupil: "That one [pointing to the last one]."

Analysis and Comments: This was an appropriate task, as Orin had no time concepts as applied to people or animals. He was able to generalize quickly, however. The animal mixed with people seemed to confuse him, and he pointed to the woman as "the youngest." Practice will continue with mixed groups and groups of various sizes.

For Self-instruction: Devise a teaching procedure and performance evaluation method for this pupil: Darlene, eleven years old, specific learning disability. Darlene could not tell time. She could not tell the minute hand from the hour hand on the clock, and did not know how many minutes there are in an hour. Upon completion of the lesson Darlene will be able to tell time to the nearest minute.

Perceptual-Motor Skills

22/Auditory Acuity

DEFINITION: The ability to receive and differentiate auditory stimuli.
ILLUSTRATION: Pupil responds functionally to wristwatch tick, hidden sound toys, and general normal conversational directions. Pupil has no significant decibel loss.
EDUCATIONAL RATIONALE: The ability to receive and to respond to auditory stimuli is a result of the integration of experience and neurological organization. The training of children in listening skills with emphasis on the development of good habit patterns of auditory attention and motivation should be stressed.

SUGGESTED PROGRAM IDEAS

1. Gross Awareness
   a. Screening: Present wristwatch to each ear and train child to listen and raise his hand when he no longer hears the tick. Whisper commands to child from varying directions for each ear. Click coins by each ear. Present commands in normal voice in front of room and note response. Obtain audiometric screening on doubtful cases.
   b. Preferred seating: Place the child with listening difficulties in central position near the front.
   c. Amplification: For the pupil with suspected hearing loss and inattention, use portable auditory training unit for selected units of work.
   d. Instrument play: Present rattle, drum, cymbal, bell, horn, whistle, triangle, etc., to child for free play. Condition child to turn when teacher sounds the instrument behind the pupil's back.
   e. Common noises: Present pictures and recordings of trains, boats, airplanes, thunder, hammering.
   f. Animal sounds: Use pictures and recordings of animal noises (*The Farmer Says*).
   g. Nature sounds: Pupils lie on grass and listen to sounds of birds, wind, grass moving, etc.

2. Fine Sound Awareness
   a. Tape recordings: Record pupils engaged in following activities and play back frequently for identification: clapping hands softly, shaking a sand rattle, dropping marbles in a jar, pouring water in a glass, rustling and crumpling paper, heart beat with stethoscope, hard breathing with stethoscope, graded sound cylinders, etc.
   b. Imitation games: With pupil's back turned, teacher bounces ball three times, snaps fingers, taps desk with pencil, coughs, taps glass with spoon, etc. Child turns and imitates what he heard. Tape record and compare sounds.
   c. Relaxation game: Teach children to place their heads in arms on desk, shut their eyes, relax, and listen to "quiet sounds." Tape record relaxation time. Follow up by having children relate what they heard and by playing back tape.

3. Speech Awareness
   a. Listening games: Teach imitation and games through records such as *Let's Listen* (grades 1–3). Play Simon Says, Who Am I? and similar games.
   b. Talking books: Show pupil how to operate talking books such as *Mother Goose Nursery Rhymes*. Use recorded story records and tapes for general audio stimulation.
   c. Whisper games: Children whisper instructions in one another's ears and follow through. Teacher uses cardboard tube to enhance whispered instructions.
   d. Poems and stories: Teach rote poems, rhymes, and action stories.

  e. Telephone: Provide simple telephones or walkie-talkie for stimulating experimentation by children.

  f. Singing: Teach choral singing. Use records and listening post and sing folk songs, etc.

  g. Special training: Children with significant hearing loss should be taught speech and lip reading with speech therapy if needed. Deaf children should be taught finger spelling together with speech reading. Adolescent nonoral deaf children should be taught formal manual signs and speech reading.

  h. Taped speech: Pupil attends to tape recorded story while teacher reads contrasting story.

REFERENCES

Kastein, Shulamith, "An Analysis of the Development of Language in Children with Special Reference to Dysacusis." *The Special Child in Century 21,* edited by Jerome Hellmuth, pp. 139–172. Seattle: Special Child Publications, 1964.

Wenger, M. A.; Jones, F. M.; and Jones, M. H. "Audition." *Physiological Psychology,* pp. 151–189. New York: Holt, Rinehart & Winston, 1956.

Related Programs

- *Learning to Listen* (auditory training record from John Tracy Clinic), Children's Music Center, Inc., 5373 W. Pico Boulevard, Los Angeles, Calif.
- *Let's Listen* (grades 1–3, record), Educational Record Sales, 157 Chambers Street, New York, N.Y.
- *Ear Training for Middle Grades, What is Listening?* (records), Educational Record Sales
- Barry, Hortense. "Auditory Awareness." *The Young Aphasic Child: Evaluation and Training,* p. 32. Washington, D.C.: Alexander Graham Bell Association for the Deaf, 1961.
- Cruickshank, William, ed. "Listening Games." *A Teaching Method for Brain-Injured and Hyperactive Children,* p. 182. Syracuse: Syracuse University Press, 1961.
- *Child's World of Sounds* (record), Bowmar Records, 622 Rodier Drive, Glendale, Calif.
- *Familiar Sounds* and *Animal Sounds* (audio flashcard sets), Electronic Futures, Inc., 57 Dodge Avenue, North Haven, Conn.

Instructional Materials

- *Echorder Automatic Speech and Language Training Aid,* RIL Electronics Corp., Street Road and Second Street Pike, Southampton, Pa.
- Transistorized True Binaural Auditory Trainer (portable model), Ambco Electronics, 1224 W. Washington Boulevard, Los Angeles, Calif.
- Wooden Sound Cylinders, Creative Playthings, Princeton, N.J.
- Step Bells, Constructive Playthings, 1040 E. 85th Street, Kansas City, Mo.
- *Mother Goose Nursery Rhymes,* Audio Creations, 235 Broadway, Millbrae, Calif.
- Stethoscope, Lakeshore Equipment Co., 1144 Montague Avenue, San Leandro, Calif.
- Phonic Mirror (for identifying, isolating, discriminating, producing, and monitoring through reinforcement of speech sounds), H. C. Electronics, Inc., 250 Camino Alto, Mill Valley, Calif.
- Screening Audiometer, Eckstein Brothers Auditory, 4807 W. 118th Place, Hawthorne, Calif.
- *Listen to My Seashell* (book), Children's Music Center, Inc.
- *Mr. Sound Says* and *The Farmer Says,* Sears, Roebuck and Co.

Further Evaluation

- General evaluation of pupil response to normal classroom auditory stimulation
- Myklebust, Helmer R. *Auditory Disorders in Children: A Manual for Differential Diagnosis.* New York: Grune & Stratton, 1958.
- Reichstein, Jerome, and Rosenstein, Joseph. "Differential Diagnosis of Auditory Deficits—A Review of the Literature." *Exceptional Children.* 31 (1964):71–82.

PRESCRIPTIVE ILLUSTRATION

Priority Teaching Objective: Cecil, nine years old, aphasic. At the completion of the

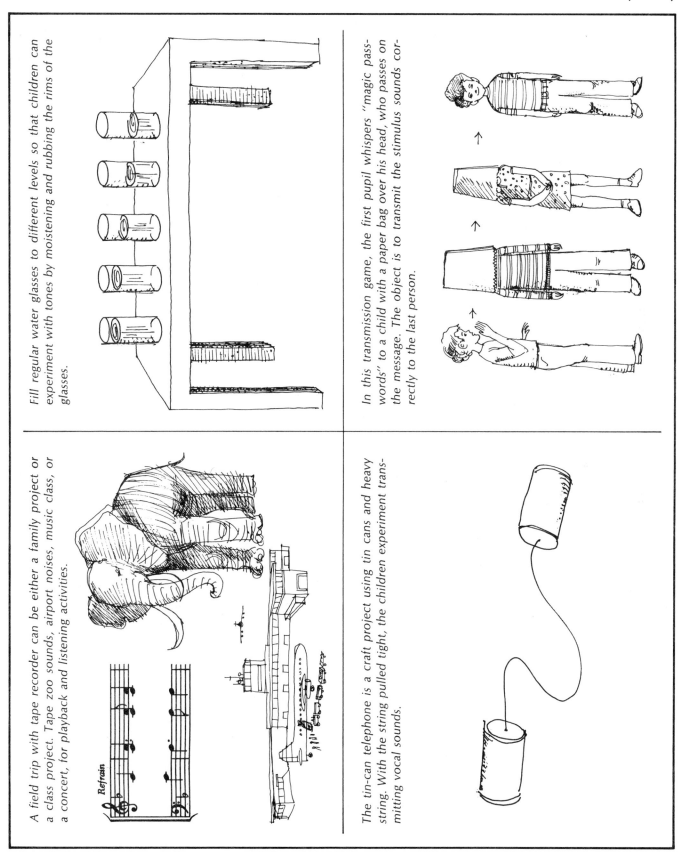

Fill regular water glasses to different levels so that children can experiment with tones by moistening and rubbing the rims of the glasses.

In this transmission game, the first pupil whispers "magic pass-words" to a child with a paper bag over his head, who passes on the message. The object is to transmit the stimulus sounds correctly to the last person.

A field trip with tape recorder can be either a family project or a class project. Tape zoo sounds, airport noises, music class, or a concert, for playback and listening activities.

Refrain

The tin-can telephone is a craft project using tin cans and heavy string. With the string pulled tight, the children experiment transmitting vocal sounds.

All programs should be modified or extended to meet the needs of individual pupils.

lesson, Cecil will be able to repeat correctly thirty-four of thirty-nine similar sounding words as presented by the teacher with her lips hidden from view.

Pretest Tasks: Cecil's teacher said the following words one at a time and asked him to repeat them correctly: an, tan, ran, pan, can, fan, man. Cecil was able to repeat only "ran" correctly.

Specific Teaching Procedures: "Cecil, listen carefully to the word I am going to say and then repeat it for me: an. What was the word?"

Pupil: "An."

"That's right. Now look at my lips and tell me what I am saying this time: tan. What was it?"

Pupil: "Tan."

"Good! Now I am going to cover my lips so you cannot see them. Listen to the words, then tell me what I said: tan; an. What did I say?"

Pupil: "Tan, an."

"Fine. Now let's do the same with these. Listen carefully to them and then give them back to me: an, tan, ran. What were they?"

Pupil: "An, tan, ran."

(Lesson sequence: pan, can, fan; can, fan, man; at, sat, cat, rat; rat, pat, fat, mat; in, tin, pin, win, bin; all, tall, call, ball, fall, hall, wall; run, sun, bun, fun, gun; it, sit, mit, fit, pit, bit, hit.)

Performance Evaluation: Cecil was able to repeat correctly thirty-seven of the thirty-nine words when each word was presented separately and he could respond immediately. He was also able to sequence three words correctly.

Analysis and Comments: The lesson was appropriate but should now be made more demanding by requiring sequencing.

For Self-instruction: Devise a teaching procedure and performance evaluation method for this pupil: Margaret, five years old, hard of hearing. Margaret will be able to identify three different "sound patterns" played on a xylophone. She will raise her hand when she hears the correct pattern.

23/Auditory Decoding

DEFINITION: The ability to understand sounds or spoken words.

ILLUSTRATION: Pupil can follow simple verbal instructions; can indicate by gesture or words the meaning or purpose of auditory stimuli, such as animal sounds, nouns, or verbs.

EDUCATIONAL RATIONALE: Children need to be taught to listen carefully and to understand and respond to oral stimulation and instructions. Training activities should stress behavioral responses and simple "yes-no" answers rather than long verbal replies.

SUGGESTED PROGRAM ACTIVITIES

1. Sound Identification
   a. Matching: Place picture of train, cow, dog, gun, etc., on chalkboard; teacher then says sound ("choo-choo," "moo," etc.), and child points out appropriate picture. Use *The Sound Says* and *Mr. Farmer Says* for additional matching exercises.
   b. Tone matching: Teach children to match step bells or piano notes by holding hands high for high notes, squatting for low notes, etc.
   c. Instrument sounds: Arrange pictures of musical instruments and use records or actual instrument to teach sound. Play sound on tape or record and have child point out appropriate picture.
   d. Noises: Child turns his back while teacher claps hand, blows whistle, hits with hammer, crumples paper, etc. Child then turns around and duplicates noise.
   e. Tapping: With child's back turned, teacher taps glass, box, can, drum, etc. Child turns around and points out object tapped.
   f. Contrasting sounds: Teacher walks noisily, then tiptoes; walks rapidly, then slowly; talks in high voice, low voice. Child then describes the sound—loud, fast, high, etc.

2. Understanding Questions
   a. Yes or no: Child responds to questions with a "yes" or "no" or nods head. Verbs—"Do birds crawl? Do cars move? Do worms walk?" Sex—"Is a boy a man? Are girls females? Is John a woman?" Purpose—"Are crayons to color? Are chairs to fly? Is food to eat? Are bicycles to ride? Are pencils to paint?"
   b. Alike or different: Teacher instructs pupil to indicate whether the second word is the same as or different from the stimulus word: *dog—fog, shush—slush, ape—ape, coat—boat, throw—threw,* etc.
   c. True or false: Read a story or textbook assignment aloud. Prepare a series of true-or-false questions to be presented in spelldown fashion.
   d. Clues: Arrange assorted objects or pictures on table. Teacher says, "What is big, round, and bounces," ". . . small, long, and sharp?" etc. Child points out object.
   e. Question games: Ask varied-length questions and have child repeat questions.

3. Understanding and Following Directions
   a. Action records: Play rhythm and activity records such as *Dance-a-Story* and teach children to carry out directions.
   b. Charades: Children divide into teams and select names of books, movies, events (Pinocchio, Mary Poppins, Halloween, etc.) to act *out* for the other side to guess. Show how to open the door, cut with a knife, sweep the floor, etc.

c. Simple directions: "Open the door. Walk around the room. Find me the arithmetic book on the second shelf. Put your hand on your head and skip to the desk and back," etc.

d. Book exercises: "Locate page 320. Show me the third paragraph on this page. Point out the first word in the last paragraph on page 1."

e. Sounds and voice training exercises: Teach lessons from *Play it by Ear—Auditory Training Games* from the John Tracy Clinic (also for direct use with parents as a source of homework exercises).

f. Drawing and marking exercises: Prepare special ditto work sheet and record instructions for listening post use: i.e., "Mark the first circle in the top row," etc.

g. Speech games: Play Speecho and other speech discrimination games.

h. Symbol association: Arrange mixed letters, numbers, and simple words in chalk tray. Teacher says "a," "I," "cat," etc., and child points out symbol. "Show me the letter that comes before *N*. Give me the number that comes after 14," etc. Use phonetic records and formal phonic training program.

i. Nonsense stories: Read stories and insert nonsense words. Have child spot the word.

REFERENCES

Kirk, Samuel. "Children with Auditory Handicaps." *Education of Exceptional Children,* pp. 151–166. Boston: Houghton Mifflin, 1962.

Montessori, Maria. "Exercises for the Discrimination of Sounds." *The Montessori Method,* pp. 203–214. New York: Schocken Books, 1964.

Related Programs

- *Listen* and *These Are Sounds About You* (record and filmstrip), Guidance Associates, Pleasantville, N.Y.
- *What's Its Name; A Guide to Speech and Hearing Development,* Palfrey's Educational Supply Co., 7715 E. Garvey Boulevard, Rosemead, Calif.
- Ronnei, Eleanor C. *Learning to Look and Listen.* New York: Columbia University Teachers College, 1951.
- *Who Said It?* (record), Educational Activities, Inc., P.O. Box 392, Freeport, N.Y.
- *Play It by Ear—Auditory Training Games* (sound section), John Tracy Clinic, 806 W. Adams Boulevard, Los Angeles, Calif.
- Barry, Hortense. "Discrimination." *The Young Aphasic Child: Evaluation and Training,* pp. 32–34. Washington, D.C.: Alexander Graham Bell Association for the Deaf, 1961.
- *Sights and Sounds—Feeling and Perceiving* (record), Curtis Audio-Visual Materials, Independence Square, Philadelphia, Pa.
- *Follow-through with Sounds,* Knowledge Aid Co., 8220 N. Austin Avenue, Morton Grove, Ill.
- Goldstein, Herbert, and Levitt, Edith. *A Reading Readiness Workbook in Auditory Discrimination.* Parkinson Program for Special Children. Chicago: Follett Publishing, 1965.
- *Auditory Training Program,* Developmental Learning Materials, 3505 N. Ashland Avenue, Chicago, Ill.
- *Listening and Learning* (kit with records), Houghton Mifflin Co., 2 Park Street, Boston, Mass.

Instructional Materials

- Recorder, Creative Playthings, Princeton, N.J.
- *Mr. Sound Says, The Farmer Says,* Sears, Roebuck and Co.
- Step Bells, Constructive Playthings, 1040 E. 85th Street, Kansas City, Mo.
- *Poems Children Enjoy,* Palfrey's Educational Supply Co.
- Speecho (phonetic game), Palfrey's Educational Supply Co.
- Sound and Articulation Game, Palfrey's Educational Supply Co.
- *Dance-a-Story* (record), Educational Record Sales, 157 Chambers Street, New York, N.Y.
- *Sounds for Young Readers* (record—phonetic and auditory discrimination sounds), Educational Record Sales
- "Talking Page" (auditory discrimination modules), Responsive Environments Corp., Englewood Cliffs, N.J.

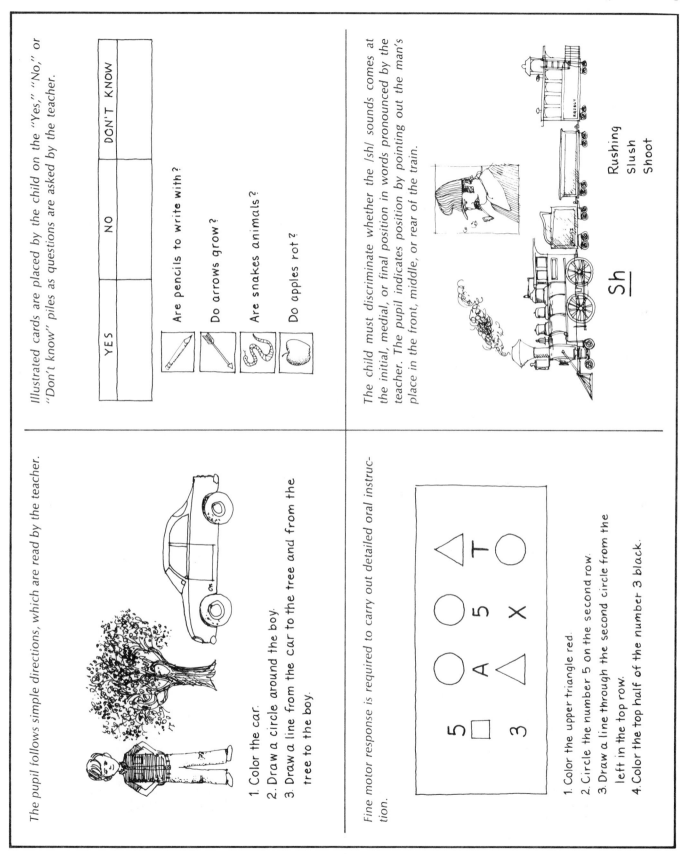

Illustrated cards are placed by the child on the "Yes," "No," or "Don't know" piles as questions are asked by the teacher.

YES	NO	DON'T KNOW

Are pencils to write with?

Do arrows grow?

Are snakes animals?

Do apples rot?

The child must discriminate whether the /sh/ sounds comes at the initial, medial, or final position in words pronounced by the teacher. The pupil indicates position by pointing out the man's place in the front, middle, or rear of the train.

Rushing
Slush
Shoot

Sh
—

The pupil follows simple directions, which are read by the teacher.

1. Color the car.
2. Draw a circle around the boy.
3. Draw a line from the car to the tree and from the tree to the boy.

Fine motor response is required to carry out detailed oral instruction.

5 ◯ ◯ △
□ A 5 T
3 △ X ◯

1. Color the upper triangle red.
2. Circle the number 5 on the second row.
3. Draw a line through the second circle from the left in the top row.
4. Color the top half of the number 3 black.

All programs should be modified or extended to meet the needs of individual pupils.

- Wepman Auditory Discrimination Test, Language Research Associates, 950 E. 59th Street, Chicago, Ill.
- Valett Developmental Survey of Basic Learning Abilities: auditory discrimination
- Illinois Test of Psycholinguistic Ability: auditory decoding subtest

PRESCRIPTIVE ILLUSTRATION

Priority Teaching Objective: Betty Anne, five years old, educationally handicapped. Upon completion of this lesson, Betty Anne will be able to decode all ten pairs of words used in the pretest, according to difference or similarity.

Pretest Tasks: Betty Anne was auditorily presented with a list of ten word pairs. After the teacher read each pair, Betty Anne was to respond by deciding if the two words of each pair were alike or different. The word pairs marked (*) below are those which she identified incorrectly:

bog—dog	hay—hay*	money—bunny*	would—should*	light—light
cat—rat	did—hid	chase—chase	may—pay	fat—sat

Specific Teaching Procedures: "Betty Anne, I am going to say a pair of letters. I want you to repeat the pair of letters after me and then tell me if they sound alike or different. If I say /b/ — /d/, you repeat the sounds and say 'different' because they sound different from each other. What are you to do?"

Pupil: "I say the sounds and then tell you if they are alike or different when I hear them."

"Good. For every pair of sounds you correctly identify as different or alike, I will put a chocolate peanut in your cup. Repeat these sounds after me and tell me if they are alike or different."

/b/ — /d/	/l/ — /l/	/d/ — /h/	/ch/ — /ch/	/m/ — /p/
/c/ — /r/	/h/ — /h/	/m/ — /b/	/w/ — /sh/	/f/ — /s/

Performance Evaluation: "Very good, Betty Anne, you earned nine candies because you made only one mistake: /b/ — /d/ are different, not alike."

Pupil: "/b/ — /d/, /b/ — /d/."

The task was only partially appropriate as it seemed too easy for Betty Anne. On the second try she correctly identified all ten pairs. The total lesson took ten minutes.

Analysis and Comments: Betty Anne was well motivated and concentrated quite hard to listen and repeat the sounds. The practice exercises will be modified to include very similar sounds such as /b/ — /d/, /p/ — /b/, /s/ — /sh/, two-syllable words, and complicated sounds.

For Self-instruction: Devise a teaching procedure and performance evaluation method for this pupil: Leroy, ten years old, hard of hearing. Leroy will be able to listen carefully and respond correctly by explaining what is wrong with four of the five sentences below:

We read from dishes.	We swim in the street.
A ball is a square.	We cook on a bed.
Boys wear dresses.	

24/Auditory-Vocal Association

DEFINITION: The ability to respond verbally in a meaningful way to auditory stimuli.

ILLUSTRATION: Pupil can associate wtih verbal opposites, sentence completion, or analogous verbal responses.

EDUCATIONAL RATIONALE: Children must be taught to listen and to respond verbally in meaningful ways through the use of association, logical inference, and judgment. Expressive fluency should be recognized as a secondary goal.

SUGGESTED PROGRAM IDEAS

1. Primary Association
   a. Place association: "For the next minute, tell me all the things you can think of that belong in the grocery store [sports shop, school, etc.]. Who are the pupils who sit around you?"
   b. Word association: "Tell me all the words you can think of when I say 'boy' [money, camp, clothes, cookies, etc.]."
   c. Sentence completion: Teach pupil to listen to beginning sentence stimulus and then to complete it by association. "The color of this book is —————. My name is —————. My favorite television program is —————. When summer comes, I —————. I am now ————— years old. Candy is —————. When my birthday comes, —————."
   d. Free association: Provide stimulating toys such as toy telephones, puppets, dolls, etc., and tape recorders for children to record and play back.
   e. Guided association: Use TV films, filmstrips, and colored pictures to stimulate general discussion and pupil association.

2. Analogous Association
   a. Prepositional analysis: "Is my hand under the desk? Are parks to live in?" Have pupil explain his reply.
   b. Class differences: "Which of the following words does not belong—birds, bees, flies, cars [John, Mary, Bill, George; apples, hamburgers, steak, wieners, etc.]?" Repeat exercise, requiring verbal listing of things that *do* go together.
   c. Verbal-opposite training: "Name the opposite of boy [man, day, morning, early, big, heavy, young, etc.]." Have pupils give their own stimulus words for association and discussion of relationships.
   d. Analogy games: Teach verbal association to analogies such as: "In the morning it is light, in the evening it is —————. [Birds are in the sky and fish are in the —————. Fire is hot and ice is —————," etc.].
   e. Descriptive analysis: Tell a brief one-paragraph story and then ask questions: "Did the boy run? Was the bicycle red?" etc.
   f. Logical analysis: Play question games with leading questions: "It is big, yellow, and in the sky. It has fur, whiskers, and chases mice," etc.

3. Integrative Activities
   a. Jokes and riddles: Teacher presents joke or riddle followed by discussion of its meaning or solution given by pupil.
   b. Story discussion: Read aloud poems or part of a funny story such as Dr. Seuss books. Teacher writes discussion outline (Who? What? Where? When? Why?

How?) on the board and presents questions one at a time. Have two students work together to create a story and tell it to the class.

c. Radio-television: Listen to selected programs and follow with verbal association activities.

d. Programmed material: Read aloud selected lessons from the Continental Press *Reading-Thinking Skills* Series, and have pupils discuss.

e. Listening post reports: Have pupils listen to recorded stories and then follow up with both individual reports and panel discussions.

f. General conversation: Engage pupil in conversation regarding previous day's activities, present school work, hobbies, sports interests, etc. Tape record conversation and play back. Encourage and reward extended comments and vocal association to ideas.

REFERENCES

Herdy, Miriam Pauls. "Communication and Communication Disorders." *The Teacher of Brain-Injured Children,* edited by William Cruickshank, pp. 131–136. New York: Syracuse University Press, 1966.

Montessori, Maria. "Language and Knowledge of the World." *Dr. Montessori's Own Handbook,* pp. 123-131. New York: Schocken Books, 1965.

Related Programs

- *Let's Listen: Auditory Training for Speech Development and Reading Readiness* (record), Ginn and Co., Boston, Mass.
- *Song Dramatization for Children* (record), Educational Record Sales, 157 Chambers Street, New York, N.Y.
- *Reading-Thinking Skills* (preprimer through grade 4 series), Continental Press, Elizabethtown, Pa.
- *Riddles, Rhymes, and Stories,* Giant Activity Book, Continental Press
- Hogan, Sister James Lorene. *The ABC of Auditory Training.* University City, Mo.: St. Joseph's Institute for the Deaf, 1961.
- *Listening Games* by Guy Wagner et al., Teachers Publishing, 866 Third Avenue, New York, N.Y.

Instructional Materials

- Walkie-talkie or real telephone sets
- Listening post and earphones
- John Tracy Clinic Correspondence Course for Parents of Little Deaf Children (for use by parents of preschool children)
- Jokes from newspapers, magazines, and joke books
- Poetry and poem books
- Dr. Seuss books: *The Cat in the Hat, If I Ran the Circus, On Beyond Zebra*
- Tape recorder
- Radio and television sets
- Selected science fiction stories for reading aloud and stimulating verbal association
- *What Is Listening* (record), Children's Music Center, Inc., 5373 W. Pico Boulevard, Los Angeles, Calif.

Further Evaluation

- Wechsler Intelligence Scale for Children: Similarities subtest
- Detroit Verbal-Opposites Test
- Incomplete sentence tests (oral presentation)
- Illinois Tests of Psycholinguistic Ability: auditory-vocal association subtest
- Teacher evaluation of conversational associations

PRESCRIPTIVE ILLUSTRATION

Priority Teaching Objective: Ruby, ten years old, educable mentally retarded. Upon com-

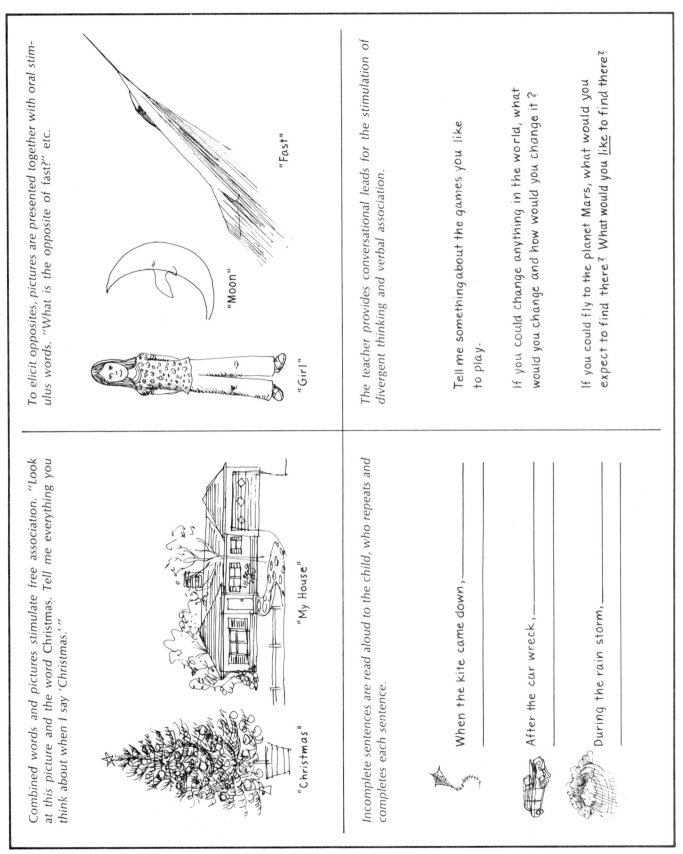

To elicit opposites, pictures are presented together with oral stimulus words. "What is the opposite of fast?" etc.

"Fast"

"Moon"

"Girl"

The teacher provides conversational leads for the stimulation of divergent thinking and verbal association.

Tell me something about the games you like to play.

If you could change anything in the world, what would you change and how would you change it?

If you could fly to the planet Mars, what would you expect to find there? What would you *like* to find there?

Combined words and pictures stimulate free association. "Look at this picture and the word Christmas. Tell me everything you think about when I say 'Christmas.'"

"Christmas"

"My House"

Incomplete sentences are read aloud to the child, who repeats and completes each sentence.

When the kite came down, _____

After the car wreck, _____

During the rain storm, _____

All programs should be modified or extended to meet the needs of individual pupils.

pletion of this lesson, Ruby will be able to respond verbally with an opposite word to an auditory stimulus word for three out of three stimulus words.

Pretest Tasks: Ruby was shown a group of objects that represented opposite concepts. She was then asked the opposite of hard (soft), the opposite of big (little), and the opposite of empty (full). She was unable to respond with an appropriate response to any of the three items.

Specific Teaching Procedures: "Ruby, we are going to work with some objects that are very different. Can you name them?"

Pupil: "Rock, cotton, glass, sticks."

"Good. Now, Ruby, I want you to match the opposite items. Opposite means that one thing is very different from another. For instance, the opposite of cold is hot and the opposite of boy is girl. What is the opposite of hot?"

Pupil: "Cold."

"That's right. What is the opposite of boy?"

Pupil: "Girl."

"Now we will find some objects here that are opposites. I am going to point to one of these objects [rock]. This is a rock and it is hard. Can you find something that is the opposite of hard—something that is not hard?"

Pupil: "Cotton is soft."

"Yes, the opposite of hard is _____."

Pupil: "Soft."

"Good. If you do not know the opposite, then I will tell you. For each correct answer, you will get a check on your sheet."

Performance Evaluation: On the posttest Ruby got all of the items correct. The lesson took twenty minutes.

Analysis and Comments: Ruby has a good attitude. She likes individual instruction. She was able to generalize from the object to its verbal meaning, once given the name of the object. She has much trouble in school with concepts and retention.

For Self-instruction: Devise a teaching procedure and performance evaluation for this pupil: Kenneth, eight years old, educationally handicapped. Upon completion of the lesson Kenneth will be able to identify the word that does not belong in a series (such as *grass, tree, chair, flower*) and explain why it does not belong. Ten sets of words will be presented in the posttest.

Perceptual-Motor Skills

25/Auditory Memory

DEFINITION: The ability to retain and recall general auditory information.
ILLUSTRATION: Pupil can act out (charades) Santa Claus, simple plots of common nursery rhymes ("Jack and Jill"), can describe yesterday's experiences, meals, television and story plots.
EDUCATIONAL RATIONALE: Children must be taught that what they are hearing is important and that they will be expected to recall and use auditory information following training activities. Pupils should be rewarded for increasing their auditory memory span as evidenced through individual improvement records.

SUGGESTED PROGRAM IDEAS

1. Beginning Activities
   a. Animal sounds: "Make a sound like a dog [pig, duck, cat, horse, lion, etc.]."
   b. Game rules: "Tell me how you play tag [Ring around the Rosie, checkers, card games, chess, etc.]."
   c. Giving simple instructions: "Billy, explain to Johnny what we do in school during the mornings and what we usually do about this time of day. Mary, explain our class rules to Barbara," etc.
   d. Daily activities: "What do we do at the beginning of school in the morning [at 11 o'clock, at 1 o'clock, at 3 o'clock, etc.]?"
   e. Favorite music: "Tell me about your favorite records—what are the titles and why do you like them? Name for me as many different records or songs as you can."
   f. Instruments: "Tell me the names of as many different instruments as you can."
   g. Sports: "Tell me the names and sports of as many athletes as you can."

2. Middle Stage Activities
   a. General information: "Tell me what you did last night. What did you get on your last birthday? What did you do last weekend?"
   b. Following general instructions: "Turn to the spelling [arithmetic, etc.] work you were doing yesterday and do the next assignment. Find the last story that you have completed in your reading book."
   c. Food: "What did you have for breakfast [for supper last night, for lunch yesterday, for dinner last Sunday, etc.]? What goes with salt? Tell me as many foods as you can think of."
   d. Charades: Teach children how to listen to a nursery rhyme or story such as "Jack and Jill," and then to recall and act out the basic plot.
   e. Spelling: "Tell me as many spelling words as you can remember from last week's spelling test. Now write down as many of these words as you can remember."

3. Advanced Activities
   a. Phonic Association: Use alphabet cards: "What is the sound of this letter?" Use picture cards: "What sound does the name of this picture begin with?" etc.
   b. Phonic integration: Place alphabet cards against chalkboard. Tell pupil a sound (/sh/, /b/, etc.); have him select proper card and use the sound in a word and sentence.
   c. Story repetition: Read short and simple story to pupil. After every few sentences, stop and have child recall general idea of what has been read.
   d. Grammar recall: Teach correct grammar, such as proper use of past tense, by saying,

"Last Saturday I went to the store. I bought a loaf of bread." Have child repeat. Extend to practice with present and future tense verbs, etc.

e. Detailed stories: Use listening post records or tape-recorded stories of considerable length. Train children to listen carefully as they will be asked to relate story in detail. Tape record immediate recall of class and follow up with taped recall one day and one week later.

f. Play "I'm packing Santa's toy bag": "Here is an airplane, here is a ball, here is a car," etc.

REFERENCES

Cronbach, Lee J. "Meaningful Learning." *Educational Psychology*, pp. 350–371. New York: Harcourt, Brace & World, 1963.

Strauss, Alfred, and Kephart, Newell. "Auditory Perception." *Psychopathology and Education of the Brain-Injured Child*, Vol. 2, pp. 81–89, 109–111. New York: Grune & Stratton, 1955.

Related Programs
- *Golden Mother Goose, The Big Golden Book of Poetry, Finger Play Poems for Children*, Palfrey's Educational Supply Co., 7715 E. Garvey Boulevard, Rosemead, Calif.
- Barry, Hortense. "Auditory Memory." *The Young Aphasic Child: Evaluation and Training*, p. 36. Washington, D.C.: Alexander Graham Bell Association for the Deaf, 1961.
- *Sounds I Can Hear* (record), Scott, Foresman and Co., Glenview, Ill.
- Cruickshank, William, ed. "Hearing and Distinguishing Sounds." *A Teaching Method for Brain-Injured and Hyperactive Children*, pp. 183–185. Syracuse: Syracuse University Press, 1961.
- *Rhymes and Rhyming Words* (audio flashcard set), Electronics Futures, Inc., 57 Dodge Avenue, New Haven, Conn.
- *Auditory Discrimination—Rhyming Words Workbook*, Milliken Publishing Co., 611 Olive Street, St. Louis, Mo.
- *Developing Auditory Awareness and Insight* by Selma Harr, Med. Instructional Materials, 1415 Westwood Boulevard, Los Angeles, Calif.
- *The Auditory Stimulator—A Program for the Development of Attention, Listening and Memory Skills* by Joseph Kaplan, Educational Performance Associates, 563-F Westview Avenue, Ridgefield, N.J.
- *Furst Memory Course*, Memory Studies, 835 Diversey Parkway, Chicago, Ill.

Instructional Materials
- Milton Bradley Aids: Alphabet Poster Cards, Palfrey's Educational Supply Co., 7715 E. Garvey Boulevard, Rosemead, Calif.
- Phonic charts and materials
- Cut-out magazine pictures of animals, instruments, sports activities, musical instruments
- John Tracy Clinic Correspondence Course for Parents of Little Deaf Children
- Listening post and tape recorder
- *Bambi, Black Beauty, Four Winnie-the-Pooh Stories, Goldilocks and the Three Bears, Jack and the Beanstalk, Grimm's Fairy Tales, Paul Bunyan, Snow White, Story Teller Series* (story records), Educational Record Sales, 157 Chambers Street, New York, N.Y.
- Record player and assorted musical records and songs
- Leap and Listen, Facilitation House, Box 611, Ottawa, Ill.

Further Evaluation
- Elementary tests of English grammar
- Sentence completion items
- Illinois Test of Psycholinguistic Ability: auditory reception subtest
- Peabody Picture Vocabulary Test
- *Screening Test for Auditory Reception*, Academic Therapy Publications, San Rafael, Calif.

PRESCRIPTIVE ILLUSTRATION

Priority Teaching Objective: Mike, ten years old, regular fourth grade. Upon completion

The pupil imitates the teacher's phrases with use of correct grammar.

Teacher: I will be _____ years old next year.
Pupil: I will be _____ years old next year.

Teacher: He is a little boy. I am a grown woman.
Pupil: He is a little boy. I am a _____.

Teacher: Tomorrow I may go to the store. I might buy some candy.
Pupil: Tomorrow I may go to the store. I might buy _____.

When the teacher has presented the stimulus sound, the pupil uses it in a complete sentence.

b s p d
sl gl fl dr
cr th

The pupil gives a detailed response to the teacher's instructions. The reply is written down and may be typed out for the pupil's future reference.

Tell me all about what you saw on television last night. Tell me as much as you can because I am going to write it down for you.

The teacher points to the sound /tr/ while presenting it orally. The pupil is required to associate the correct picture with this beginning sound.

Tr

of the lesson, Mike will be able to select nine out of ten word endings orally presented to him in a posttest.

Pretest Task: Mike was presented ten 3 X 5 cards with the following word endings printed on them: -and, -an, -ike, -ook, -at, -ill, -ame, -ell, -all, -ot. He was asked to select the card that had the ending like the word I said to him (sand, man, like, book, cat, hill, game, bell, fall, and got). Of the ten, he missed hill, bell, fall, and game.

Specific Teaching Procedures: "Mike, in this lesson I am going to hand you a letter like this b. You place it in front of each of these cards with word endings and then I'll say what the word says. Then you tell me if it is a real word or not."

"Watch and listen. The b is now in front of this word ending (-ell). I say bell and now you say real or not, OK? Now tell me what you are to do."

Pupil: "I'm going to put the little letter here in front of each word and you are gonna say the word. Then I say yes or no."

"You tell me if it is a real word or not, all right?"

Pupil: "Yes, that's right."

"Let's start with this b: b-all, b-ill, b-all, b-ame." (Sequence repeated with d, s, g, f.)

Performance Evaluation: "Good work, Mike; you made only one error. Do you know where?"

Pupil: "I think I said fame was not a real word!"

Analysis and Comments: The lesson took eight minutes and was only partially appropriate, although Mike got all ten correct in his posttest. His attitude was good, and he actually did better than I had anticipated since he lacks self-confidence to the point where he is always reluctant to try. He was quite pleased with himself. The lesson will be extended to include initial blends, then to the addition of suffixes.

For Self-instruction: Devise a teaching procedure and performance evaluation method for this pupil: Karl, twelve years old, educationally handicapped. At the completion of the lesson, Karl will be able to name all of the chess pieces, explain how they move, and how the game of chess is won.

Perceptual-Motor Skills

26/ Auditory Sequencing

DEFINITION: The ability to recall in correct sequence and detail prior auditory information.

ILLUSTRATION: Pupil can imitate specific sound patterns, follow exactly a complex series of directions, repeat digit and letter series.

EDUCATIONAL RATIONALE: Pupils need instruction in attending to specific directions and in the identification and location of sound patterns and sequences. Drill and meaningful practice should be an integral part of the total remedial program.

SUGGESTED PROGRAM IDEAS

1. Beginning Activities
   a. Following specific directions: "Listen carefully. I want you to go to the bookcase, bring me a book, open it to page ten, put it on this table, open the door, and then come and sit down.
   b. Singing: "Do you know any song or part of a song you could sing for me, such as 'America,' 'Old MacDonald,' or 'Silent Night'?"
   c. Music patterns: Teacher makes simple rhythmic pattern on drum, box, etc., and child repeats. Repeat and extend using triangles, tone blocks, and musical bells.
   d. Dot-dash: On chalkboard, write pattern: •–/•–•–. Also say or tap pattern. Erase and have pupil repeat.
   e. Time activities: "What comes before Wednesday [after Friday, before March, after June, etc.]?" Give practice exercises in days of week, months of year.
   f. Personal data: "What is your address [when is your birthday, what are the names and ages of everyone in your family, etc.]?" Teach basic information required.
   g. Alphabet: Repeat alphabet.
2. Middle Stage Activities
   a. Numbers forward: "Say: 1–5, 6–9–3, 4–8–1–7, 3–2–7–6–5–1."
   b. Numbers backward: "Listen and say these numbers backward: 3–7, 6–9–1, 5–8–2–3, 7–4–9–2–5," etc.
   c. Telephone number game: Children tell their numbers and others repeat.
   d. Letters forward: "Say: A–B, C–X–0, T–L–B–M, Y–N–N–D–Q," etc. Extend exercises with letters backwards. Use anagrams and have pupil lay out the letters in correct sequence.
   e. Recall: "What comes before M [after T, before 5, after 17, before 42, etc.]?"
   f. Sound location: "Listen for the sound /d/ and tell me whether it comes at the beginning, middle, or end of the word: blood, riddle, drip." Have pupil make up words and exercises.
   g. Mixed symbols: "Listen carefully and repeat: X–3–2–boy–15, Car–20–man–Y–7–T, Pow–7–Zit–1," etc.
   h. Pupil sequence: Assign pupils numbers, call sequence, have them line up accordingly.
   i. Nonsense series: Repeat nonsense words.
3. Advanced Activities
   a. Extended sentences: "Listen carefully and repeat exactly what I say: Today is _____, 197__." "The big dog with a bone in its mouth ran down the street and up the hill," etc.

b. Spelling: Teacher spells out various words, then the pupil writes them on chalk-board or paper.

c. Poetry: Have child recall simple poems ("Jack and Jill," "Humpty Dumpty," etc.). Teach poems and rhymes of increasing length and difficulty.

d. Sequence stories: First child says, "I saw a dog." Next child adds a sentence and passes it on until series cannot be recalled.

e. Joke telling: Tell simple jokes and have pupil repeat them. Extend exercise to more complicated jokes and riddles.

REFERENCES

Myklebust, Helmer R. *Auditory Disorders in Children: A Manual for Differential Diagnosis.* New York: Grune & Stratton, 1954.

Related Programs

- Lowell, Edgar, and Stoner, Marguerite. *Play It by Ear—Auditory Training Games.* Los Angeles: John Tracy Clinic, 1963.
- Barry, Hortense. *The Young Aphasic Child: Evaluation and Training,* p. 36. Washington, D.C.: Alexander Graham Bell Association for the Deaf, 1961.
- Psychoeducational Resource Programs No. 23 (Auditory Decoding), 31 (Visual Memory), 32 (Visual-Motor Memory)
- *Listen and Do* (16 recordings and worksheets), Houghton Mifflin Co., 110 Fremont Street, Boston, Mass.
- Van Witsen, Betty. "Auditory Perceptual Skills." *Perceptual Training Activities Handbook,* pp. 41–43. New York: Columbia Teachers College, 1967.
- Kratoville, Betty Lou. *Listen, My Children, and You Shall Hear.* Danville, Ill.: Interstate Printers and Publishers, 1968.
- *Auditory Discrimination in Depth,* Teaching Resources, 100 Boylston Street, Boston, Mass.
- *Auditory Stimulator—A Program for the Development of Attention, Listening and Memory Skills* by Joseph Kaplan, Educational Performance Associates, 563-F Westview Avenue, Ridge-field, N.J.
- Boning, Richard A. *Following Directions.* Specific Skill Series. Rockville Centre, N.Y.: Barnell Loft, Ltd., 1963–1967.

Instructional Materials

- Listening post and record player, earphones and amplifier
- Rhythm Bells, Constructive Playthings, 1040 E. 85th Street, Kansas City, Mo.
- Double-headed Skin Tom-Tom, Constructive Playthings
- Triangle with Striker, Constructive Playthings
- Tone Blocks, Constructive Playthings
- Junior Orchestra Cymbal wtih Mallet, Constructive Playthings
- John Tracy Clinic Correspondence Course for Parents of Little Deaf Children (for use by parents of preschool children)
- Sentence or phrase strips
- *The Big Golden Book of Poetry, Golden Nursery Tale Book, Jokes and Riddles* (book), Palfrey's Educational Supply Co., 7715 E. Garvey Boulevard, Rosemead, Calif.
- Tape recorder
- Buzzer Board and Patterns, Developmental Learning Materials, 3505 N. Ashland Avenue, Chi-cago, Ill.

Further Evaluation

- Stanford-Binet L-M: repeating digits and memory for sentence items
- Wechsler Intelligence Scale for Children: digit span subtest
- Illinois Test of Psycholinguistic Ability: auditory sequential memory subtest
- Gessell, Arnold. "Immediate Memory Tests." *The First Five Years of Life: A Guide to the Study of the Preschool Child,* pp. 175–180. New York: Harper and Brothers, 1940.
- Screening Test for Auditory Perception, Academic Therapy Publications, San Rafael, Calif.

With the pupil blindfolded to increase auditory attention, rhymes are presented in broken sequence and finally in meaningful sequence.

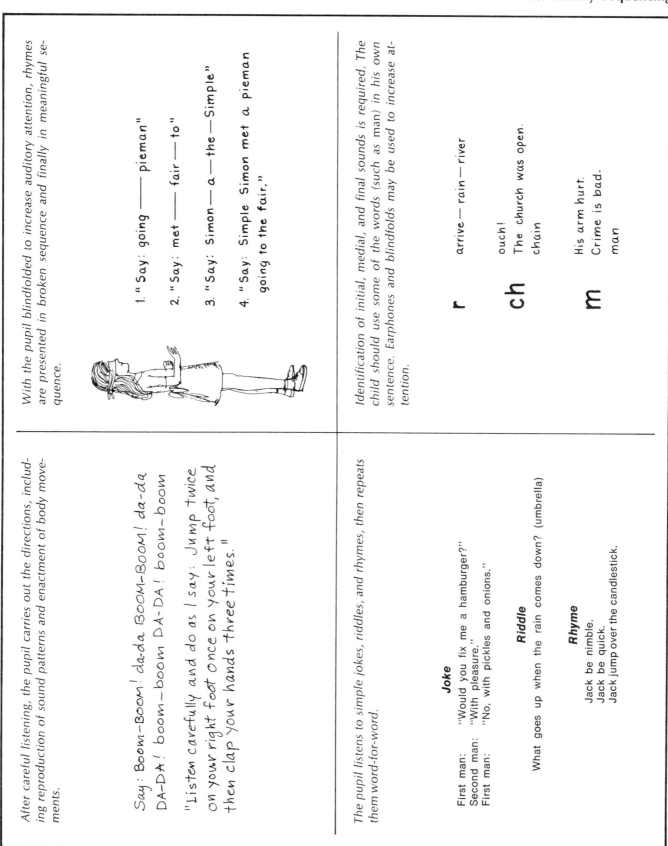

1. "Say: going —— pieman"

2. "Say: met —— fair — to"

3. "Say: Simon — a — the — Simple"

4. "Say: Simple Simon met a pieman going to the fair."

Identification of initial, medial, and final sounds is required. The child should use some of the words (such as man) in his own sentence. Earphones and blindfolds may be used to increase attention.

r arrive — rain — river

ch ouch!
The church was open.
chain

m His arm hurt.
Crime is bad.
man

After careful listening, the pupil carries out the directions, including reproduction of sound patterns and enactment of body movements.

Say: Boom-Boom! da-da Boom-Boom! da-da DA-DA! boom-boom DA-DA! boom-boom

"Listen carefully and do as I say: Jump twice on your right foot once on your left foot, and then clap your hands three times."

The pupil listens to simple jokes, riddles, and rhymes, then repeats them word-for-word.

Joke

First man: "Would you fix me a hamburger?"
Second man: "With pleasure."
First man: "No, with pickles and onions."

Riddle

What goes up when the rain comes down? (umbrella)

Rhyme

Jack be nimble.
Jack be quick.
Jack jump over the candlestick.

All programs should be modified or extended to meet the needs of individual pupils.

Priority Teaching Objective: Spencer, nine years old, specific learning disability. Upon completion of this lesson, Spencer will be able to repeat seven of nine number, letter, and word sequences.

Pretest Tasks: Spencer was given the following series of number, letter, and word sequences:

ties–10–20–top

1–a–Spencer–2–man–*b*

log–30–*s*–dog–*d*–7

In each series Spencer made at least one mistake.

Specific Teaching Procedures: "Spencer, I am going to say several more number, letter, and word sequences. I want you to listen carefully and repeat them after me. For each sequence you repeat correctly you get two points on your credit card:

9–2–0–5	a–c–e–g	king–ring–sing–ping
2–5–3–0–1	z–j–b–f–v	apple–Ann–ate–able–apricot
4–7–5–8–10–6	w–d–h–m–u–s	car–boat–dog–cat–boy–man

Performance Evaluation:

(correct)	(correct)	ring–king–sing–bing
(correct)	v–j–b–e–z	apricot–apple–able
4–7–5–7–8–10	h–m–w–g–s–u	boy–man–vat–dog–car

"Very good. Those were hard. You earned six points. Do you remember where you made some of your mistakes?"

Pupil: "On the last ones with words. They were hard."

Analysis and Comments: This was a very appropriate and demanding lesson which took ten minutes. Spencer's attitude was only fair; he was not paying attention to the tasks. He seemed mad at me for some reason and kept moving his chair further away and would not look at me.

For Self-instruction: Devise a teaching procedure and performance evaluation method for this student: Hank, eighteen years old, educationally handicapped. Hank will be able to explain the introduction to the *Declaration of Independence*, and then repeat it in correct sequence during a class presentation.

Perceptual-Motor Skills

27/Visual Acuity

DEFINITION: The ability to see and to differentiate meaningfully and accurately objects in one's visual field.

ILLUSTRATION: Pupil can see without noticeable fatigue, holds material at appropriate working distance, has no significant loss of acuity on Snellen or Illiterate E chart.

EDUCATIONAL RATIONALE: What an individual sees is the result of a psychophysical process which integrates gravitational forces, conceptual ideation, spatial-perceptual orientation, and language functions. Children should be provided varied visual experiences and practice in their interpretation and utilization.

SUGGESTED PROGRAM IDEAS

1. Visual Exploration
   a. Food: Place apple, cookie, candy, etc., at some distance from the child. Explain that it is something good to eat and that he may have it if he looks at it and describes it. Gradually extend distance to twenty feet.
   b. Toys: Place a mechanical toy, doll, etc., at some distance from the child. Explain that it is something that is fun to play with and that he may use it if he looks at it and describes it. Gradually extend distance to twenty feet.
   c. Light scope: Encourage exploration with the taleidescope and description of natural forms and objects through mirror reflections. Present kaleidoscope with different frames for viewing.
   d. Magnifiers: Explore hands, clothes, toys, books, pictures, animals, etc. View varied textures, shapes, elements. Use telescope to explore distant objects.
   e. Color exploration: View primary solid colors, paints, crayons. Play with color paddles and superimpose colors. Experiment with prisms.
   f. Visual orientation: Place same-color crayon in pupil's hand, on desk, in chalk tray, on floor, across room, etc., with other crayons. Have child point out location of "his color," whatever it may be.

2. Visual Description
   a. Sighting activities: Point out an object at some distance and have pupil sight and describe it. Use cardboard tube to sight and describe object. Teach use of simple telescope.
   b. Personal description: Teacher gives visual description of a child in the classroom and asks pupil to point out that child.
   c. Object identification: Place a number of different objects on the table in front of the child and in the chalk tray at varying distances. Teacher describes object and requires pupil to point to it.
   d. Visual field description. Child looks out the window and describes all that he sees. Tape record his report and play it back to him.
   e. Picture analysis: Using large pictures, the teacher says: "Point out the frog. Point to the house. Find the bird," etc.
   f. Activity description: One child does specific things moving about in different parts of the room; another pupil describes it.
   g. Picture story: Ask child to describe picture in story book.
   h. Films and television: Child watches movie or television and then describes what he saw. Others also describe and compare perceptions.

i. Flashlight beam: Focus light on objects in dark room and have pupil describe them.

3. Visual Interpretation

a. Miscroscope activities: Teach monocular and binocular use with substage light. Have pupil describe in advance what he is looking for, what he expects to see, and then what he actually sees.

b. Charades: Children act out "dog," "Santa Claus," "writing," "washing," "eating," etc. A pupil watches, identifies, and interprets.

c. Sequence interpretation: Show picture, such as a table immediately after a meal has been served, and ask child what preceded it, what might come next, etc.

d. Size interpretation: Child is presented varying-sized nails, circles, balls, sticks, pencils, etc. Ask pupil to point out all "small nails, large sticks, big circles, little balls," etc.

e. Special interest projects: Pupil sits looking ahead while objects are gradually moved into his peripheral field until he can clearly *describe* them. Change objects and directions.

REFERENCES

Buktenica, Norman A. *Visual Learning*. San Rafael, Calif.: Dimensions Publishing, 1968.

Getman, G. N. "The Visuomotor Complex in the Acquisition of Learning Skills." *Learning Disorders,* Vol. 1, edited by Jerome Hellmuth, pp. 49–76. Seattle: Special Child Publications, 1965.

McLaughlin, Samuel C. "Visual Perception in Strabismus and Amblyopia." *Psychological Monographs, General and Applied,* Vol. 78, No. 12. Washington, D.C.: American Psychological Association, 1964.

Related Programs

- *Visual Perceptual Skills* and *Visualization* (filmstrips), Educational Record Sales, 157 Chambers Street, New York, N.Y.
- Stereo Reader Programs, Keystone Manufacturing Co., Meadville, Pa.
- Frostig, Marianne, and Horne, David. "Perceptual Constancy Exercises." *The Frostig Program for the Development of Visual Perception: Teacher's Guide,* pp. 60–65, 120–134. Chicago: Follett Publishing, 1964.
- Professional synoptics training for amblyopia and other special training as may be required
- Van Witsen, Betty. "Visual Training." *Perceptual Training Activities Handbook,* pp. 11–29. New York: Columbia Teachers College, 1967.

Instructional Materials

- EZY-REDE Bar Magnifier, Apex Specialties Co., 1115 Douglas Avenue, Providence, R.I.
- Giant Tripod Magnifier, Creative Playthings, Princeton, N.J.
- Large Prism, Creative Playthings
- Tri-Color Viewer, Creative Playthings
- Cardboard Snellen Charts for School Use, American Medical Association, 535 N. Dearborn Street, Chicago, Ill.
- Hand magnifiers of various sizes
- View Master (stereopticon) and slides from photography shop
- Teleidescope and kaleidoscope
- Microscope and telescope
- Tape recorder

Further Evaluation

- Teacher judgment of pupil behavior, e.g., closeness of reading material, losing place while reading, fatigue while reading, rubbing eyes, reports of double vision, blurring, jumping, etc.
- Visual acuity evaluation by school nurse
- Professional optometric and opthalmological examination
- Illinois Test of Psycholinguistic Ability: visual reception subtest
- Keystone Visual-Survey Service Tests, Keystone View Company, Meadville, Pa.

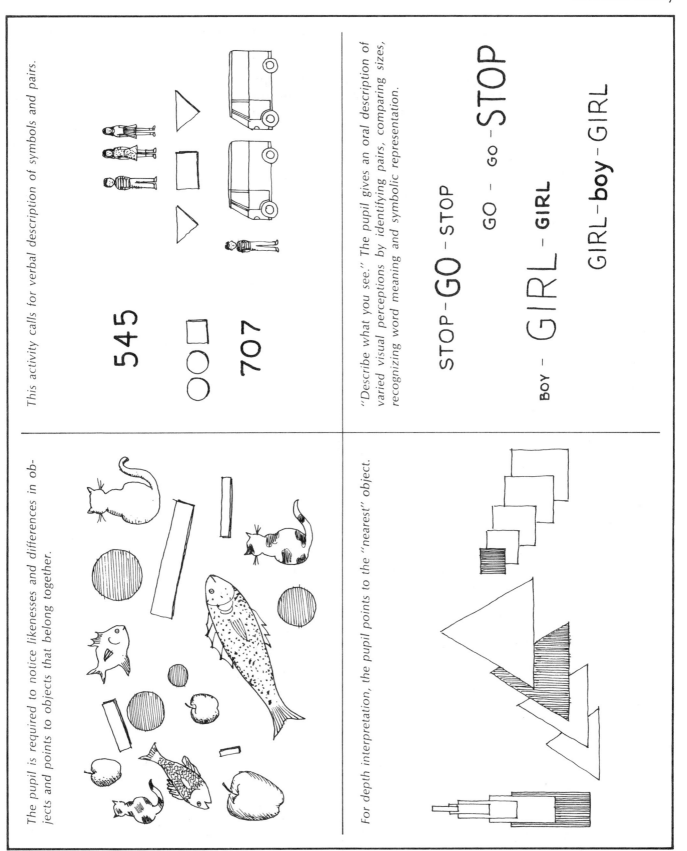

This activity calls for verbal description of symbols and pairs.

545

707

The pupil is required to notice likenesses and differences in objects and points to objects that belong together.

"Describe what you see." The pupil gives an oral description of varied visual perceptions by identifying pairs, comparing sizes, recognizing word meaning and symbolic representation.

STOP - GO - STOP

GO - GO - STOP

BOY - GIRL - GIRL

GIRL - boy - GIRL

For depth interpretation, the pupil points to the "nearest" object.

All programs should be modified or extended to meet the needs of individual pupils.

Priority Teaching Objective: Juanita, ten years old, educable mentally retarded. Using her right and left eyes separately, Juanita will be able to identify, by pointing and naming, two-thirds of the objects presented on a special poster.

Pretest Tasks: Juanita was shown a story-book picture including approximately forty-five objects. She was asked to pick out as many objects as she could from the picture by pointing and naming them. Of the possible forty-five forms, Juanita named eleven objects that were human forms: a little boy, a fat lady, a little girl, a man, etc.

Specific Teaching Procedures: "Juanita, we are going to look at this story picture, which is different from the first one. This time we are going to look through this spy [magnifying] glass at the picture. It should help you go slower, look more carefully, and see more things in the picture. See how I use the spy glass. I put the glass over this part of the picture, and then point and describe some of the things I see."

"For each different thing you see and describe you will be able to take one of these green stickers and stick it on your card. Now tell me what you are to do."

Pupil: "I'm to look carefully through the spy glass at each part of the picture and tell you as many things as I can find."

Performance Evaluation: Juanita slowly picked out thirty-eight of the forty-four forms on this picture. She omitted some, such as clouds and trees. She took fifteen minutes to complete the task.

Analysis and Comments: This was a fairly appropriate task in that the procedure and sticker reinforcements helped Juanita to pay attention. Although her reported visual acuity is 20/30 in the right eye and 20/40 in the left eye, it appears that much of her acuity problem may be due to lack of sustained attention to detail. She will be given exercises in figure-ground discrimination and visual scanning to improve visual performance.

For Self-instruction: Devise a teaching procedure and performance evaluation method for this pupil: Neil, eight years old, educationally handicapped. Neil will be able to identify by name eight of ten objects presented to him one at a time, to the right or left side of his head, while he is looking into a wall mirror.

28/Visual Coordination and Pursuit

DEFINITION: The ability to follow and track objects and symbols with coordinated eye movements.

ILLUSTRATION: With head steady, pupil can move eyes to fixate on stable objects in varied places, pursue moving objects such as finger positions, follow pictures and word stories left to right without jerky movements.

EDUCATIONAL RATIONALE: Coordinated eye movements are essential in order to attend to sequentially arranged symbolic learning material such as reading matter. Child should be provided systematic instruction in visual coordination and occular control activities.

SUGGESTED PROGRAM IDEAS

1. General Coordination
   a. Walking: Pupil sits at end of room with head steady and visually follows teacher or student who walks back and forth at the other end of room.
   b. Skipping: Pupil sits and tracks another person who skips around the perimeter of the room, then skips back and fourth and in figure eight.
   c. Object focus: Teacher sits in front of pupil and says: "Look at the flag on the wall while I count five. Look at my desk. Look at the door," etc.
   d. Ball roll: Teacher rolls a utility ball away from the pupil while child tracks it. Pupil rolls ball in different directions and tracks while counting aloud until the ball stops.
   e. Gliders: Pupil makes paper and balsa wood gliders. Holding head still, he follows glider flight as it is thrown by another person. Sail paper plates and track them.
   f. Racing cars: Use wind-up mechanical cars or racing cars on track. Visually follow one car at a time around the track.
   g. Electric train light: Pupil sits in corner of dark room and tracks electric train by following headlight of the engine.

2. Specific Directional Training
   a. Horizontal-lateral: Sit in front of pupil with thumbtack in pencil eraser about eighteen inches from the midline of the nose. Slowly move to the left while pupil counts to ten.
   b. Vertical: Follow same procedure starting at midline. Extend to right and left sides. Remind pupil not to move head.
   c. Diagonal: Begin at midline and move in all directions. Change angles and starting points.
   d. Rotary: Begin at midline of nose and have pupil track small circular movements. Extend size and positions of circles. Take old phonograph records and make cardboard extensions with luminescent dots. Use in dark room at different speeds (slow, 33⅓ to fast, 78) with pupil counting different number of revolutions.
   e. Varied patterns: With increasing control, pupil should track basic form patterns, free movements, with changing depth perception, etc.
   f. Reinforcement procedures: Track small penlight. Track balls of various sizes held by teacher. Track balls held jointly by teacher and pupil. Track flashlight spotted on and off wall in dark room. Repeat with monocular as well as binocular exercises.
   g. Make large 100-number chart for specific focus training.
   h. Sequential arrangements: Arrange blocks, paper balls, etc. in sequential order by size.

3. Extended Activities

    a. Game targets: Sit midline side of ping-pong, volleyball, badminton, or tennis game, and track ball, counting until play stops.

    b. Thumb focus: Hold right and left thumbs in front of body, shoulder high, eighteen inches apart. Following commands, "right, left, right, left," focus the eyes on the thumb indicated. Repeat after changing thumb positions.

    c. Pencil tracking: Hold pencil straight out in dominant hand. Focus "pencil-teacher, pencil-clock, pencil-flag." Practice on objects to the north, south, east, west, up and down, etc.

    d. Suspended tennis ball: Suspend tennis ball from ceiling on string. Hold a rolling pin (with stripes of various colors painted on it) in both hands and bounce ball from selected colors.

    e. Chalkboard tracking: Pupil slowly follows chalk line and points with finger as line is drawn from left to right.

    f. Paper tracking: Teacher sits in front of pupil and slowly draws line pattern on paper from left to right as pupil tracks and follows with finger.

    g. Word and sentence tracking: Pupil tracks reading material on large chart and in books following penlight or pointer as directed by teacher.

REFERENCES

Getman, Gerald N., and Hendrickson, Homer H. "The Needs of Teachers for Specialized Information on the Development of Visuomotor Skills in Relation to Academic Performance." *The Teacher of Brain-Injured Children,* edited by William Cruickshank, pp. 155–168. Syracuse: Syracuse University Press, 1966.

Related Programs

- *Visual Perceptual Skills* and *Visual Motor Coordination* (filmstrips), Educational Record Sales, 157 Chambers Street, New York, N.Y.
- Kephart, Newell C. *The Slow Learner in the Classroom,* Chapter 9. Columbus, Ohio: Charles E. Merrill, 1962.
- Getman, G. N.; Kane, E. R.; Halgren, M. R.; and McKee, G. W. *Developing Learning Readiness.* Manchester, Mo.: Webster Publishing, 1968.
- Smith, Donald, ed. *Michigan Visual Tracking Program.* Ann Arbor: Ann Arbor Publishers, 1967.
- *Pathway School Program/1* (eye-hand coordination exercises), Teaching Resources, 100 Boylston Street, Boston, Mass.
- *Perceptual Development Programs,* Audio Dynamic Research, 1219 E. Eleventh Street, Pueblo, Colo.
- Geake, R. *Visual Tracking: A Self-instruction Workbook.* Ann Arbor: Ann Arbor Publishers, 1962.

Instructional Materials

- Moving target toy gun set
- Balloons
- Basketball, utility ball, softball, baseball, golf ball
- Penlight, flashlight
- Thumbtacks, pencils, primary lined paper
- Luminescent tape or paint
- Ping-pong set
- Old three-speed record player and records
- Assorted toys, picture cards, alphabet cards, number cards
- Primary story charts and racks
  Large-print reading books for easy tracking
- Cardboard boxes for painting and use as needed

Further Evaluation

- Teacher evaluation of occular movements during reading
- Subjective evaluation of visual pursuit tasks
- Professional opthalmological and optometric examination

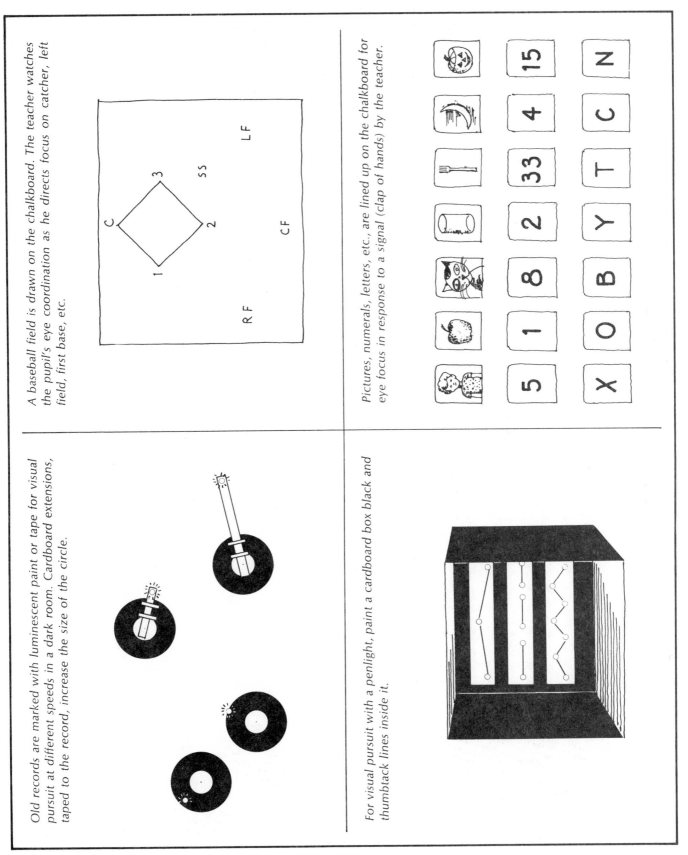

A baseball field is drawn on the chalkboard. The teacher watches the pupil's eye coordination as he directs focus on catcher, left field, first base, etc.

Pictures, numerals, letters, etc., are lined up on the chalkboard for eye focus in response to a signal (clap of hands) by the teacher.

Old records are marked with luminescent paint or tape for visual pursuit at different speeds in a dark room. Cardboard extensions, taped to the record, increase the size of the circle.

For visual pursuit with a penlight, paint a cardboard box black and thumbtack lines inside it.

All programs should be modified or extended to meet the needs of individual pupils.

Priority Teaching Objective: Jonnette, eight years old, reading disability. Upon completion of this lesson, Jonnette will be able to successfully track and follow two out of three number-line-letter patterns presented.

Pretest Tasks: Jonnette was presented the stimulus figures below on full-page worksheets. She was unable to visually specify the correct number-line-letter pattern 1→K; 2→O; 3→T.

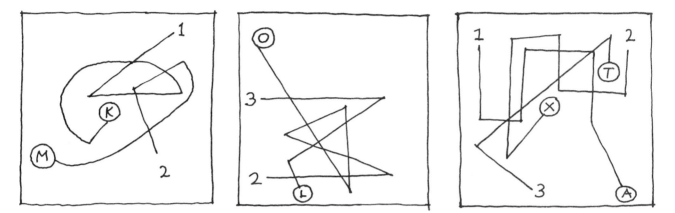

Specific Teaching Procedures: "Jonnette, we are going to learn to follow some line patterns with our eyes. Watch me on the chalkboard as I draw the letter A here, followed by a long line which ends with the letter B. Now you take the chalk and draw, over my letter A, the line and the letter B. Good!"

"This time I will draw the number 1 followed by a zig-zag line and then write this letter (Y) at the end of the line. What is the name of the last letter I drew?"

Pupil: "Y."

"That's correct. Now watch closely because I'm going to draw some other numbers, lines, and letters on the board. After each drawing, I want you to tell me the name of the letter I draw and then put your finger on it for me."

"Fine. Now we are going to do the same thing with these paper worksheets. See, I start again here in the corner with the number 1, then I draw this line, and now you tell me the letter I write."

"On this sheet we have a drawing already made. Look at the number 1. Now carefully follow the line with your eyes to the end and tell me the name of the letter. That's right! Now trace it with your finger starting at the number 1."

Performance Evaluation: The posttest was the same as the pretest. Jonnette carefully studied each worksheet and got them all correct. During the practice exercises she seemed to do much better by using her finger to reinforce visual tracking.

Analysis and Comments: This was an appropriate and difficult series of exercises for Jonnette. They will be continued with much more time given to chalkboard training. She will also be asked to make some of her own designs for tutoring Allen, who has a similar visual coordination problem.

For Self-instruction: Devise a teaching procedure and performance evaluation for this student. Rudy, fifteen years old, visual coordination reading disability. Upon completion of the training program, Rudy will be able to complete page 16 of the *Visual Tracking* program workbook by Geake and Smith, with no more than two mistakes in alphabet tracking on both exercises.

Perceptual-Motor Skills

29/Visual-Form Discrimination

DEFINITION: The ability to visually differentiate the forms and symbols in one's environment.

ILLUSTRATION: Pupil can match identical pictures and symbols such as abstract designs, letters, numbers, and words.

EDUCATIONAL RATIONALE: The ability to see likenesses and differences in one's environment is prerequisite to symbolic differentiation and interpretation as required in reading. Basic educational programs should include opportunities to point out, indicate, and comment on the details and differences perceived in one's visual field.

SUGGESTED PROGRAM IDEAS

1. Basic Discriminatory Activities
   a. Gross differences: Teacher points out varied objects in classroom, yard, field trip, and comments on visual differences; pupils are then required to view objects visually and elaborate on differences. Use filmstrip *Look About You* for introductory discussion.
   b. Color matching: Using crayons and colored papers, have pupils match colors.
   c. Concrete objects: Place pencil clip, pen, pencil, stick, nail, and bolt on the table; present child with a second pencil and ask him to point out the other one that "looks similar to this one." Extend exercise with varied objects. Point out tall and short class members.
   d. Class differences: Present a series of buttons of different sizes and colors; present a duplicate and have pupil point out the match. Extend exercise with different dolls, blocks, toy cars, marbles, coins, books, etc.
   e. Directional differences: Lay out four identical books—three facing in one direction and the fourth reversed; have pupil point out and comment on difference. Extend directional exercises with papers, pencils, nails, etc.
   f. Geometric forms: Present three wooden blocks and one cylinder; pupil points out the one that is different. Repeat with triangles, spheres, and rectangles.
   g. Concrete patterns: Arrange four checker patterns—three identical and one slightly different; have pupil point out differences. Repeat using sticks, blocks, nails, paper, dominoes, etc.
   h. Play dominoes and arrange matching sequences.
2. Pictorial Designs
   a. Animal pictures: Arrange series of identical and similar pictures for pupil to point out and describe.
   b. Basic forms: Make cards of basic geometric forms for matching.
   c. Size discrimination: Use animal and form pictures with one card a different size and teach discrimination.
   d. Picture discrimination: Use large colored picture books with varied objects and say: "Point to the cookies. Show me the boy. Put your finger on the balloon," etc.
   e. Perception cards: Use commercial cards and plaques for visual matching.
   f. Abstract designs: Teach matching and differentiation of design cards.
   g. Filmstrips: Introduce visual discrimination filmstrip series.
   h. Formal exercises: Use formal programs such as Continental Press *Visual Discrimination 1*, followed by Fitzhugh *Spatial Organization 1*.

      i. Missing parts: Show pictures of bicycles, people, etc., with parts missing. Pupil points out and describes missing parts.

3. Symbolic Discrimination
   a. Primary differentiation: Present design, number, or letter series, with one different.
   b. Size differentiation: Present series of identical designs, numbers, or letters, with one smaller or larger than the others.
   c. Rotation: Symbols are identical but one is rotated for identification.
   d. Cursive and manuscript series: Present letter series requiring identification of odd letter.
   e. Basic word patterns: Present series (e.g., boy–boy–girl–boy) for pattern discrimination. Use primary word list.
   f. Formal exercises: Use Fitzhugh *Spatial Organization 3* and Continental Press *Visual Discrimination* 2 programs.
   g. Fine discriminations: Teach discrimination of inversions, reversals, substitutions, i.e, saw–sam, was–saw, saw–san, etc.

REFERENCES

Pickford, R. W. "Vision." *Annual Review of Psychology,* Vol. 8, edited by Paul Farnsworth. Palo Alto, Calif.: Annual Reviews, 1957.

Teacher's Guide and Supplement for Visual Discrimination, Level One and Level Two. Elizabethtown, Pa.: Continental Press, 1958.

Related Programs

- *Visual Perceptual Skills* and *Visual Discrimination and Matching* (filmstrips), Educational Record Sales, 157 Chambers Street, New York, N.Y.
- *Let's Look at First Graders: A Guide to Understanding and Fostering Intellectual Development in Young Children* (concepts of space and time), Educational Testing Service, Princeton, N.J.
- *Look About You* (record and filmstrip), Guidance Associates, Pleasantville, N.Y.
- *Visual Discrimination 1 and 2,* Continental Press, Inc., Elizabethtown, Pa.
- *Spatial Organization Workbooks 1 and 3.* The Fitzhugh Plus Program. Galien, Mich.: Allied Educational Council, 1966.
- *Likenesses and Differences* (audio flashcard set), Electronics Future, Inc., 57 Dodge Avenue, North Haven, Conn.
- *Detect: A Sensorimotor Approach to Visual Discrimination,* Science Research Associates, Inc., 259 E. Erie Street, Chicago, Ill.
- Manolakes, George, et al. *Try: Experiences for Young Children,* Task 3. New York: Noble and Noble, 1967.
- Goldstein, Herbert, and Levitt, Edith. *A Reading Readiness Workbook in Visual Discrimination.* Parkinson Program for Special Children. Chicago: Follett Publishing, 1966.

Instructional Materials

- Checker kit for pattern exercises
- Perception Plaques, Constructive Playthings, 1040 E. 85th Street, Kansas City, Mo.
- Geometric Insets, Constructive Playthings
- Judy Matchettes, The Judy Company, 310 N. Second Street, Minneapolis, Minn.
- Judy Geometric Forms, The Judy Company
- Butterfly Board, Airplane Board, Lakeshore Equipment Company, 1144 Montague Avenue, San Leandro, Calif.
- 3-D Art, Palfrey's Educational Supply Co., 7715 E. Garvey Boulevard, Rosemead, Calif.
- Origami, Palfrey's Educational Supply Co.
- Picture Readiness Game, Match Sets I and II, Match Me, Primary Kiddie Kards, Full-color Picture Dictionary Cards, Palfrey's Educational Supply Co.
- People Puzzles, Shapes Puzzles, Animal Puzzles, Developmental Learning Materials, 3505 N. Ashland Avenue, Chicago, Ill.

Building blocks, sticks, and checkers are used in varying arrangements requiring the pupil to notice the differences in patterns.

The pupil should detect the differences in these groups of word symbols. No reading of words should be required.

CAT CAT TAC

TOY TOY TOY

FEEL LEFE FEEL

The pupil must detect slight directional differences in an arrangement of needles and toy money.

A size and directional program, using letters and numbers, can be printed on cards, dittos, or chalkboard.

3 3 3 3 3

C C C C Ɔ C C C

8 8 8 8 8 8 8 8

T ⊥ T T T T

All programs should be modified or extended to meet the needs of individual pupils.

Further Evaluation
- Sanford Binet L-M: Visual discrimination tests (Manual, pp. 74–75, 78–79, 82)
- Gesell School Readiness Tests: Visual Test 1, orientation of forms
- Valett Developmental Survey of Basic Learning Abilities: visual discrimination
- Frostig Developmental Test of Visual Perception: form constancy and position in space tests

PRESCRIPTIVE ILLUSTRATION

Priority Teaching Objective: Ron, seven years old, transitional first grade. Ron will be able to match twenty-seven of thirty symbol discrimination tasks (letters, designs, words) under a three-second time exposure for each design.

Pretest Tasks: When Ron was shown a series of ten symbol discrimination tasks such as the following, he was able to match only three of them:

Specific Teaching Procedure: "Ron, in this lesson we are going to go through each row on the worksheet, matching up the one letter, design, or word that is exactly like the first one on the row. We will go slowly letting you take as much time as you need to find the correct symbol. Then we will go through the list again, going as fast as you can, having only a short time of three seconds to find each correct symbol."

"Now watch me as I do the first row. I will use this paper scanner so the letter V shows through the opening. Now I move the scanner across the worksheet to find another V. There it is, so I will stop and point to it. This is how you should do each row, looking carefully at the first symbol and then quickly finding the one that matches it."

"Now tell me what you are to do."
Pupil: "I will find each row, like this with the card, then I will look at the first thing closely, and then try to find another one just like it in the row, and go as fast as I can."

Performance Evaluation: "Very good, you got the first rows that you did slowly all correct. On the second try, when we went faster, you missed a few. Can you remember any of the ones you couldn't find in a hurry?"
Pupil: "Yes, I can find some of the ones I couldn't get fast [points out several errors]. They look alike sometimes, and it takes me longer, and I get mixed up on the hard ones."

Analysis and Comments: On a posttest Ron got twenty-one of thirty correct in fifteen minutes. His attitude was good, and he was well motivated. He does not respond well under time limits. More difficult form discrimination items should be given, but the time should be increased to four or five seconds per symbol.

For Self-instruction: Devise a teaching procedure and performance evaluation method for this pupil: Barry, ten years old, perceptually handicapped. Upon completion of the lesson Barry will be able to cut out four different forms and paste them on the appropriate sections of a form-matching design (such as four different parts on the outline of a tree). He will be successful in completing five out of six such designs.

30/Visual Figure-Ground Differentiation

DEFINITION: *The ability to perceive objects in foreground and background and to separate them meaningfully.*

ILLUSTRATION: *Pupil can differentiate picture of self and friends from group picture, differentiate objects in "front" and "back" part of pictures and mockups, differentiate his name from among others on paper and blackboard, perceive simple forms and words imbedded in others.*

EDUCATIONAL RATIONALE: *The differentiation of meaningful objects in the environment requires visual concentration, attention, and stability. Children should be trained in the skills of visual scanning, peripheral discrimination of boundaries, and detecting significant details; pointing, matching, describing, and kinesthetic-motor modalities should be used in the remedial education program.*

SUGGESTED PROGRAM IDEAS

1. Beginning Activities
   a. Reduce stimuli: If necessary, provide an individual study booth for the pupil in order to restrict the perceptual environment. Present one activity at a time and break down to component parts for visual differentiation.
   b. Doll house: Present toy doll house, furniture, and dolls for free play and placement.
   c. Toy farm: Pupil watches and participates in farm arrangement.
   d. Object differentiation: "Point out the doll in front of the house. Point out the toy picture on the wall in the play house. Point out the big house on the hill across the street."
   e. Form differentiation: "Point out the square things in this room. Point out the round things in this box. Point out the triangular-shaped objects on the shelf," etc.
   f. Tracing: Trace two- and three-dimensional forms with fingers. Trace objects on paper. Use stencils to trace designs. Shade or color both the figure and the background. Copy pictures and designs. Watch others copy and trace and then finger trace their work.
   g. Photograph activity: Finger trace pupils, parents, etc., in foreground and background of pictures.
2. Middle Stage Activities
   a. Puzzle play: Begin with Judy Senior Puzzles with good figure-ground contrast. Extend activity to include advanced picture puzzles with much figure-ground confusion.
   b. Sorting activities: Sort similar objects such as clothes, buttons, assorted paper, marbles, etc.
   c. Verbal description: Use picture books, nature walks, slides, etc., and have child point to the "bug on the leaf, the bird in the sky," etc.
   d. Missing parts: Use Continental Press and similar materials to teach visual organization and integration of separated pieces of pictures and designs.
   e. Cutting: Cut out persons and objects from magazine pictures. Replace figures on background as a puzzle. For hidden and elaborate figures, cut away details and unnecessary parts to emphasize the basic figure.
   f. Single out figure on ground: Draw small square on large circle and point out square as figure and circle as ground. Extend to include outline of a man in front of a tree,

117

car in front of a house, cat in front of a fence, etc. Have pupil differentiate and trace with fingers.

   g. Complex collage: Have pupils create picture collages and point out and describe various figures and objects.

3. Advanced Activities

   a. Overlapping figures: Draw overlapping mixed figures and designs for pupil to visually differentiate upon request. Use finger tracing, coloring, and cutouts for training.

   b. Superimposed lines: Draw heavy lines over black and white figures for visual discrimination.

   c. Hidden figures: Draw hidden-figure outlines or purchase activity books with hidden-figure puzzles. Locate, trace, and color the figures.

   d. Gestalt completion: Cut up black silhouette pictures of animals and objects and paste on white paper with pieces separated by space. Use for visual identification exercises.

   e. Marble board and blocks: Use red and black marbles on grey marble board to create complex designs for tracing and imitation. Halsam design blocks can be used to give practice in creating and separating figures on varied backgrounds.

   f. Symbolic material: Shade over words, letters, and numbers. Separate and mix letters in the pupil's name and require visual integration for reading.

   g. Word scanning: Have pupil locate a given word on a dictionary page or in a book.

REFERENCES

Strauss, Alfred A., and Kephart, Newell C. "Psychopathology of Perception." *Psychopathology and Education of the Brain-Injured Child,"* pp. 47–89. New York: Grune & Stratton, 1955.

Related Programs

- Hackett, Layne C., and Jensen, Robert G. *A Guide to Movement Exploration.* Palo Alto, Calif.: Peek Publications, 1967.
- *Visual Perceptual Skills* and *Figure Ground Perception* (filmstrips), Educational Record Sales, 157 Chambers Street, New York, N.Y.
- Frostig, Marianne, and Horne, David. "Figure-Ground Perception Exercises." *The Frostig Program for the Development of Visual Perception,* pp. 79–83. Chicago: Follett Publishing, 1964.
- *Independent Activities, Levels 1 and 2* (identifying missing parts), Continental Press, Elizabethtown, Pa.
- Barry, Hortense. "Training for Figure-Ground Disturbance." *The Young Aphasic Child: Evaluation and Training,* pp. 36–50. Washington, D.C.: Alexander Graham Bell Association for the Deaf, 1961.
- *Fairbanks/Robinson Program 1* (Section G, figure-ground discriminations), Perceptual-Motor Development, Teaching Resources, 100 Boylston Street, Boston, Mass.
- ETA Visual Perception Kit, Educational Teaching Aids, A. Daigger Co., 159 W. Kinzie Street, Chicago, Ill.

Instructional Materials

- Toy doll house and furniture
- Pegboard and Pegboard Discovery Guides, Lakeshore Equipment Co., 1144 Montague Avenue, San Leandro, Calif.
- Judy Senior Puzzles, The Judy Company, 310 N. Second Street, Minneapolis, Minn.
- Color Cubes Set, Playskool Manufacturing Co., 3720 N. Kedzie Avenue, Chicago, Ill.
- Modern Form Set, Palfrey's Educational Supply Co., 7715 E. Garvey Boulevard, Rosemead, Calif.
- Assorted picture puzzles with figure-ground contrast
- Forms and form boards for tracing and matching
- Color and hidden-figure puzzle books
- Hidden Forms Puzzles from *Humpty Dumpty magazine,* The Better Reading Foundation, Inc., Thompson Lane, Box 538, Nashville, Tenn.
- Figure-Ground Transparencies, Speech and Language Materials, Inc., P.O. Box 721, Tulsa, Okla.

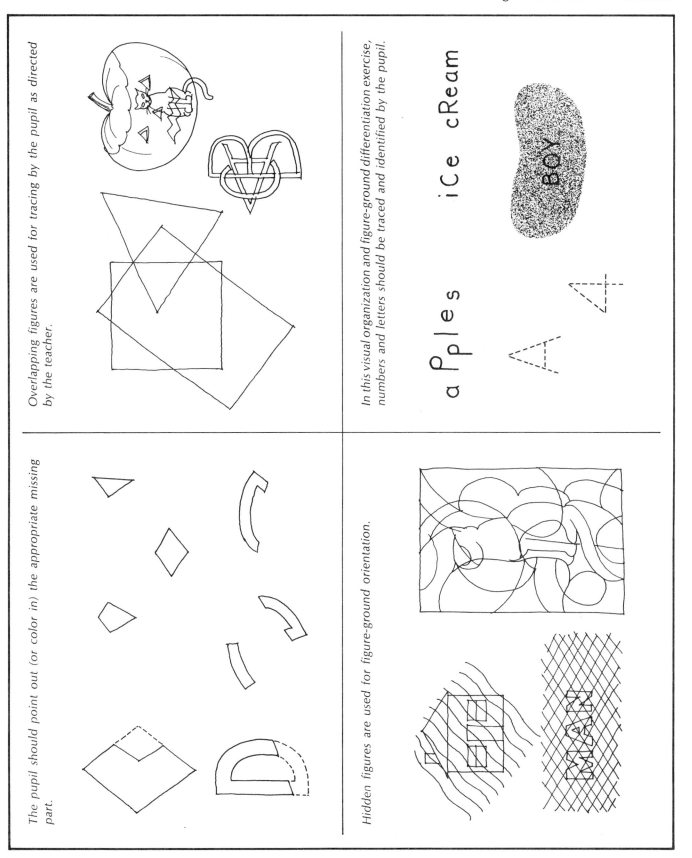

Overlapping figures are used for tracing by the pupil as directed by the teacher.

In this visual organization and figure-ground differentiation exercise, numbers and letters should be traced and identified by the pupil.

The pupil should point out (or color in) the appropriate missing part.

Hidden figures are used for figure-ground orientation.

All programs should be modified or extended to meet the needs of individual pupils.

Further Evaluation

- Ayres Southern California Figure-Ground Visual Perception Test, Western Psychological Services
- Frostig Developmental Test of Visual Perception: Test II, figure-ground
- The Hooper Visual Organization Test, Western Psychological Services
- Strauss Marble Board Test
- Raven Progressive Matrices, Western Psychological Services
- Illinois Test of Psycholinguistic Ability: visual closure subtest

PRESCRIPTIVE ILLUSTRATION

Priority Teaching Objective: Paul, six years old, educable mentally retarded. Paul will be able to find hidden shapes and pictures on a worksheet, discriminating the stimulus form with 100 percent accuracy (on selected Frostig worksheets).

Pretest Tasks: Paul was given the Frostig Developmental Test of Visual Discrimination. He achieved moderately well until he was presented four overlapping figures, which he was unable to distinguish. He could not differentiate figure from ground when finding shapes in a highly complex background.

Specific Teaching Procedures: "Paul, here is a picture that has four little birds—like this one—hiding in it. See how I put my finger on the bird and trace it. Now I am going to take this blue crayon and color in the bird. Now it is a pretty blue bird and is easy to see. We are going to find the other birds the same way. Tell me how we are going to do it, Paul."

Pupil: "Find the little birds with my finger and then color them in. They're hiding and it isn't easy."

"That's right. You may have the paper to take home when you find as many birds as you can and color them in. Now go ahead."

Performance Evaluation: "Very good! You found all of the birds except one. What did you think of that?"

Pupil: "That was fun—but they were hard to trace!"

Analysis and Comments: Paul got eight of the nine birds on the worksheet, and it appeared to be a very appropriate task. He had to search carefully to find all of the required shapes. This is the first time I have heard Paul verbalize so freely over a school learning task, as he is usually tense and uncommunicative when presented his assignments. The hidden-picture exercises will be continued on a more difficult level and supplemented with overlapping figures, which should be much more difficult for him.

For Self-instruction: Devise a teaching procedure and performance evaluation method for this pupil: Steve, eleven years old, educationally handicapped. Steve will be able to identify thirty out of thirty-five words in a field of nonsense words and obtrusive stimuli.

Perceptual-Motor Skills

31/Visual Memory

DEFINITION: The ability to recall accurately prior visual experiences.

ILLUSTRATION: Pupil can recall from visual cues where he stopped in book, can match or verbally recall objects removed or changed in the environment, can match briefly exposed symbols.

EDUCATIONAL RATIONALE: Visual recall and retention must be sufficiently developed to insure success in reading and related abstract learning tasks. Training should be provided in the recall of material through pointing, matching, and verbal description from memory.

SUGGESTED PROGRAM IDEAS

1. Simple Recall Activities
   a. Show and hide: Place coin, pencil, tack, button, clip, nail, and pen on table. After placing, count to ten with pupil watching. Child turns his back, and one item is removed and placed in a box with several other objects. The pupil is to turn around and find the missing object.
   b. Plastic people: Arrange five or six different cowboys, Indians, soldiers, etc., on the table. Cover objects and show one duplicate to the pupil for five seconds. Remove the duplicate, uncover original objects, and have child point out the match.
   c. Magazine picture match: Briefly show the pupil a cut-out object from a magazine picture; show duplicate picture intact and have pupil point out original object.
   d. Immediate verbal recall: Pupil closes eyes and describes his clothes, bulletin board, etc.
   e. General verbal recall: Have the child describe in detail what he had for breakfast, what a bee looks like, how the principal looks, what he saw on TV, etc.
   f. Comic strip characters: Cut out and arrange different poses of a comic strip character. Briefly expose child to one duplicate, remove. Have child point out match.
   g. Opaque projector: Arrange assorted objects in front of child. Project one on screen with projector, remove. Have pupil find duplicate object. Use basic forms and designs for similar practice.
   h. Names: Have various pupils stand up and another child name them as they stand.
2. Symbol Training
   a. Perception cards: Arrange dotted perception cards in chalk tray. Briefly expose model. Then remove and have pupil point out duplicate. Repeat exercises, occluding one eye at a time.
   b. Domino matching: Use large dominoes for exposing and recalling visual patterns.
   c. Form boards: Present form from magnetic form board, remove. Have pupil locate duplicate.
   d. Concentration games: Place deck (or partial deck) of cards face down. Two pupils turn over one card at a time and recall and remove duplicate cards (two eights, two aces, etc.), Keep record of pupil's score and reward improved performance.
   e. Directional matching: Use directional arrows and designs for recall matching.
   f. Frostig program: Teach recall of motor and spatial sequence materials.
   g. Filmstrip training: Teach exercises from the Visual Memory Filmstrip series.
   h. Object sequencing: Arrange several individual picture cards in chalk tray. Cards are then removed, shuffled, and given to pupil to rearrange in original sequential order.

i. Reproduce highway signs and symbols on ditto sheets. Pupils play with parents when traveling—first to check all signs wins.

3. Word and Number Training

  a. Numbers: Present five or six number cards. Briefly expose pupil to a duplicate. Remove duplicate and have child match by recall.

  b. Alphabet letters: Teach alphabet recall using cards, link letters, plastic letters, etc. Use both capital and lowercase letters.

  c. Words: Make word cards for *boy, girl, in, cat, up, home;* present cards and briefly expose one duplicate. Remove and match. Be sure *not* to teach names or spelling because visual recall is all that is demanded at this point.

  d. Number and letter sequences: Arrange varied cards in chalkboard tray and expose pupil to them for ten seconds. Shuffle, again expose pupil to them for ten seconds. Shuffle and have child rearrange.

  e. Page recall: Open small picture or story book to a given page and have pupil scan it for a few seconds. Close book and then request the child to find the page through visual memory.

  f. Word phrases: Make several three- or four-word sentence strips. Arrange in front of pupil and have him match a duplicate by memory. Shuffle the sequence and have pupil rearrange.

  g. Tachistoscopic training: Use filmstrip programs for brief visual exposure, matching, and verbal association and recall.

REFERENCES

Getman, G. N. "Practice in Visual Memory." *Physiology of Readiness.* Minneapolis, Minn.: Programs to Accelerate School Success, 1964.

Strauss, Alfred, and Kephart, Newell. *Psychopathology and Education of the Brain-Injured Child,* pp. 148–156. New York: Grune & Stratton, 1955.

Related Programs

- *Visual Perceptual Skills* and *Visual Memory (filmstrips),* Educational Record Sales, 157 Chambers Street, New York, N.Y.
- Frostig, Marianne, and Horne, David. "Position in Space: Recall of Motor Sequence" and "Spatial Sequences." *The Frostig Program for the Development of Visual Perception,* pp. 51–60, 61–68. Chicago: Follett Publishing, 1964.
- "Concentration" card and object games of all kinds requiring visual retention.
- Elementary Tachist-O-Flasher Kit (seeing skills, instant words, instant word phrases, number recognition), Learning Through Seeing, Inc., Sunland, Calif.
- *Missing Parts* (audio flashcard sets), Electronics Futures, Inc., 57 Dodge Avenue, North Haven, Conn.

Instructional Materials

- Pairs Word Game, Memory Arithmetic Game, Educational Concentration, Palfrey's Educational Supply Co., 7715 E. Garvey Boulevard, Rosemead, Calif.
- Duplicate letter, number, and word cards, comic strips, sentence and phrase strips
- Perception Cards, Large Number Cards, Palfrey's Educational Supply Co.
- Opaque projector
- Jumbo Color Dominoes, Palfrey's Educational Supply Co.
- Magnetic Basic Form Board, Magnetic Alphabet and Spelling Board, Palfrey's Educational Supply Co.
- Hard-board and felt pens for making designs and symbols
- Plastic cowboys and Indians
- Link Letters, Palfrey's Educational Supply Co.
- Picture Sequence Cards, Milton Bradley Co., 74 Park Street, Springfield, Mass.
- *Fairy Tales Crossword Puzzles,* Ideal School Supply Co., 11000 S. Lavergne Street, Oak Park, Ill.

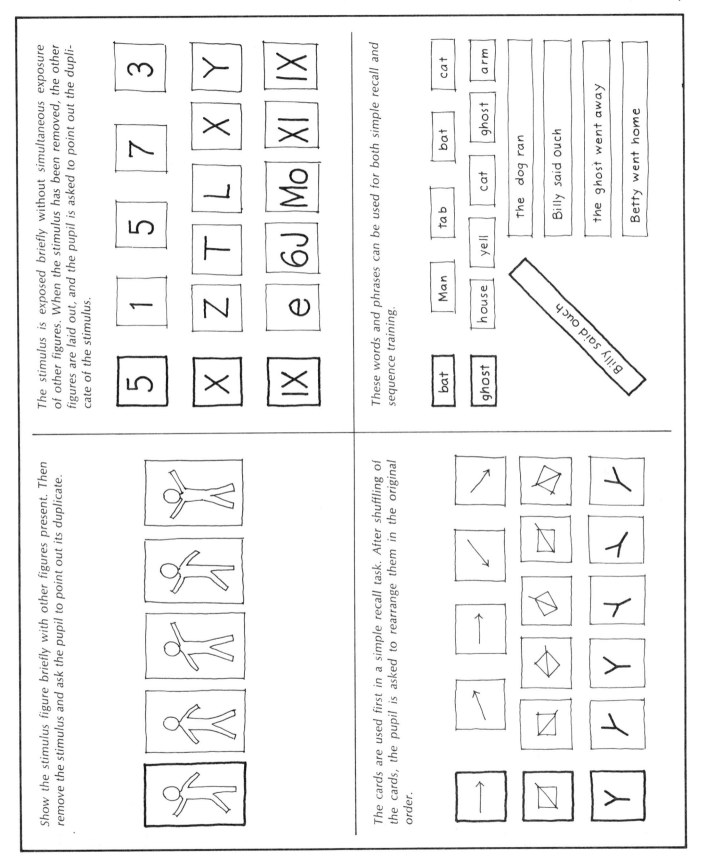

The stimulus is exposed briefly without simultaneous exposure of other figures. When the stimulus has been removed, the other figures are laid out, and the pupil is asked to point out the duplicate of the stimulus.

These words and phrases can be used for both simple recall and sequence training.

Show the stimulus figure briefly with other figures present. Then remove the stimulus and ask the pupil to point out its duplicate.

The cards are used first in a simple recall task. After shuffling of the cards, the pupil is asked to rearrange them in the original order.

All programs should be modified or extended to meet the needs of individual pupils.

- Spraing's Bender Recall Test
- Valett Developmental Survey of Basic Learning Abilities: visual retention.
- Gesell Development School Readiness Kit: Visual Test 1, memory of orientation of forms
- Illinois Test of Psycholinguistic Ability: visual sequential memory subtest

PRESCRIPTIVE ILLUSTRATION

Priority Teaching Objective: George, fourteen years old, educationally handicapped. George will be able to recall from memory a design that has been presented visually for ten seconds and to pick it from four choices differing only in their position in space. He will successfully complete eight out of ten of the visual memory tasks presented to him.

Pretest Tasks: George was presented five stimulus design cards (one at a time) such as the following. He was unable to remember and identify any of them when they were subsequently presented on a four-symbol work sheet.

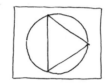

Specific Teaching Procedures: "George, today we are going to begin to work with more difficult memory tasks. You have done very well so far. The designs that I show you today will be pointed in many different directions. You know it is important to remember what direction letters and numbers face. We will begin with this one. You see how the leaf design faces this way. Now I am going to cover it and count to ten. Then we will take the cover off this side of the work sheet and you are to look over all four designs carefully and then check the one that you were to remember."

"Fine; now these symbols will become more difficult because they are abstract and do not look like anything you know. Study them carefully before you pick out the one you think is correct."

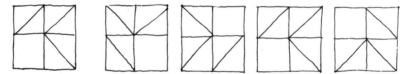

Performance Evaluation: George was presented a series of twenty visual-memory designs. Each was exposed to him for about a ten-second period before it was covered for ten seconds. The work sheet was then presented to George, and he was asked to mark the correct design from his memory. George correctly matched fourteen of the designs. The task was quite difficult for him, and he was tempted to quit when the designs became increasingly abstract. His motivation was only fair.

Analysis and Comments: The lesson was too complex for George. It was too much of a jump from earlier visual-memory training. The tasks should be simplified with longer practice periods.

For Self-instruction: Devise a teaching procedure and performance evaluation method for this pupil: Allan, seven years old, autistic. In the morning during "news time," I noticed that Allan was unable to remember or relate anything that happened to him from the previous day. He would parrot someone else's remarks. I decided to begin work on building direct recall of immediate experiences using concrete objects. Upon completion of this first lesson, Allan will be able to identify by name the missing object, when first shown three objects (small doll, toy cow, toy car) and then having one removed.

Perceptual-Motor Skills

32/Visual-Motor Memory

DEFINITION: The ability to reproduce motorwise prior visual experiences.

ILLUSTRATION: Pupil can draw designs and symbols following brief exposure, can reproduce letters, numbers, simple words on demand, can portray prior objects or events through gestures or drawings, can reproduce varied patterns and identify hidden materials.

EDUCATIONAL RATIONALE: The ability to recall what one has learned or experienced and to act on this information is essential to all sequential tasks in education. Without an adequate visual-motor memory span, tasks must constantly be learned anew with great loss of time and efficiency. Retention of sequential visual-motor patterns is an essential element of this learning ability.

SUGGESTED PROGRAM IDEAS

1. Forms
   a. Present pupil the following series of designs drawn on hardboard, expose for five seconds, remove, and have child reproduce from memory: vertical line, circle, square, triangle, diamond.
   b. Extend memory reproductions to more complex designs integrating the above forms. If pupil has difficulty, use tracing techniques and longer exposure to insure success.
   c. Arrange toy house or farm scene. Remove toys and have child reproduce scene.

2. Objects
   a. Display simple items such as airplane, dog, doll, book, pencil, coin, shoestring, and block. Have pupil study objects for one minute. Cover objects and remove one, placing it in box with other assorted objects. Remove cover and have pupil find and present removed object.
   b. Gradually extend above activity to include "academic" materials only, such as varied textbooks, workbooks, papers, math and science materials, and instructional aids.
   c. Using walnut shells and green peas, teach pupil moving shell game and have him reproduce movements.

3. Patterns
   a. Arrange bead patterns on string, expose to pupil for ten seconds, remove and have child rebuild pattern from memory. Gradually extend length and complexity of patterns.
   b. Follow the above procedure using buttons or building blocks in different colors and sizes. Arrange various paper forms and colors in memory sequences to be followed. Arrange toys and other objects in sequence patterns.
   c. Pupil folds 8½" × 11" paper into four sections and numbers them. Have him draw a circle in the first section, a triangle in the second, a square in the third, and a rectangle in the fourth.
   d. With alphabet and number cards, build this sequence: 76/in/go/boy/girl/54/ good/house/school/932. Being certain not to use verbal clues such as names of letters, have the pupil reproduce the symbol patterns. Extend the list as necessary.
   e. Show toothpick or matchstick pattern; have the pupil reproduce the pattern.
   f. Flash license plates and have the pupil write the license numbers from memory.
   g. Write a nonsense word on the chalkboard; erase and have pupil reproduce it.

125

REFERENCES

James, William. "Memory." *The Principles of Psychology*, Vol. 1. New York: Dover Publications, 1950.

Related Programs

- Frostig, Marianne, and Horne, David. "Position in Space: Recall of Motor Sequences." *The Frostig Program for the Development of Visual Perception*, pp. 51–60. Chicago: Follett Publishing, 1964.
- Visual-Memory Lessons from *Visual Readiness Skills, Levels 1 and 2*, Continental Press, Elizabethtown, Pa.
- The Letter Form Board, Houghton Mifflin Co., Department M, 110 Tremont Street, Boston, Mass.
- Getman, G. N., et al. "Practice in Visual Memory." *Developing Learning Readiness*. Manchester, Mo.: Webster Publishing, 1968.
- *Motor Coordination and Hand-Eye Coordination* (Workbook D-93), Milliken Publishing Co., 611 Olive Street, St. Louis, Mo.
- *Developing Visual Awareness and Insight* by Selma Herr, Med. Instructional Materials, 1415 Westwood Boulevard, Los Angeles, Calif.
- *Perceptual Skill Builder,* Perceptual Development Program, Audio Dynamic Research Inc., 1219 E. 11th Street, Pueblo, Colo.
- Seriation Program (Piaget), Learning Research Associates, Inc., 1501 Broadway, New York, N.Y.

Instructional Materials

- Mousetrap Game, Ideal School Supply Co., 11000 S. Lavergne Street, Oak Park, Ill.
- Magnetic alphabet board, Child Guidance
- Toy money set
- Assorted kindergarten beads
- Milton Bradley Aids: Educational Concentration, Memory Arithmetic Game, Palfrey's Educational Supply Co., 7715 E. Garvey Boulevard, Rosemead, Calif.
- Spot the Set and Shape Matching Cubes, Childcraft Equipment Co., Inc., 155 E. 23rd Street, New York, N.Y.

Further Evaluation

- Frostig Developmental Test of Visual Perception: position in space tests
- Graham-Kendell Memory for Designs
- Bender Visual-Motor Recall Test
- Pupil writes name and address
- Illinois Test of Psycholinguistic Abilities: visual sequential memory and manual expression subtests

PRESCRIPTIVE ILLUSTRATION

Priority Teaching Objective: Brenda, nine years old, educable mentally retarded. Brenda will be exposed to nine toothpick designs for five seconds each, and will then be able to reproduce the designs without error.

Pretest Tasks: Brenda was presented the following designs, made of toothpicks pasted on black paper. She was given a black paper and six toothpicks. She was then exposed to each design for five seconds and asked to duplicate it on the black paper with her toothpicks. Of the nine designs presented, she missed the seven checked:

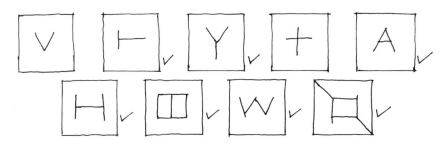

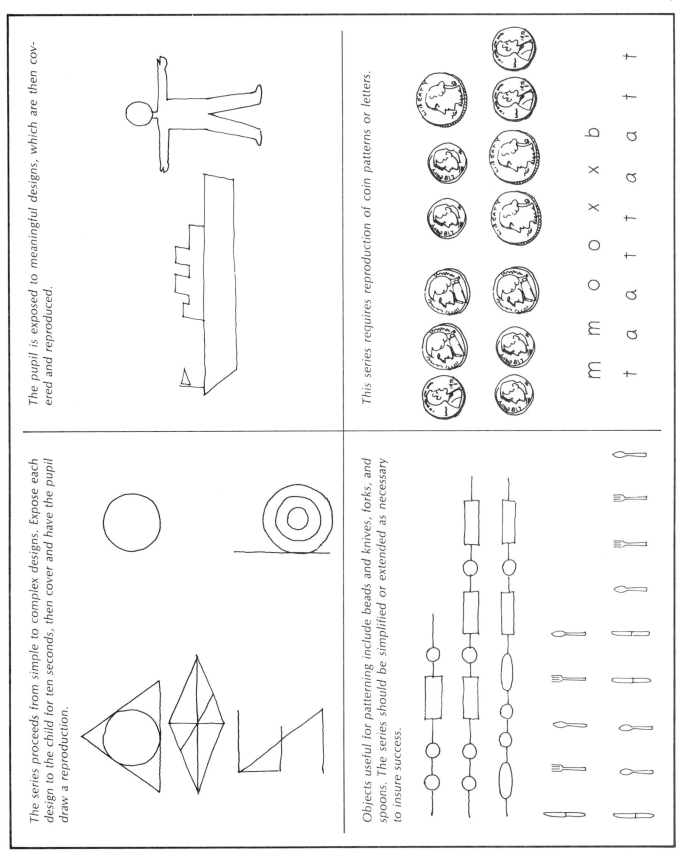

The pupil is exposed to meaningful designs, which are then covered and reproduced.

This series requires reproduction of coin patterns or letters.

The series proceeds from simple to complex designs. Expose each design to the child for ten seconds, then cover and have the pupil draw a reproduction.

Objects useful for patterning include beads and knives, forks, and spoons. The series should be simplified or extended as necessary to insure success.

All programs should be modified or extended to meet the needs of individual pupils.

Specific Teaching Procedures: "Brenda, in this lesson we are going to make designs with toothpicks. I will show you a design for a short time. You will then make the design with your toothpicks on the black sheet of paper."

"Watch me and see how I look at the card. Now I turn the card over and make the design. Now, Brenda, tell me what you are going to do."

Pupil: "I'm going to make things on the black paper with toothpicks."

"Good. For each design you remember correctly, you will get a check on your bank credit card."

"I will show you the first card here. Look carefully. Good. Now we turn it over. Now make the design you just saw."

Performance Evaluation: Brenda was presented twelve practice items of increasing difficulty. She got eight correct and earned eight points. She was able to identify the ones she missed and to reproduce them correctly with longer exposure. The posttest was the same as the pretest, and she only made two errors as follows:

Analysis and Comments: This was a partially appropriate lesson. Some of the designs were too easy and others much too difficult for Brenda. She was well motivated, but failed to meet the teacher's performance expectations. Future designs will be reproduced in pencil to reinforce the toothpick arrangements.

For Self-instruction: Devise a teaching procedure and performance evaluation method for this pupil: Todd, seven years old, regular second grade. Todd will be able to reproduce from memory a series of letters. Each series will be exposed to him for five seconds, and he will then write the series on the blackboard. He will be expected to reproduce five of the six series correctly.

33/Visual-Motor Fine Muscle Coordination

DEFINITION: The ability to coordinate fine muscles such as those required in eye-hand tasks.

ILLUSTRATION: Pupil can write legibly, trace, and imitate precise body movements without difficulty; can cut, manipulate, and judge fine physical responses without gross errors.

EDUCATIONAL RATIONALE: The coordination of visual perception of stimuli with fine motor responses required in many educational tasks is prerequisite to academic success.

SUGGESTED PROGRAM IDEAS

1. Reproduction of Simple Forms
   a. Draw vertical line, circle, square, triangle, and diamond on chalkboard. Have pupils come to board and trace forms with fingers. Pupils then draw forms on chalkboard and chalk in the designs, followed by tracing perimeter, first with finger and then again with chalk.
   b. Pupils then copy forms on drawing paper using felt pens or crayons, fill in designs, and again trace perimeter. Cut out forms and place on paper; trace again and cut out for practice.
   c. Provide open stencils of forms for precise tracing followed by coloring and cutting. Use hardboard forms for precise perimeter tracing, coloring, and cutting.
   d. Cut out sandpaper forms and sort them.

2. Completion of Fine Motor Tasks
   a. Teacher prepares gadget board with extensive series of locks, latches, plugs, zippers, levers, and varied buttons and snaps of all kinds. Pupils manipulate objects with increasing skill.
   b. Pupils can string beads and proceed to threading needles, buttons, macaroni, etc.
   c. Complete paint-by-number picture.
   d. Make finger-painting pictures.

3. Complex Designs
   a. Prepare an extended series of forms which become increasingly complex. Follow procedures in No. 1 above, with pupils proceeding from board work to seatwork, first using tracing techniques, and then proceeding to copy work. Advanced designs should be similar to letter or number symbols.
   b. Prepare series of abstract mazes and follow-the-number picture completion designs. Have pupil first follow cues and then copy the design from memory.
   c. Have pupil write name both in cursive and manuscript, trace, enlarge, color over, cut out, and paste.
   d. Sew a design on cloth.
   e. Teach embroidery, crocheting, and weaving.

REFERENCES

Getman, G. N. "The Visuomotor Complex in the Acquisition of Learning Skills." *Learning Disorders,* Vol. 1, pp. 49–76. Seattle: Special Child Publications, 1965.

Related Programs

- Frostig, Marianne, and Horne, David. "Perceptual Constancy." *The Frostig Program for the Development of Visual Perception.* Chicago: Follett Publishing, 1964.
- Visual-Motor Skills (books), Continental Press, Elizabethtown, Pa.
- Touch-typing programs (primary type)
- Zweig-Bruno Stereo-tracing Exercise Pads, Keystone View Co., Meadville, Pa.
- *Visual Discrimination Skills* (transparency-duplicating book), Milliken Publishing Co., St. Louis, Mo.

Instructional Materials

- Pick-up sticks
- Marble games
- Picture-BB completion toys
- Etch-a-Sketch
- Paint-by-number sets
- Giant Activity Books: *Follow the Dots, Play with Dots,* Palfrey's Educational Supply Co., 7715 E. Garvey Boulevard, Rosemead, Calif.
- Double-Handled Scissors, Developmental Learning Materials, 3505 N. Ashland Avenue, Chicago, Ill.
- Lacing Boards, Developmental Learning Materials
- Beginner's Loom, Educational Teaching Aids, 159 W. Kinzie Street, Chicago, Ill.
- Keystone Integrator for Perceptually Handicapped, Keystone View Co., Meadville, Pa.

Further Evaluation

- Bender Visual-Motor Gestalt Test
- Frostig Developmental Test of Visual Perception: eye-motor coordination, spatial relations
- Spraing's Perceptual Analysis Test: visual-motor sections
- Ayres Southern California Motor Accuracy Test
- O'Connor Finger Dexterity Test

PRESCRIPTIVE ILLUSTRATION

Priority Teaching Objective: Arne, seven years old, educable mentally retarded. Arne will be able to complete five incomplete pictures of increasing difficulty (star, house, dog, hat, ship) by drawing in the missing lines with correct proportion.

Pretest Tasks: Arne was presented three incomplete pictures: a ball, a table, and a boy. He attempted to complete all pictures but with great difficulty, poor proportion, and many incomplete lines and errors.

Specific Teaching Procedures: "Arne, we are going to begin work on some drawings. Look at all of these pictures. Each one has something missing, and it is very hard to tell what some of the pictures are."

"You remember seeing this picture of an incomplete ball yesterday, don't you? You remember that you took your pencil and drew in the missing part of the ball to complete the picture."

"Here is the face of a girl. Look carefully and you will see that one eye is missing from her face. I will complete the eye by drawing in these lines here. Now you do the same with this picture of a girl's face. That's good!"

"Now look at this picture. What is it?"

Pupil: "A cup."

"Yes, but you see some lines are missing. Now you go ahead and finish the picture."

"Let's go ahead and do some more of them [donut, tree, glass, bicycle, airplane]."

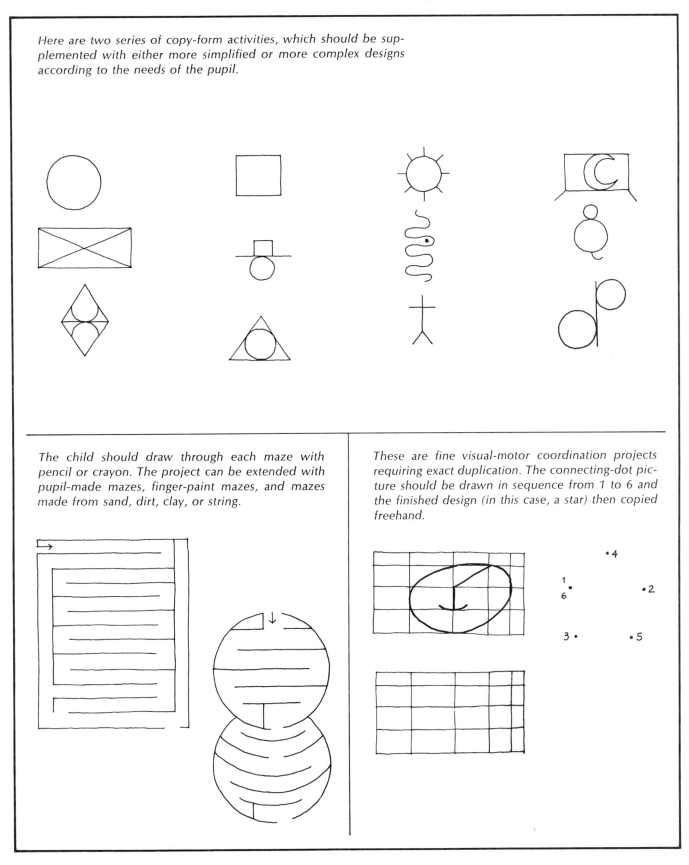

Here are two series of copy-form activities, which should be supplemented with either more simplified or more complex designs according to the needs of the pupil.

The child should draw through each maze with pencil or crayon. The project can be extended with pupil-made mazes, finger-paint mazes, and mazes made from sand, dirt, clay, or string.

These are fine visual-motor coordination projects requiring exact duplication. The connecting-dot picture should be drawn in sequence from 1 to 6 and the finished design (in this case, a star) then copied freehand.

All programs should be modified or extended to meet the needs of individual pupils.

Performance Evaluation: Arne was able to identify all of the worksheets except the donut. He had difficulty with the bicycle—leaving out some details—and the airplane was finished out of proportion. On the projected five-item posttest he did much better, although several lines on the ship were left incomplete.

Analysis and Comments: The items were appropriate but should be sequenced more carefully for continued practice.

For Self-instruction: Devise a teaching procedure and performance evaluation method for this pupil: Nelson, ten years old, neurologically handicapped. Upon completion of the lesson Nelson will be able to complete all of the following tasks (on a gadget board) within a three-minute period: 1. Plug in and turn on the light. 2. Open the bolt latch to the door lock. 3. Use the key to unlock the door. 4. Use two nuts and two bolts to bolt two metal plates together.

Perceptual-Motor Skills

34/Visual-Motor Spatial-Form Manipulation

DEFINITION: The ability to move in space and to manipulate three-dimensional materials.

ILLUSTRATION: Pupil can build block houses and designs, draw three-dimensional pictures, complete shop and craft projects, integrate form and space puzzles.

EDUCATIONAL RATIONALE: The perception of forms in space, and the ability to judge motor skills required to manipulate objects relative to one another, are basic to the solution of nonverbal performance problems encountered in everyday life.

SUGGESTED PROGRAM IDEAS

1. Basic Forms
   a. Present pupil geometric forms of cones, spheres, cubes, cylinders, triangular prisms, and pyramids. Have child feel, play, build spontaneous structures, and group forms.
   b. Collect varied balls and blocks; group and relate to basic geometric forms. With large building blocks, encourage child to experiment with building projects using many forms.
   c. Squeeze colored clothespins open and closed, into design on small rope.
   d. Screw and unscrew assorted jar lids.

2. Form Patterns
   a. Construct simple projects with large building blocks and have pupil imitate pattern. Pupil constructs mosaic tile pictures. Construct pegboard and marble board designs. Develop progressive Tinker Toy construction projects. Using modeling clay, create basic forms and construct simple bowls and objects.
   b. Using toy farm, pupil plays with animals and arranges them in space; with clay, creates additional animals and people, using toys as models.
   c. With hammer, nails, and handsaw, pupil cuts, nails, and joins wood in both spontaneous play and in imitation of simple projects.
   d. Practice yo-yo tricks.
   e. Sew assorted buttons on cloth in arranged patterns.
   f. Arrange difficult pegboard designs.
   g. Manipulate pipe cleaners into designs and figures.
   h. Take photograph of desk and table arrangements including books, pencils, etc. Have child copy photograph.

3. Symbol Manipulation
   a. Give pupil small and large wooden, plastic, and hardboard letters and numbers for use in free play. Have child combine symbols in free play with other three-dimensional forms. Pupil then groups all forms including symbols. Arrange symbols in spatial (but nonmeaningful) relationships and have pupil imitate.
   b. Arrange symbols by looking in a mirror.
   c. Construct mobiles of letters, numbers, and three-dimensional forms.

REFERENCES

Montessori, Maria. *Dr. Montessori's Own Handbook.* New York: Schocken Books, 1965.

Related Programs

- Frostig, Marianne, and Horne, David. "Spatial Relationships" and "Spatial Sequences." *The Frostig Program for the Development of Visual Perception*, pp. 1–4, 61–68. Chicago: Follett Publishing, 1964.
- Adaptive physical education programs
- Three-dimensional toy puzzles
- Montessori Cylinder Blocks, A. Daigger and Co., 159 W. Kinzie Street, Chicago, Ill.
- *Fairbanks/Robinson Program 1, Perceptual-Motor Development* (Section J), Teaching Resources, 100 Boylston Street, Boston, Mass.

Instructional Materials

- Geometric Solids, Constructive Playthings, 1040 E. 85th Street, Kansas City, Mo.
- Farmer set and three-dimensional animals
- Tinker Toys
- Building blocks
- Mosaic play tile and parquetry sets
- Small wooden pegboard, marble board
- Judy Hundred Pegboard, The Judy Company, 310 N. Second Street, Minneapolis, Minn.
- Small and large wooden letters and numbers
- Pythagoras (game), Constructive Playthings
- Yo-yo games
- Interlocking Cubes, I.D.A., P.O. Box 55, Citrus Heights, Calif.
- Alphabet Children's Blocks from toy stores
- Erector Set, Sears, Roebuck and Co.
- Geometric Insert Board, Childcraft Equipment Co., Inc., 155 E. 23rd Street, New York, N.Y.
- ETA Triangle Pattern Boards, A. Daigger and Co.
- Tooti Launchers, Creative Ideas Co., 5328 W. 142nd Place, Hawthorne, Calif.

Further Evaluation

- Nebraska Test of Learning Aptitude: block building
- Strauss Marble Board Test
- Frostig Developmental Test of Visual Perception: spatial relations
- Ayres Space Test

PRESCRIPTIVE ILLUSTRATION

Priority Teaching Objective: Anthony, twenty-one years old, trainable mentally retarded. Upon completion of the lesson, Anthony will be able to match and construct six out of eight block designs using yellow, orange, blue, green, red, and purple blocks. The designs will be presented on individual cards sequenced according to difficulty (see illustration).

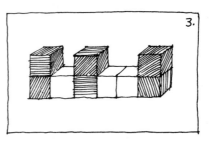

Pretest Tasks: Anthony was shown a series of eight block-design cards and asked to reproduce them using the colored blocks. He was able to construct designs 4 and 6 correctly but erred with all others.

Specific Teaching Procedures: "Anthony, we are going to learn how parts can be arranged together to make something. We will use these colored work blocks to begin with. You have worked with design cards before, so these will not be new to you."

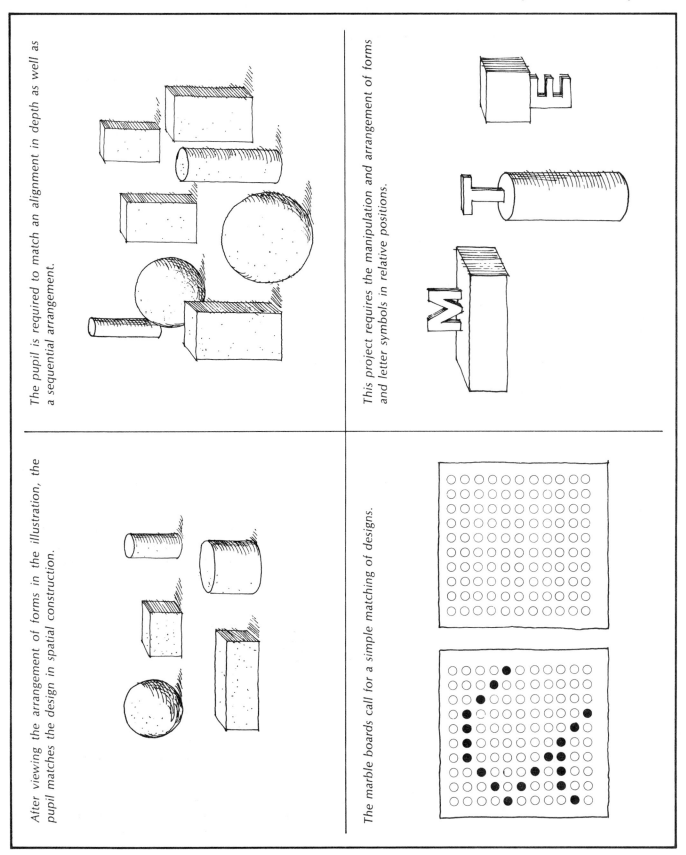

The pupil is required to match an alignment in depth as well as a sequential arrangement.

This project requires the manipulation and arrangement of forms and letter symbols in relative positions.

After viewing the arrangement of forms in the illustration, the pupil matches the design in spatial construction.

The marble boards call for a simple matching of designs.

All programs should be modified or extended to meet the needs of individual pupils.

"I'm going to show you some cards like this one. Notice how the design has different colors, and the blocks are arranged in different ways. First, I'm going to build a tower right next to the card. As I build the tower, I will say each color. Then I want you to repeat the color to me. Then after I finish my tower, I want you to build one just like it. Watch me carefully. I pick up the green block. Now you say 'green.' "

Pupil: "Green."

"Now I pick up the red. You copy mine and show me how you would do it."

"Good. Now for each design you get right and work hard on, you will get this plus mark on your work card, which will give you more money on pay day. Here are the other designs. Do each one as carefully as you can."

Performance Evaluation: "Very good, Anthony; you earned six plus marks. Do you know of anything you did wrong?"

Pupil: "I missed four."

Analysis and Comments: The task was only partially appropriate. Anthony's performance was sporadic with much distractibility. Total time required was fifteen minutes. The exercises should be extended to include more two-dimensional designs.

For Self-instruction: Devise a teaching procedure and performance evaluation method for this pupil: Jesse, seven years old, visually handicapped. Jesse will be able to arrange a number of small wooden figures (animals, people, trees, houses) on a table in the same spatial relationships as presented in a stimulus photograph.

Perceptual-Motor Skills

35/Visual-Motor Speed of Learning

DEFINITION: The ability to learn visual-motor skills from repetitive experience.

ILLUSTRATION: Pupil can respond with increasing speed to rote learning tasks such as copying digit or letter sequences, spelling, specific arithmetic processes, and gross motor skills such as jumping over a rope.

EDUCATIONAL RATIONALE: Most visual-motor skills can be improved through refined practice and drill. The specific skill to be learned must be broken down into its component movements or processes and a systematic approach developed to accomplish the task to the point of overlearning. Both meaningful practice and drill must be utilized in order for the skill to be developed for functional use.

SUGGESTED PROGRAM IDEAS

1. Gross Motor Skills
   a. Present the pupil with a low-slung rope or yardstick. Show him how to jump over with two feet together. Gradually raise height until practice and effort is required to accomplish task efficiently.
   b. Have pupil string colored clothespins on line in time contest with self. Pair off with pupil of similar ability for speed contest in stringing and unstringing.
   c. Time pupil in filling and emptying large Judy Pegboard including simple and abstract designs; reward pupil for improving time performance.
   d. String beaded necklaces while timed.

2. Sorting
   a. Arrange box of assorted nails, nuts, bolts, and screws. Have pupil sort objects into proper boxes, keeping record of time. Reward pupil for improving time in subsequent sorts.
   b. In a similar fashion, use letters and numerals of various sizes. Require speed in sorting into proper groups.
   c. Sort pictures into categories (animals, transportation, words, clothes, etc.).

2. Copying
   a. Develop series of simple abstract symbols for copy speed tasks. Pupil then moves to copying random letters and numbers. Use tape recorder to improve speeds by having pupil respond to directions of varied complexity.
   b. Arrange a symbol code requiring more complete visual-motor coordination. Gradually move to speed copying of nonsense syllables and more meaningful codes.
   c. Time pupil at simple copy work from board and at rote arithmetic. Reward him for improved speed of accurate performance.
   d. Copy letter and word sequences on typewriter and maintain speed record.
   e. Fill in multiplication answers quickly on ditto sheet, using reference answer card.

REFERENCES

Cronbach, Lee J. "Skills." *Educational Psychology,* pp. 270–313. New York: Harcourt, Brace & World, 1963.

Related Programs

- *Physical Fitness Activities*, Album 14 (record), Educational Record Sales, 157 Chambers Street, New York, N.Y.

- Psychoeducational Resource Program No. 17: Reaction-Speed Dexterity
- *Visual Readiness Skills*, Levels 1 and 2 (times learning and relearning), Continental Press, Elizabethtown, Pa.
- *Following Directions and Sequence* (transparency-duplicating book), Milliken Publishing Co., St. Louis, Mo.

Instructional Materials

- Labyrinth, Creative Playthings, Princeton, N.J.
- Judy Hundred Pegboard, The Judy Company, 310 N. 2nd Street, Minneapolis, Minn.
- Varied puzzles (for speed construction)
- Large beads and laces (for speed)
- Jack and ball set (for timed performance and accuracy)
- Racket-Wack by Marx (indoor tennis), Sears, Roebuck and Co.
- Adjustable Floor Puncher, Sears, Roebuck and Co.
- Tooti Bounce, Tooti Toss, Tooti Launcher, Creative Ideas Co., 5328 W. 142nd Place, Hawthorne, Calif.
- Table tennis

Further Evaluation

- Wechsler Intelligence Scale for Children: coding subtest
- Purdue Pegboard
- Professional optometric evaluation
- Sequential time periods required to complete specific classroom assignments

PRESCRIPTIVE ILLUSTRATION

Priority Teaching Objective: Peter, thirteen years old, educationally handicapped. Upon completion of the lesson, Peter will be able to match twelve of fifteen word patterns within the time allocations. Each word will be presented on a 3″ × 5″ card with ten seconds allowed for Peter to find and arrange the cardboard letters in correct sequence.

Pretest Tasks: Peter was presented a ten-word pretest, consisting of ten three-letter words, each exposed for ten seconds. He was slow in responding and was unable to complete any of the first four words before the next word was exposed. He did, however, complete three of the ten words presented (*dad, fun, top*).

Specific Teaching Procedures: "Peter, we are going to work to increase your speed and accuracy in doing your work. First, we are going to work on putting words together as fast as we can."

"Here is a tray of many alphabet letters. See how each letter is printed on a small piece of cardboard. We can put the letters together to spell words like this: If I take the letter *P*, then an *e*, a *t*, an *e*, and then an *r* and put them next to each other like this, I have spelled your name. Now you do it."

"That is good. Next, look at this card. It has three letters on it and spells something: what does it spell?"

Pupil: "Cat—I think!"

"That was right. Now you pick out the letters from your tray and arrange them as quickly as you can. You must hurry, as I will count to ten slowly and then I will show you another card. When you have arranged each word on the tray, just leave it there and then make the new word below it. Here is the next word [*dog, man, boy, cap, and, band, stop, book, love, good*]."

Performance Evaluation: On the posttest, Peter arranged eleven of the fifteen words correctly on the alphabet tray within the time limitations. The lesson was appropriate and appeared demanding as it was difficult for Peter to search the tray for the letters.

A coding project requires speed in copying one-digit, letterlike designs.

REFERENCE CODE

Time____

This activity requires perception and direct copying of simple forms with a time record of accomplishment.

Time____

Another activity requires rote repetition of a letter and number series.

REFERENCE CODE

Time____

A more complex two-digit code involves the mixing and interchange of letters and numbers.

REFERENCE CODE

Time____

All programs should be modified or extended to meet the needs of individual pupils.

Analysis and Comments: At the beginning of the task, Peter searched for each letter separately. By the fourth word, he had retained the image of the entire word and was searching for two or more letters at once. His speed and accuracy seemed to improve as he moved along, although he did tend to lose concentration near the end of the lesson.

For Self-instruction: Devise a teaching procedure and performance evaluation method for this pupil: Leann, eight years old, neurologically handicapped. Leann will be able to listen to a ten-minute tape recording and follow the directions to draw specified designs within time allocations. She will be able to complete eight of the nine drawings as directed on the tape (ball, flower, house, etc.).

Perceptual-Motor Skills

36 / Visual-Motor Integration

DEFINITION: The ability to integrate total visual-motor skills in complex problem solving.

ILLUSTRATION: Pupil can play complex team sports, swim, draw accurate pictures including people, may play musical instrument, write extended letters, move freely about neighborhood and community.

EDUCATIONAL RATIONALE: The degree of integration of visual-motor skills is evidenced in complex tasks requiring coordination of eyes, hands, and large muscles. Varied educational experiences need to be planned in these areas to provide opportunity for closure and integration to develop.

SUGGESTED PROGRAM IDEAS

1. Drawing People
   a. Request pupils to draw pictures of themselves and one another. Then have them draw picture of teacher. Next, have them draw pictures of families. For child with unusual difficulties, point out body parts and request pupil to include them in the drawing.
   b. Extend drawings to paintings on large art paper. Have class work on painting large pictures of class with each person named. Have pupil draw or paint part of a figure with another pupil completing the picture.
   c. Have pupils draw pictures to a story.

2. Picture Completion Puzzles
   a. Cut up pictures of people and have pupils reassemble and glue. Have pupils make own human puzzles at home by pasting human pictures on cardboard to cut up and assemble. Pupils can make puzzles of scenes, common objects, etc., in similar way. Gradually progress to assembly of commercial puzzles, from simple Judy puzzles to complex jigsaw puzzles with group participation.
   b. As class project, design mural of large fish or animal and have class construct paper mosaic with groups working together on the project. Have each pupil draw a map of his neighborhood and construct a paper mosaic of it.
   c. Scribble figures: Pupils draw scribbles on chalkboard; other pupils "complete them" to make recognizable figure (animal, person, etc.).

3. Symbolic Learning
   a. Write simple words and sentences in both manuscript and cursive on the chalkboard and have pupils copy them in crayon on art paper; have pupils cut up paper into puzzle and reassemble.
   b. Plan class party and paint large signs in cursive writing for the party. Following the party, cut up signs and use them as puzzles. Print numbers on large paper, cut up, and reassemble. Join together symbols in a series to duplicate stimulus form presented to the child. Play acting charades and drawing charades to communicate predetermined ideas.
   c. Teach simple tunes on piano or instruments using music.
   d. Develop nonverbal language using signs, formulas, etc.

REFERENCES

Cruickshank, W.; Bentzen, F.; Ratzeburg, F.; and Tannhauser, M. *A Teaching Method for Brain-Injured and Hyperactive Children*, pp. 186–195. Syracuse: Syracuse University Press, 1961.

Related Programs

- Sutphin, Florence. *A Perceptual Testing and Training Handbook for First Grade Teachers.* Winterhaven, Fla.: Winterhaven Lions Research, 1964.
- *Parents' Home Training Guide Kit* for Winterhaven Perceptual Training Program.
- Frostig, Marianne, and Horne, David. "Position in Space: Assembly of Parts." *The Frostig Program for the Development of Visual Perception.* Chicago: Follett Publishing, 1964.
- *ERIE Program 1, Perceptual-Motor Teaching Materials,* Teaching Resources, 100 Boylston Street, Boston, Mass.
- *Reading: Visual Motor Performance Unit 1,* Paul S. Amidon & Associates, Inc., 1035 E.C. Plymouth Building, Minneapolis, Minn.
- *Draw It with Shapes,* Facilitation House, Box 611, Ottawa, Ill. . .

Instructional Materials

- Etch-a-Sketch
- Weaving and loom kits
- *What To Do for Kindergarten and Primary Art* and *What To Do in Elementary Handcraft* (Hayes books), Lakeshore Equipment Co., 1144 Montague Avenue, San Leandro, Calif.
- Paddle-tennis games
- Judy Alpha-Forms, The Judy Company, 310 N. Second Street, Minneapolis, Minn.
- Judy Senior Puzzles, The Judy Company
- Pythagoras (game), Constructive Playthings, 1040 E. 85th Street, Kansas City, Mo.
- Color Cubes, Playskool Manufacturing Co., Chicago, Ill.
- Bingo games
- Walt Disney Wooden Puzzle Cubes, Sears, Roebuck and Co.
- Seven Educational Puzzles, Sears, Roebuck and Co.
- Spirograph, Cuisenaire Company of America, 9 Elm Avenue, Mt. Vernon, N.Y.
- Manolakes, George, et al. *Try: Experiences for Young Children.* New York: Noble and Noble, 1967.
- Tooti Toss and Launcher, Perceptual Development Set, Creative Ideas Co., 5328 W. 142nd Place, Hawthorne, Calif.
- Cubasco Animal Puzzle Blocks, Mead Educational Services, Atlanta, Ga.
- Tangram Puzzle and Book Set, Toy Review, P.O. Box 2001, Lincoln Center, Mass.

Further Evaluation

- Wechsler Intelligence Scale for Children: object assembly and block design tests
- Goodenough, and Goodenough-Harris Draw-a-Man Tests
- Bender Visual-Motor Gestalt
- Copying simple words, sentences, paragraphs
- Beery-Buktenica Developmental Test of Visual-Motor Integration, Follett Publishing

PRESCRIPTIVE ILLUSTRATION

Priority Teaching Objective: Jessica, thirteen years old, educationally handicapped. Jessica will be able to look at a series of twenty incomplete symbols, verbally identify each symbol, recognize the missing part, orally explain what is missing, and then draw in the missing part. She should successfully complete eighteen of the twenty symbols at her own rate of speed.

Pretest Tasks: On the pretest task of fifteen symbols, Jessica got four correct. It was obvious that she was not thinking of what she was doing and failed to attempt to develop an image of the symbol or words she was working with.

Specific Teaching Procedures: "Jessica, when you have finished these lessons, you will be able to look at symbols such as words and pictures, tell me what they are and what is missing, and then complete the symbol for me."

"For example, here is a card with some letters on it except that one of the letters is partially missing. Look carefully; you can see the letters *H, A, P, P,* and part of the letter *Y.* Altogether it spells *happy.* The part of the letter *Y* that is missing is the middle part of this

The pupil copies sentences in manuscript and cursive as accurately as possible.

I LIKE BIRTHDAY PARTIES.

I like birthday parties.

The pupil traces any letters and sequences found in the stimulus.

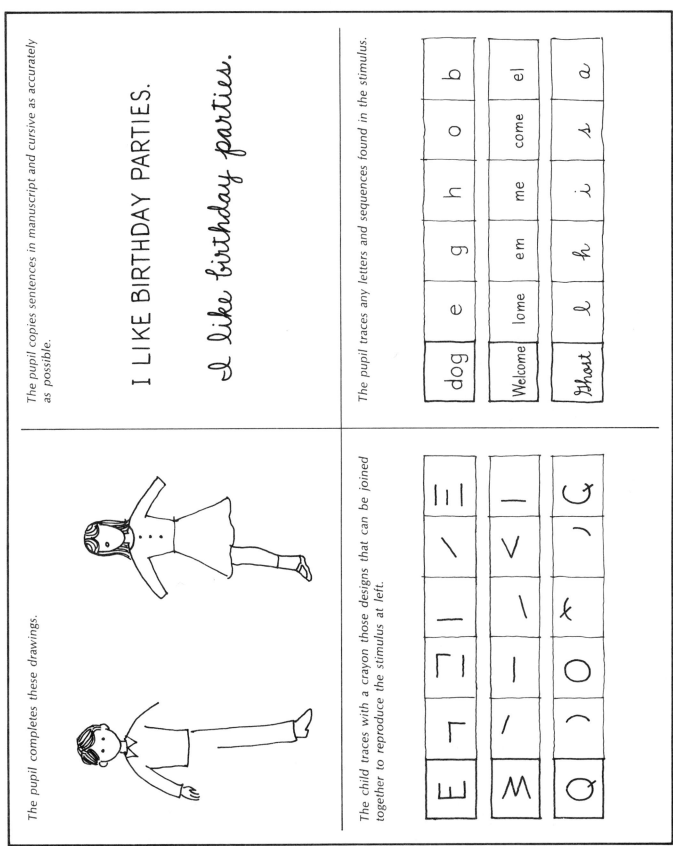

The pupil completes these drawings.

The child traces with a crayon those designs that can be joined together to reproduce the stimulus at left.

All programs should be modified or extended to meet the needs of individual pupils.

bottom line, so I will draw that in with my pencil. See now, how the entire word is complete."

"Here is the next one. What do you think it is?"

Pupil: "A stop sign, but part of the letter *O* is missing."

"That's right. You go ahead and finish it."

"Now here are some other incomplete words and symbols for you to finish." (Manuscript words incomplete: *father, school, candy, mail.* Symbols incomplete: U.S. flag, cross, railroad crossing, bicycle.)

Performance Evaluation: On the posttest, Jessica completed seventeen of the twenty symbols without difficulty. She enjoyed working at the task and was pleased with her success.

Analysis and Comments: The lesson was an appropriate one, as it helped Jessica to think about what she was to do and then to concentrate on the missing parts. It should now be expanded to include missing parts of cursive words and short sentences.

For Self-instruction: Devise a teaching procedure and performance evaluation method for this pupil: Kathy, ten years old, educable mentally retarded. Kathy will be able to arrange the flannel board felt pieces into recognizable objects as follows: cat, boat, human face, flag, wagon.

Language Development

37/Vocabulary

DEFINITION: The ability to understand words.

ILLUSTRATION: Pupil has a basic receptive vocabulary in accord with chronological age and educational opportunity.

EDUCATIONAL RATIONALE: Vocabulary develops as a result of experience and neurological integration. Children must be provided varied educational opportunities as a basis for language development. Directive teaching of basic nouns through concrete aids, imitation, and reinforcement techniques should be followed by sequential instruction in verbs, adverbs, and adjectives.

SUGGESTED PROGRAM IDEAS

1. Jargon—Imitative Vocabulary
   a. Develop pupil responsiveness by having him imitate actions: sit down, touch nose, touch mouth, clap hands, stamp feet, clap hands and say BANG, hit drum and say BOOM, etc. Go slowly and reward pupil after every correct imitative response. Play action stories, such as Lion Hunt, to involve pupil.
   b. Show picture of cow (*moo*), dog (*arf-arf*), cat (*meow*), and lamb (*baa-baa*). Play record of sounds. Have pupil repeat sounds after teacher. When simple sounds are learned, extend program to other animal sounds such as horse, lion, etc.
   c. Using nonsense words and syllables (*bink, la, bu*), have pupil repeat; reward correct responses. Use action words with accompanying activity (*bang, zoom, wow, ugh, beep, help,* etc.), with imitation. Use random number series (*one, nine, five, three*) in the same way. If necessary, use portable auditory trainer with earphones to insure sound reception.

2. Pragmatic Vocabulary
   a. Using imitative procedures and reward, show pupil picture of himself, repeat his name several times while pointing to picture, and request response. Expand to pictures and names of family members, teacher, and one or two other pupils.
   b. Collect common objects such as shoe, cup, spoon, button, nail, pencil, paper, book, etc. Present objects to pupil, have him feel objects, then request names. Use drill to memorize names. Develop large pictures of common objects and nouns and continue program without reference to concrete object itself. Using Dolch Picture Word Cards, systematically show picture, present the word, and then say the word, with verbal imitation by the pupil.
   c. Introduce tape recorder along with road signs; play Road Game—child pretends to drive car, reads signs into recorder; play back child's responses. Label things in room or in child's bedroom and have child verbalize words with recorded feedback. Learn color words, body parts, city, state, numbers, and alphabet letters.
   d. Teach health and safety sight vocabulary: *stop, go, poison, police, fire,* etc.

3. Symbolic Vocabulary
   a. With pupil arranging toy farm, teach names of all animals and objects. Print vocabulary names on large cards with crayons. Begin development of basic Dolch word box by pupil. Use kinesthetic tracing and sand letters to reinforce vocabulary if needed.
   b. Have pupil cut out pictures for picture-manuscript vocabulary file and add to it

145

daily. Extend vocabulary to abstract words (*love, like, help, good,* etc.) with picture associations and discussion of meanings. Transfer procedure to include simple sentences (I am Tom.), choral responses, and poems. Use picture dictionary.

c. Pupils make "people-work" cards by pasting pictures of workers and naming their occupations ("doctor," "soldier," "farmer," "carpenter," etc.).

REFERENCES

Bargs, Tina. *Language and Learning Disorders of the Pre-Academic Child, with Curriculum Guide.* New York: Appleton-Century-Crofts, 1968.

Louvas, O.; Berberich, J.; Perloff, B.; and Schaeffer, B. "Acquisition of Imitative Speech by Schizophrenic Children." *Science,* November 1965.

Wood, Nancy. *Delayed Speech and Language Development.* Englewood Cliffs, N.J.: Prentice-Hall, 1964.

Related Programs

- *Peabody Language Development Kits,* Levels P–3, American Guidance Service, Inc., Publisher's Building, Circle Pines, Minn.
- *Useful Language,* Levels 1–3, Continental Press, Elizabethtown, Pa.
- *My Puzzle Books I and II, Readiness for Reading, Who Gets It?, Match Sets I and II* (Dolch programs), Lakeshore Equipment Co., 1144 Montague Avenue, San Leandro, Calif.
- Sullivan, M. W., and Buchanan, Cynthia Dee. *Programmed Reading.* Manchester, Mo.: Webster Publishing, 1968–1969.
- Goldstein, H., and Levitt, E. *A Simplified Reading Readiness Program.* Urbana, Ill.: R. W. Parkinson, 1964.
- *Language Games* by Guy Wagner et al., Teachers Publishing, 866 Third Avenue, New York, N.Y.
- *Language Concepts* and *Number Concepts,* Fitzhugh Plus Program, Allied Education Council, Galien, Mich.
- *Word Bank,* Mott Basic Language Skills Program, Allied Education Council
- *Speech Sound Series* by Kay Mosier, Keystone View Co., Meadville, Pa.
- *Language Concepts Through Drawing* by Robert Gill and S. Engelmann; *Language Concepts in Song,* by S. Engelmann, Instructional Media of America, Inc., 175 Fifth Avenue, New York, N.Y.
- *Distar Language 1,* Science Research Associates, 259 E. Erie Street, Chicago, Ill.

Instructional Materials

- *Singing Action Games* (record), Educational Record Sales, 157 Chambers Street, New York, N.Y.
- *Building Verbal Power* (record), Educational Record Sales
- *Let's Sing About the Alphabet* (record), Education Record Sales
- *Dr. Seuss Presents* (record to accompany books), Eduational Record Sales
- *What's Its Name?* (language development book), Palfrey's Educational Supply Co., 7715 E. Garvey Boulevard, Rosemead, Calif.
- Dolch Materials: Group Word Sounding Game, Basic Sight Cards, Sight Phase Cards, Picture Word Cards, Popper Words Sets I and II, Lakeshore Equipment Co.
- Milton Bradley Aids: Link Letters, Picture Word Builder, Sentence Builder, Educational Password, Lakeshore Equipment Co.

Further Evaluation

- Stanford Binet L-M: vocabulary tests
- Wechsler Intelligence Scale for Children: vocabulary
- Detroit Tests of General Aptitude: verbal-opposites test
- Hills-Mills Vocabulary Scale
- Peabody Picture Vocabulary Tests
- Dolch Basic Sight Word Test

PRESCRIPTIVE ILLUSTRATION

Priority Teaching Objective: Sandy, twenty-three years old, developmental center for the mentally retarded. Sandy's language, both receptive and expressive, is severely limited;

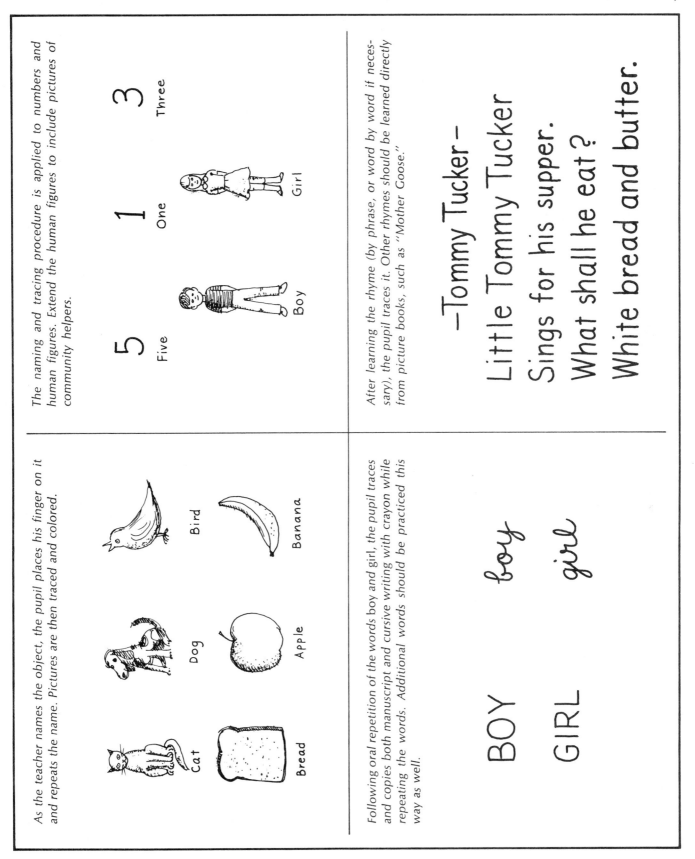

The naming and tracing procedure is applied to numbers and human figures. Extend the human figures to include pictures of community helpers.

5   1   3
Five One Three

Boy   Girl

After learning the rhyme (by phrase, or word by word if necessary), the pupil traces it. Other rhymes should be learned directly from picture books, such as "Mother Goose."

—Tommy Tucker—
Little Tommy Tucker
Sings for his supper.
What shall he eat?
White bread and butter.

As the teacher names the object, the pupil places his finger on it and repeats the name. Pictures are then traced and colored.

Bird   Dog   Cat

Banana   Apple   Bread

Following oral repetition of the words boy and girl, the pupil traces and copies both manuscript and cursive writing with crayon while repeating the words. Additional words should be practiced this way as well.

boy
girl

BOY
GIRL

All programs should be modified or extended to meet the needs of individual pupils.

however, through repetitive instruction she has been able to recognize and name a few common objects in her everyday environment. Upon completion of this lesson, Sandy will be able to point out a hammer, work card, screwdriver, apple, and pliers. She will also be able to name these objects upon request.

Pretest Tasks: Sandy was unable to identify any of the five objects (hammer, work card, screwdriver, apple, and pliers) laid out on the work center; she needs to learn those basic objects with which she will have daily contact.

Specific Teaching Procedures: "Sandy, it is time to learn a new game. Remember when we would hide things and then find them again? Today we are going to do something like that."

"This is a cup, and this thing is a checker. I am going to put the cup in your hand. Here it is. What did I put in your hand?"

Pupil: "Cup."

"Good; now here is the checker; say 'checker.'"

Pupil: "Checker."

"Now watch. I will put this candy here on the table and then put the *cup* over it. Now I put this shoe box over the cup and another box over the checker. You find the cup for me and you can have the candy under it. Give me the *cup*."

"That was good, Sandy; you did that fast. Now we will do the same with other things."

(The hammer, a small saw, screwdriver, apple, and pliers were randomly paired and presented two times with objects Sandy already knew: book, pen, orange, doll, cup. The same procedure was followed in teaching all of the names.)

Performance Evaluation: "Wow, Sandy! That was fantastic . . . very good! Do you know why you got all that candy?"

Pupil: No response.

Analysis and Comments: After one half-hour the pretest was given again. Sandy identified the pliers, hammer, and apple without difficulty but failed to respond to "saw" and "screwdriver." Her attitude was quite good, and it was obvious she could learn through such basic drill. More unfamiliar objects in the workshop will be taught to her in the same way.

For Self-instruction: Devise a teaching procedure and performance evaluation method for this pupil: Marie, ten years old, educable mentally retarded. Upon completion of the lesson, Marie will be able to identify the correct picture of a noun orally presented to her, from three Dolch picture cards arranged before her. She will achieve 80 percent accuracy of all 220 words presented to her.

Language Development

38/Fluency and Encoding

DEFINITION: The ability to express oneself verbally.

ILLUSTRATION: Pupil can communicate verbally, has average fluency of speech without undue hesitation or stuttering, uses coherent sentence structure.

EDUCATIONAL RATIONALE: Fluent verbal expression and communciation develop gradually as a result of experience and verbal stimulation. When the child has the need to express himself and feels free to do so, he should be rewarded and encouraged to engage in extended forms of verbal communication.

SUGGESTED PROGRAM IDEAS

1. Free Expression
   a. Have the child participate in marching eurythmics and activity games, gradually involving sounds ("Simon says: Clap your hands. Say BOO," etc.). Repeat sound patterns (la-la-la-la-la-la/ba-ba-ba-ba, etc.) together.
   b. Place varied pictures in box, pull them out quickly, having pupil imitate names. Generalize to naming objects from box. Then, extend to using sentences, "This is a ——————. I have a ——————. Here is a ——————." Using sentences, name objects in room.
   c. Have children create and arrange Indian village, toy cities, etc., and describe evolving creation.

2. Rhyming-Singing
   a. Using record of nursery rhymes, have pupil follow along; then have child repeat rhymes after teacher. Develop recitation of simple rhymes and poems.
   b. Select records of fun songs; sing, involving pupil. Following the song, have pupil repeat song and describe what happened. Use filmstrips with songs and poems to increase motivation for response.
   c. Place objects or pictures that rhyme in a bag (deer, gear, fear, etc.) and have pupils ask: "Is it a ——————?"

3. Free Association
   a. Take field trip to zoo, train ride, etc., to be followed by game of Twenty Questions, relating to experiences. Arrange photographs of pupil on field trip and have pupil recall experience.
   b. Obtain family pictures and slides; involve pupil in describing events. Use tape recorder to record pupil comments, play back, and further extend associations to feedback.
   c. Using cartoons ("Peanuts") or sequential puzzle series, have pupil describe events. Extend procedure to describing story from picture cues in a book. Generalize to complex pictures from magazines and newspapers.
   d. Talk to pupil over toy telephone, requesting comments on family pictures; use toy walkie-talkie to extend activity. Have pupil associate sounds and stories to animal puppets and put on simple play requiring interaction with other pupils. Involve pupils in dramatization of nursery rhymes, poems, fairy tales, with free verbal interaction.
   e. Have class help plan complex activity such as making an art mural, putting on a play, etc. Have pupil describe his involvement and explain overall events. Involve pupil in planning for future events. Have pupils free associate to incomplete sentence stories.

f. Tape record children's choral reading, TV commercials, free verse, and creative poetry about personal feelings and experiences.

g. Round robin stories: Teacher begins story that is picked up and expanded by successive pupils.

REFERENCES

Barry, Hortense. *The Young Aphasic Child*. Washington, D.C.: Alexander Graham Bell Association for the Deaf, 1961.

Chukovsky, Kornei. *From Two to Five*. Berkeley, Calif.: University of California Press, 1963.

John, Vera, and Goldstein, Leo. "The Social Context of Language Acquisition." *The Disadvantaged Child*, Vol. 1. Seattle: Special Child Publications, 1967.

Related Programs

- *Let's Look at First Graders: A Guide to Understanding and Fostering Intellectual Development in Young Children* (basic language skills units), Educational Testing Service, Princeton, N.J.
- *Peabody Language Development Kits*, Levels 1–2, American Guidance Service, Inc., Publishers' Building, Circle Pines, Minn.
- *Songs for Children with Special Needs*, Volumes 1, 2, 3 (records), Educational Record Sales, 157 Chambers Street, New York, N.Y.
- *Rhythms and Songs for Exceptional Children* (record), Educational Record Sales
- *Rhyming*, Levels 1–2, Continental Press, Elizabethtown, Pa.
- *Useful Language*, Levels 1–3, Continental Press
- *Language Development Experiences for Young Children*, University of Southern California, University Bookstore, Los Angeles, Calif.
- *An Experience-Centered Language Program*, Franklin Publications, Inc., 367 S. Pasadena Avenue, Pasadena, Calif.
- *Peabody Rebus Reading Program*, American Guidance Services, Inc., Publishers' Building, Circle Pines, Minn.
- *Helping Young Children Develop Language Skills* (book of activities), by Merle B. Karnes, Council for Exceptional Children, 1201 Sixteenth Street, N.W., Washington, D.C.

Instructional Materials

- *Let's Say Poetry Together* (record for choral speaking), Educational Record Sales
- *Together We Speak* (choral speech book), Palfrey's Educational Supply Co., 7715 E. Garvey Boulevard, Rosemead, Calif.
- Ginn Basic Card Sets, Unit 1, Palfrey's Educational Supply Co.
- Speed Up game, Palfrey's Educational Supply Co.
- Toy telephones
- *Mother Goose Favorites* (talking book-record), Educational Projects, Book Division Dept. PA 11-13, 488 Madison Avenue, New York, N.Y.
- *Fun With Language* (record), Bowmar Records, 622 Rodier Drive, Glendale, Calif.

Further Evaluation

- Illinois Test of Psycholinguistic Abilities: verbal expression subtest
- Michigan Picture Test and Thematic Apperception Test
- Mecham Verbal Language Development Scale
- Valett Developmental Survey of Basic Learning Abilities: language development and verbal fluency
- Eisenson Examination for Aphasia, Psychological Corp., New York, N.Y.
- Basic Concept Inventory, Follett Publishing Co., 1010 W. Washington Boulevard, Chicago, Ill.

PRESCRIPTIVE ILLUSTRATION

Priority Teaching Objective: Pat, fifteen years old, emotionally disturbed. Following three lessons in expressive poetry, Pat will be able to select one of five stimulus pictures and create free verse about it. The verse will be a coherent statement of her feelings, and she will record it by using a cassette tape recorder.

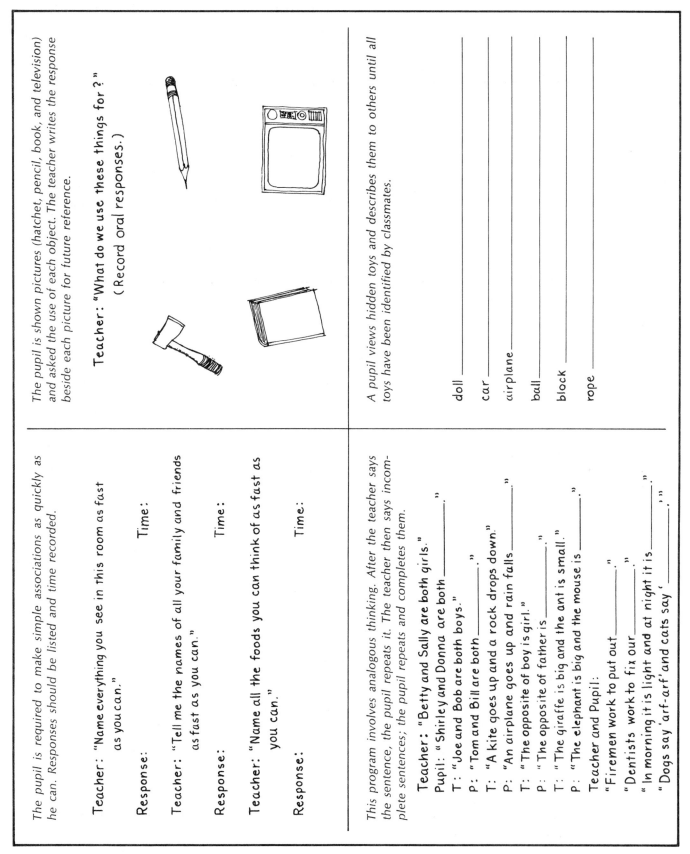

The pupil is shown pictures (hatchet, pencil, book, and television) and asked the use of each object. The teacher writes the response beside each picture for future reference.

Teacher: "What do we use these things for ?"
(Record oral responses.)

A pupil views hidden toys and describes them to others until all toys have been identified by classmates.

doll _____

car _____

airplane _____

ball _____

block _____

rope _____

The pupil is required to make simple associations as quickly as he can. Responses should be listed and time recorded.

Teacher: "Name everything you see in this room as fast as you can."

Time:

Response:

Teacher: "Tell me the names of all your family and friends as fast as you can."

Time:

Response:

Teacher: "Name all the foods you can think of as fast as you can."

Time:

Response:

This program involves analogous thinking. After the teacher says the sentence, the pupil repeats it. The teacher then says incomplete sentences; the pupil repeats and completes them.

Teacher: "Betty and Sally are both girls."
Pupil: "Shirley and Donna are both _____."
T: "Joe and Bob are both boys."
P: "Tom and Bill are both _____."
T: "A kite goes up and a rock drops down."
P: "An airplane goes up and rain falls _____."
T: "The opposite of boy is girl."
P: "The opposite of father is _____."
T: "The giraffe is big and the ant is small."
P: "The elephant is big and the mouse is _____."
Teacher and Pupil:
"Firemen work to put out _____."
"Dentists work to fix our _____."
"In morning it is light and at night it is _____."
"Dogs say 'arf-arf' and cats say '_____.'"

All programs should be modified or extended to meet the needs of individual pupils.

Pretest Tasks: At the beginning of the program, Pat, along with five other pupils in her group, was requested to write a brief poem of her feelings about herself or anything she might choose. She was unable to respond either in writing or orally to a tape recorder.

Specific Teaching Procedures: "Pat, as you know, we have been working on how to express our feelings about things in what is known as free verse or expressive poetry. We have read some poems that other class members have created. You have also heard a tape recording of poetry made by some students in last year's class."

"Now, we are going to try to express our feelings about several pictures. Here, for instance, is a picture of a young man in a dark corner crying. Now listen to this tape. This is what one student said about this picture:

> It's like the world has just slipped by
> and you were missed.
> It's like everything has just dropped,
> right when you almost had it.
> It's like almost having enough and
> then losing all.

"Here are several other pictures. Select one you might have some personal feelings about."

(Pat selected a picture of dead children outside a burning village in an Asian country.)

"Just turn the tape recorder on and let yourself go. Say just what you feel, but try to do it in verse form."

Performance Evaluation: Pat responded with hesitancy to the first lesson and looked to the teacher for permission to proceed. It appeared that she was afraid to express her real feelings. By the second lesson she was responding fairly fluently with considerable encouragement. By the end of the third half-hour lesson, she recorded an eight-line expressive poem.

Analysis and Comments: This was an appropriate lesson that seems to have "opened up" Pat. She will now be introduced to the poetry group where the stimulation may help her become even more open and expressive.

For Self-instruction: Devise a teaching procedure and performance evaluation method for this pupil: Juanita, seven years old, educable mentally retarded. Juanita will be able to use the tape recorder to record as many animals and foods as she can think of, as fast as she can. She will be able to name at least fifteen animals and ten foods within a three-minute period.

Language Development

39/Articulation

DEFINITION: The ability to articulate words clearly without notable pronunciation or articulatory problems.

ILLUSTRATION: Pupil uses words with correct pronunciation of initial, medial, and final sounds.

EDUCATIONAL RATIONALE: During preschool and kindergarten years, most children evidence articulatory difficulties, which gradually disappear as a result of maturation and experience. By the middle primary grades, however, the child with notable articulation problems may require special education and speech correction. Many articulation problems can be avoided through a consciously developed program of classroom speech improvement.

SUGGESTED PROGRAM IDEAS

1. Involvement
   a. Have pupil imitate teacher's movements: standing up, sitting down, clapping, jumping, shouting, "BOOM, BANG, WOW," etc. Request pupil to move chair, pick up pencil, scribble on paper.
   b. Introduce finger-plays ("Eensy Teensy Spider," etc.) and action stories ("Jack and the Beanstalk") to obtain motor involvement and further verbalization.
   c. Children listen for specified sounds and respond by clapping, standing, etc.
   d. Involve pupils in choral reading—story poems, etc.

2. Speech Demonstration Stories
   a. Teacher presents story such as "Jack and the Beanstalk" to pupil or class. Use pictures of story characters or puppets. Involve pupils in repeating, "fe, fi, fo, fum," etc. Ideally, teacher should center lesson on one sound that class or pupil is having difficulty with. Following the story, class participation lessons should be planned for each sound: /f/, /s/, /th/, /r/, /ch/, etc. Children eight years of age or older with notable articulation difficulties should be referred to the school speech correctionist.
   b. Demonstration lessons should make use of pictures and seasons of the year such as Christmas (Santa), Easter (Bunny), Halloween (Ghost), etc. Outstanding picture books such as the *Listen-Hear* Series should be used to supplement demonstrations.
   c. Begin to involve children in correction by having them cover their ears when they hear a wrong sound demonstrated.
   d. Have pupils imitate tongue twisters and riddle rhymes ("Peter Piper").

3. Direct Correction
   a. By this stage the pupil has been involved, is motivated to participate verbally, but has not seemed to profit from class speech improvement demonstrations. An intensive individual approach to specific articulatory correction may be needed and should be based on evaluation of initial, medial, or final sounds.
   b. Once the articulatory difficulty has been determined, a program can be planned involving isolated imitation and practice of sounds. Identify sound misarticulation by having pupil note verbalization by using mirror and by gradually imitating correctionist. Tape recordings should be made during correctional program and played back to pupil for self-evaluation.
   c. Games should be utilized to reinforce correction once pupil is conscious of purpose of such activity. Classification of like-sounding objects and pictures, use of poems

153

and rhymes, card sounding games and "talking letter" activities should be used with sounds in context. Tok-Bak Reflectors should be used when necessary to enable pupil to monitor his own voice and articulation.

REFERENCES

Carrell, James A. *Disorders of Articulation.* Englewood Cliffs, N.J.: Prentice-Hall, 1968.
Scott, Louise B., and Thompson, J. J. *Talking Time.* Manchester, Mo.: Webster Publishing, 1966.

Related Programs

* *Listening Time,* 1, 2, 3 (33⅓ rpm records emphasizing ear training and sound repetition), Educational Record Sales, 157 Chambers Street, New York, N.Y.
* *Fun with Speech,* Vol. 1, 2 (33⅓ rpm records), Educational Record Sales
* Slepian, Jan, and Seidler, Ann. *The Listen-Hear Books.* Chicago: Follett Publishing Co., 1966.
* *Speech Sound Series: Consonant Series* by Kay Mosier, Keystone View Co., Meadville, Pa.
* *The Best Speech Series,* Stanwix House, Inc., 3020 Chartiers Avenue, Pittsburgh, Pa.

Instructional Materials

* Piper, W. *The Little Engine That Could.* Platt and Munk, 1930.
* Jones, Morris Val. *Speech Correction at Home.* Springfield, Ill.: C. C. Thomas, 1957.
* *Beginning Sounds,* Levels 1–2, Continental Press, Elizabethtown, Pa.
* *The Big Book of Sounds,* Palfrey's Educational Supply Co., 7715 E. Garvey Boulevard, Rosemead, Calif.
* Milton Bradley Aids: Phonic Talking Letters, Lakeshore Equipment Co., 1144 Montague Avenue, San Leandro, Calif.
* Dolch Tak-a-Sound Matching Game, Lakeshore Equipment Co.
* Tok-Bak Voice Reflector, Western Psychological Services, 12035 Wilshire Boulevard, Los Angeles, Calif.
* What They Say: Audio-Visual-Kinesthetic Flash Card, Webster Publishing Co., Manchester, Mo.
* Speech Lingo, Speech and Language Materials, Inc., P.O. Box 721, Tulsa, Okla.
* Alphatime Huggable Letters, New Dimensions in Educational Instruction, 160 DuPont Street, Plainview, N.Y.

Further Evaluation

* Templin-Darley Articulation Test
* Riley Articulation and Language Test
* The Templin Non-diagnostic Articulation Word and Sentence Test

PRESCRIPTIVE ILLUSTRATION

Priority Teaching Objective: Harold, nine years old, educationally handicapped. When exposed to a tape recording of fifteen words presenting the /k/ sound in initial, medial, and final positions, Harold will be able to imitate and record each word and sound.

Pretest Tasks: Harold got two words correct (*king, kite*) on the twenty-word pretest. Most of his difficulty, however, appears to be with the final consonant sound.

Specific Teaching Procedures: "Harold, we are going to begin to work on pronouncing the letter *k*. I will show you some pictures and pronounce the word and letter for you, and then we will record you on this tape recorder."

"Here is a card with the letter *k* on it. The /k/ sound sounds like this [teacher demonstrates]. Now you say it for me into the tape recorder [pupil recording]."

"If you look here, you will see three pictures. One is a key, one a turkey, and one a book. Give me the key and say the word as you hand me the picture. Good; now give me the turkey and say the word. Now the book."

"If you listen carefully, you will notice that sometimes the /k/ sound is at the beginning

Pronunciation of words in context can be evaluated in this functional repetition and sentence completion task. Actual response should be noted below each stimulus sentence.

I go to this school every day.

My name is _____ and I am _____ years old.

I live at _____ with my family whose
(ADDRESS)

names are _____.

This year I am in the _____ grade and next year I will be in the _____ grade.

The teacher determines whether the pupil is aware of a specific articulatory difficulty and whether he can identify the sound in words, then isolate the symbol for the sound.

What sounds do you have trouble saying?

Tell me some words that you have trouble saying:

Write here the sounds and words you have trouble saying:

The pupil repeats noise words. Note should be made of actual response and any difficulty.

BOOM! BOOM!
POW! POW!
ZAP! ZAP!
CRASH! CRASH!
SMASH! SMASH!
BANG! BANG!

This exercise requires the use of alliteration in sentences and fluent articulation of words in the opening lines of "The Night Before Chistmas."

The boy broke the bottle and then he blew up a big balloon!

The little lazy lion looked like he loved to lick lollipops.

Sally saw seashells at the seashore.

'Twas the night before Christmas, when all through the house
Not a creature was stirring, not even a mouse!

All programs should be modified or extended to meet the needs of individual pupils.

of the word, sometimes in the middle, and sometimes at the end of the word. Look at these two pictures:

"Say each word to yourself and then hand me the picture of the word with the /k/ sound in the middle."

"Now here are three more pictures. Say the words to yourself. Hand me the one with the /k/ sound on the end of the word [stick]. Now say the word into the tape recorder."

Performance Evaluation: For the first lesson, Harold did quite well. He was not conscious of the different positions of the /k/ sound and missed four words on the posttest, three of them medial sounds.

Analysis and Comments: Harold was well motivated and responded quickly to direct speech correction. He will be continued in this program twice a week until his articulation has improved.

For Self-instruction: Devise a teaching procedure and performance evaluation method for this pupil: Alexi, ten years old, educable mentally retarded. Upon completion of the lesson Alexi will be able to mark six stimulus pictures representing nouns that begin with the initial consonant *r*. The six pictures (rocking chair, rabbit, roof, rope, rake, and ring) will be part of a single worksheet containing twenty pictures suggesting words with mixed initial consonants.

Language Development

40/Word Attack Skills

DEFINITION: The ability to analyze words phonetically.
ILLUSTRATION: Pupil can make proper phonetic associations, break down words phonetically, recognize component words.
EDUCATIONAL RATIONALE: In order to read effectively, the child must be able to associate sounds with their written symbols and to analyze new words accordingly. Context cues must also be recognized and utilized by the pupil with increasing speed and facility. Pupils should have a basic sight vocabulary prior to introducing phonics.

SUGGESTED PROGRAM IDEAS

1. Vowels and Consonants
   a. First, have pupil imitate teacher who sounds out vowels and words. Then, have pupil associate sounds by saying other words with vowels as given by teacher. Extend oral practice to consonant sounds and word listing.
   b. Use vowel flash cards or charts and teach sounds, having pupil find sound in list of simple words. Teach visual association to consonants and have pupil identify letter and sound in varied words.
   c. Show filmstrips and play records to reinforce basic phonic associations. Read stories requiring pupil to identify given sounds and letters. Proceed to making sound picture books with pupil cutting pictures from magazines as well as making his own, followed by labeling pictures with sound represented. Use vowel and consonant games such as Dolch materials.
2. Blends
   a. First introduce blends aurally as with vowels and consonants. Give practice in primary blends—/br/, /kr/, /dr/, /fr/, /gl/, /sl/, /kl/, /bl/, /sm/, /sp/, /sk/, /sw/—through verbal games and "spelldowns" with teacher providing initial stimulus (/br/—"broom") and pupil associating with another word.
   b. In similar fashion, proceed to visual identification of blends and locating them in given words. Have pupils build their own list of words, begin individual word cards for each blend, and use these in spelling. Extend to picture-book projects. Use records and phonetic blend cards and games for reinforcement.
   c. Have pupil use tape recorder for recording a story written with prescribed words. Follow story by having pupil identify on tape all blends and their words used in story. Play prerecorded story and tape pupil's analysis of story. Have him identify blends used.
3. Combinations
   a. Have pupil build word list of given sounds (whip, sing, lid, fix, dish, etc.). Develop picture-word cards of sounds in varied positions (ran, girl, car, etc.). Build lists of simple sound combinations, making words such as it, an, or, be, at, etc. Combine other letters to make new words such as b-at, c-at, m-at, p-at, etc.
   b. Study sounds and symbol configurations in basic sight vocabulary previously learned; find sight vocabulary words in larger word list on board. Pupil writes simple stories, identifying combination words used. Use incomplete sentences with missing word and have pupil select appropriate word from multiple choice list using context cues.

157

c. Construct a "sound wheel" where various word-sound combinations can be made by turning wheel consonants to make varied words on outer rim (*h-it, b-it, s-it,* etc.).

REFERENCES

Engelmann, Siegfried. "Reading for the Nonreader." *Preventing Failure in the Primary Grades.* New York: Simon & Schuster, 1969.

Scott, Louise B., and Thompson, J. J. *Phonics: In Listening, In Speaking, In Reading, In Writing.* Manchester, Mo.: Webster Publishing, 1962.

Scott, Louise B., and Thompson, J. J. *Speech Ways.* Manchester, Mo.: Webster Publishing, 1955.

Related Programs
* *The Phonovisual Method,* Phonovisual Products, Inc., Dept. EC–2, Park Lawn Drive, Rockville, Md.
* *Phonics We Use Books,* A–G, Lyons and Carnahan, 407 E. 25th Street, Chicago, Ill.
* *Curious George Learns the Alphabet* (book), Educational Record Sales, 157 Chambers Street, New York, N.Y.
* *Fun with Speech,* Vols. 1, 2 (record), Educational Record Sales
* *Sounds for Young Readers,* Vol. 1–6 (phonic records), Educational Record Sales
* *Beginning Sounds,* Levels 1–2, Continental Press, Elizabethtown, Pa.
* *Talking Time Filmstrips,* Webster Publishing Co., Manchester, Mo.
* *Reading Games* by Guy Wagner, et al., Teacher's Publishing Corp., 866 Third Avenue, New York, N.Y.
* *Phonics We Use—Learning Games Kit,* Lyons and Carnahan
* *Readiness in Language Arts,* Behavioral Research Laboratories, Box 577, Palo Alto, Calif.
* *Listen and Do* (records and worksheets), Houghton Mifflin Co., 110 Tremont Street, Boston, Mass.
* *Basic Reading Series,* J. B. Lippincott Co., East Washington Square, Philadelphia, Pa.
* *Structural Reading Series* by Catherine Stern et al., L. W. Singer Co., 33 W. 6th Street, New York, N.Y.
* *Mott Basic Language Skills Program,* Series 1–3, Allied Education Council, Distribution Center, P.O. Box 78, Galien, Mich.
* *Auditory Discrimination, Beginning Sounds,* Milliken Publishing, St. Louis, Mo.
* *The Fitzhugh Plus Program,* books 201, 202, 207, Allied Educational Council

Instructional Materials
* *Phonetic Workbook Series* by Selma Herr, Palfrey's Educational Supply Co., 7715 E. Garvey Boulevard, Rosemead, Calif.
* Dolch Materials: What the Letters Say, Take, The Syllable Game, Group Sounding Game, Consonant Lotto, Vowel Lotto, Lakeshore Equipment Co., 1144 Montague Avenue, San Leandro, Calif.
* Ideal initial and final consonant charts; blend and digraph charts; vowel charts; magic cards—consonants, blends, and vowels, Lakeshore Equipment Co.
* Milton Bradley Aids: Phonetic Drill Cards, Phonetic Quizmo, Alphabet Picture Flash Cards, You Can Read Phonetic Drill, Lakeshore Equipment Co.
* *Fun with Phonics* (exercises), Highlights for Children, Inc., 2300 W. Fifth Avenue, Columbus, Ohio
* Alphabet Puzzle Cards, Childcraft Equipment Co., Inc. 155 E. 23rd Street, New York, N.Y.
* Consonant Sounds Program, Milton Bradley Co., Springfield, Mass.

Further Evaluation
* Wide Range Achievement Test: reading
* Gilmore Reading Test
* Gray-Oral Reading Test
* Clinical appraisal of simple oral reading paragraphs
* Spache Diagonostic Reading Scales: phonics section
* Illinois Test of Psycholinguistic Ability: sound blending subtest

This exercise requires saying the stimulus sound aloud and then writing three additional words containing the stimulus sound.

at   Bat   _____ _____ _____

ing Playing   _____ _____ _____

er   Flower   _____ _____ _____

it   Sit   _____ _____ _____

The pupil completes each sentence by choosing a word from a list of words starting with the same sound.

At night I go to _____.

In the water it is fun to _____.

The yellow star in the sky is the _____ (sun swim sleep)

The boy _____ down the street. (rip roar ran red)

I hit the _____ with the bat. (bell bear bolt ball)

The pupil says the sound, says the picture word, and then writes the word below the picture.

a [apple]   f [fish]

tr [train]   ch [chair]

s [sun]   gl [globe]

In each word, the pupil circles the sound symbol identical with the stimulus at left.

n	nail	animal	sun
	run	can	snail
p	pail	apple	cap
	nap	rap	plan
ch	cheese	cheat	reach
	teacher	church	preacher
sh	shoe	smashing	wish
	dish	shoot	splash

All programs should be modified or extended to meet the needs of individual pupils.

Priority Teaching Objective: Edward, ten years, old, slow learner. Edward will be able to recognize and read phonetically the vowel sounds /ü/ and /ë/ in a list of selected words with 80 percent accuracy. (Pronunciation symbols used here are from the Merriam-Webster dictionaries.)

Pretest Tasks: Edward was given a list of words: *soon, sheep, moose, sleek, peep, stool, stoop, three,* and *eel.* Asked to read the words, he mispronounced *moose, sleek, stoop, eel,* and *bleed.*

Specific Teaching Procedures: "Edward, we are going to practice using the sounds you have just read. First, I'll write a word using two colors of chalk on the board [*moon*]. As you can see, the two vowels are white, and the first and last letters of the word are yellow. What is this word?"

Pupil: "*Moon.*"

"Right. Now I'm going to change the beginning sound, and I want you to sound it with me. I change the beginning sound to /sp/. Now I'll sound it out 'sp-ü-n' and pronounce the entire word as *spoon.*"

"Now tell me what you are going to do."

Pupil: "When you change the letters, I'm gonna sound it out and say it like you did!"

"Good. Now let's see if you can do the job on these changes [*hoop, scoop, troop, swoop, smooth, groom; feel, free, steel, speed, need, feed*]."

Performance Evaluation: "You did a good job, Edward. You only missed a couple. Do you remember where?"

Pupil: "When I said *fee* I should have said *free.* And when I meant *speed.*" (He had said *seed.*)

On a ten-word posttest, Edward missed two words, *greed* and *creek.*

Analysis and Comments: The lesson was a very appropriate one. Edward achieved expectancy and he was quite pleased with himself. Because of the type of errors made, review work needs to be done on initial sounds and blends.

For Self-instruction: Devise a teaching procedure and performance evaluation method for this pupil: Otto, eleven years old, educable mentally retarded. Otto will be able to read twelve simple sentences with contractions (*isn't, it's, can't we've, I'll, I've, you'll, man's, won't, we're, he'd, what's*). He will be able to identify each word orally and give the two words from which the contraction is made.

Language Development

41/Reading Comprehension

DEFINITION: The ability to understand what one has read.

ILLUSTRATION: Pupil can recall story and paraphrase plot, can explain or relate meaningfulness of what has been read.

EDUCATIONAL RATIONALE: Comprehension of reading material requires an accurate vocabulary knowledge and the ability to relate words meaningfully in sentence, paragraph, and story form. Comprehension develops ihrough the feedback and consideration of what one has read.

SUGGESTED PROGRAM IDEAS

1. Meaningful Vocabulary
   a. Make sure that pupil has a basic sight vocabulary and knowledge of phonics. Extend vocabulary by listing special words he wants to learn (*ghost, love, death, war, good,* etc.). Match words in manuscript and cursive writing.
   b. Develop vocabulary grouping of words and have pupils classify (animals, people, toys, houses, clothes, transportation, etc.). Write words in simple sentences. Play vocabulary games, having pupils take turns in round-robin oral story building using given words. Extend to playing the game Educational Password.
   c. Pupils print larger words and find, circle, or cut out little words from context (*go* from *goat, to* from *today,* etc.) From list of words, pupils print on cards, cut up, and integrate parts into new words.

2. Experience Sentences
   a. Use pocket chart and basic vocabulary. Have pupils make simple sentences, copy sentences on paper, and discuss. Have pupils dictate simple sentences ("Today is Billy's birthday.") while teacher writes them on board with originator's name. Follow up by having each pupil copy his own sentence for filing in his "sentence story box."
   b. From basic reading series, teacher prepares short strip sentences for individual pupil use and daily practice. Have pupils progress to reading longer sentences and phrases. Discuss sentences and have pupils draw and color their picture stories, depicting sentence meaning.
   c. Use sentence-length window-cards or markers. Read to pupils and have them imitate sentence or phrase. Gradually increase length of sentence and speed. Review meaning of sentences. Transfer to silent reading, using markers.

3. Story-Paragraph Meaning
   a. Use markers for oral reading of two or more simple sentences followed by pupil's drawing and coloring picture story. Cut and paste pictures from magazines illustrating sentence story; sentences should be copied in picture-story book. Have children relate their own experiences (weekend, holiday, etc.), with teacher writing story; pupil then copies his story and adds to picture book. In same way, build stories from field trips and other experiences. Introduce primary typewriter and have pupil type his story or a previously read story that he fully comprehends.
   b. Collect simple comic sequences ("Peanuts," etc.), and have pupils read, arrange in order, write a story, and explain story into tape recorder. Generalize use of tape recorder to having pupils follow in books as teacher reads from tape; have pupils read books on tape, listen back, and then answer questions.
   c. Extend to programmed reading materials as the Sullivan Series. With advanced readers, follow structured sequence: Verbal introduction to story/oral reading/silent

reading/pupil verbal explanation of story/pupil response to oral questions/activity project interpreting story/written test regarding total comprehension.

REFERENCES

Chall, Gene. *Learning to Read.* New York: McGraw-Hill, 1967.

Dolch, E. W. *Teaching Primary Reading,* 3rd ed. Champaign, Ill.: Garrard Press, 1960.

Kaluger, G., and Kolson, C. *Reading and Learning Disabilities.* Columbus, Ohio: Charles E. Merrill, 1969.

Related Programs
* Walt Disney's *Wonder Tales, Fantasy Stories,* and *Story Classics* (filmstrips), Educational Record Sales, 157 Chambers Street, New York, N.Y.
* *Listening Skills for Pre-Readers,* Vols. 1–4 (records), Educational Record Sales
* *Storytime Filmstrip-Record Library* (record and filmstrip fairy tale series), Educational Record Sales
* Sullivan, M. W., and Buchanan, Cynthia Dee. *Programmed Reading.* Manchester, Mo.: Webster Publishing, 1968–1969.
* *Deep-Sea Adventure Series.* Palo Alto, Calif.: Field Educational Publications, 1969–1971.
* *Reading Skill Builders,* Readers Digest Services, Inc., Pleasantville, N.Y.
* *SRA Basic Reading Series,* Science Research Associates, 259 E. Erie Street, Chicago, Ill.
* *ERE Learning System,* Responsive Environment Corp., 200 Sylvan Avenue, Englewood Cliffs, N.J.
* *Lift-Off to Reading,* Science Research Associates
* Smith, Donald, ed. *Word Tracking.* Ann Arbor, Mich.: Ann Arbor Publishers, 1967.
* *Peabody Rebus Reading Program,* American Guidance Service, Publishers Building, Circle Pines, Minn.
* *Reading* by M. W. Sullivan (programmed structural linguistics), Behavioral Research Laboratories, Box 577, Palo Alto, Calif.
* *Comprehension,* Series 2,000 (Mott Basic Language Skills Program), Allied Education Council, Distribution Center, P.O. Box 78, Galien, Mich.
* Kottmeyer, William A., and Ware, Kay. *Conquests in Reading* (workbook). Manchester, Mo.: Webster Publishing, 1963.
* McHugh, Walter J., ed. *Your Own Thing: The Contemporary Reading Series.* San Francisco: Leswing Communications, 1970.

Instructional Materials
* *Reading-Thinking Skills* (primer—grade 4), Continental Press, Elizabethtown, Pa.
* *Dr. Seuss Books,* Palfrey's Educational Supply Co., 7715 E. Garvey Boulevard, Rosemead, Calif.
* *Jokes and Riddles Book,* Palfrey's Educational Supply Co.
* *Activity Series: Adventure with Words, Adventures with Language, Adventures Beyond Our Earth,* Palfrey's Educational Supply Co.
* Giant Activity Books: *Riddles, Rhymes and Stories, Simple Tricks, Science Experiments,* Palfrey's Educational Supply Co.
* *Reading Games, Language Games,* Palfrey's Educational Supply Co.
* *Functional Basic Reading Series,* Stanwix House, 3020 Chartiers Avenue, Pittsburgh, Pa.
* Educational Password Game (available in toy stores)
* *Hayes Special Education and Language Arts,* Lakeshore Equipment Co., 1144 Montague Avenue, San Leandro, Calif.
* *Children's Digest,* The Better Reading Foundation, Inc., Bergenfield, N.J.
* *Famous Classics* (story record), Curtis Audio-Visual Materials, Independence Square, Pa.
* *Basic Reading Series,* J. B. Lippincott Co., East Washington Square, Philadelphia, Pa.
* *Distar Reading 1 and 2,* Science Research Associates, Inc., 259 E. Erie Street, Chicago, Ill.

Further Evaluation
* Gilmore Reading Test
* Gray Oral Reading Test
* Wide Range Achievement Test: reading
* Spache Diagnostic Reading Scales

The sentences should be completed from context clues.

My name is _____

The _____ in the sky is yellow.

A bird _____ with its wings.

Ice _____ is good to eat.

My _____ is a man.

General comprehension: the pupil answers questions about a story.

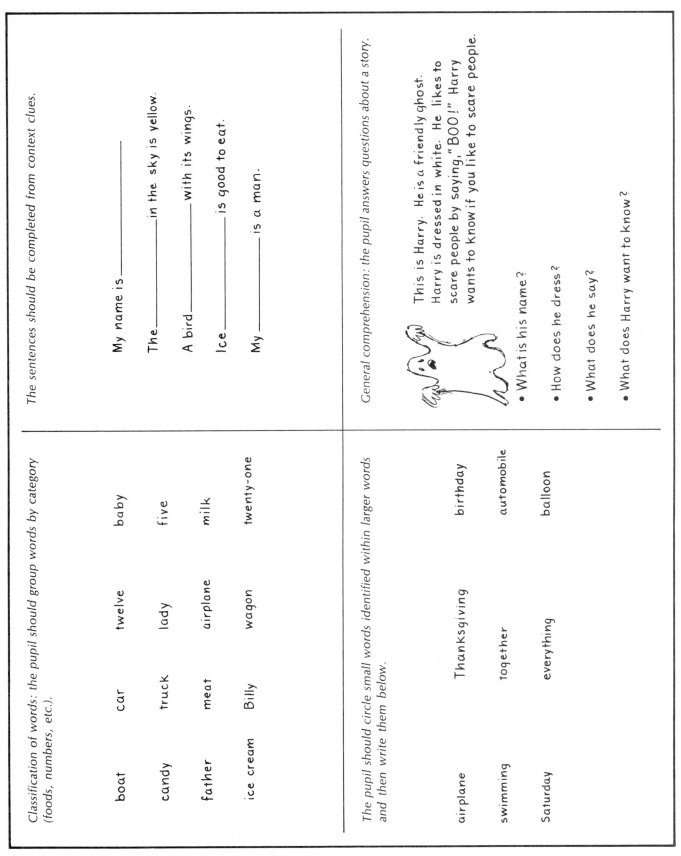

This is Harry. He is a friendly ghost. Harry is dressed in white. He likes to scare people by saying, "BOO!" Harry wants to know if you like to scare people.

- What is his name?

- How does he dress?

- What does he say?

- What does Harry want to know?

Classification of words: the pupil should group words by category (foods, numbers, etc.).

boat	car	twelve	baby
candy	truck	lady	five
father	meat	airplane	milk
ice cream	Billy	wagon	twenty-one

The pupil should circle small words identified within larger words and then write them below.

	Thanksgiving	birthday
airplane		automobile
swimming	together	
Saturday	everything	balloon

All programs should be modified or extended to meet the needs of individual pupils.

- California Reading Tests, California Test Bureau
- Durrell-Sullivan Reading Achievement Tests

PRESCRIPTIVE ILLUSTRATION

Priority Teaching Objective: Manuel, sixteen years old, educable mentally retarded. Manuel will be able to read and use in a simple sentence, four of seven words selected for the lesson; he will also be able to draw a picture for three of the seven words used.

Pretest Tasks: Manuel was asked to read seven words. He was also requested to draw a picture for each of these words:

apple	boy	dog
ball	chicken	father
bed		

Of the seven words presented, Manuel was not able to read or draw a picture for a single word. When I read each word to him, he was able to draw a picture of five of the seven and adequately defined *chicken* and *father*.

Specific Teaching Procedures: "Manuel, you're going to do something you probably have never done before. You are going to make sentences using these words, and you're going to be able to read them."

"Let's begin. I want you to make a sentence using the word *apple*. I'll write it on this chalkboard and then on this paper as you say it."

"Listen to how I would do it. The word *apple*: 'The apple is good.' Now I will write the word and sentence on the board and on your paper like this. Now tell me what you are to do."

Pupil: "YYYYeath, I make aaa sssentence for you."

"OK! Would you mind if I gave you a piece of candy for every sentence you give me to write?"

Pupil: "No."

"OK, begin with the word *apple* and make a sentence with it. I'll write what you say. Then we will do some others."

Performance Evaluation: "You made some good sentences. You may have five candies if you like. Do you remember the words you couldn't make sentences for?"

Pupil: "*Father* and . . . I don't know."

Analysis and Comments: The task was only partially appropriate for this boy because of his difficulty in expressing himself. However, he did try to express ideas for words. He needs to be drilled in a sight word vocabulary, but describing each word as he progresses. Time must be allowed for his stuttering. The Sullivan Reading program will also be used with his vocabulary development.

For Self-instruction: Devise a teaching procedure and performance evaluation method for this pupil: Jon, ten years old, educationally handicapped. Upon completion of the lesson, Jon will be able to (1) read a two-paragraph story, (2) recall and paraphrase the story by putting it into his own words, and (3) answer the five basic "W" questions: Who, What, Where, When, and Why?

Language Development

42/Writing

DEFINITION: The ability to express oneself through written language.
ILLUSTRATION: Pupil can write simple sentences and communicate ideas through paragraph, letter, story, or essay.
EDUCATIONAL RATIONALE: Writing is a basic form of language communication requiring integration of visual-motor skills and practice. Development of basic writing ability begins with training of finger and hand muscles through scribbling exercises, tracing, copying, and the increasing refinement of free writing exercises.

SUGGESTED PROGRAM IDEAS

1. Finger-Hand Coordination
   a. Begin with tracing circles in the air using full arm movements; practice with right arm, left arm, then proceeed to bilateral movements. Move to chalkboard and repeat procedure with teacher demonstration. Proceed to bilateral movements, being sure hands begin at midline of body and move away. Gradually refine to smaller circles using right hand.
   b. Present pupil with review of right-to-left exercises using scribbles, arrows, straight line drawings, etc. Transfer above procedures to paint and easels. Introduce designs of square, triangle, cross, and diamond. Proceed to finger paint, first using elbows and hands to make designs before developing finger control.
   c. Place kraft paper on floor and use crayons to make large designs. Gradually refine movements to primary large-spaced paper. Introduce letters of pupil's first name separately and have him repeat procedures using finger paint, chalk, paint, crayons, and soft pencil.

2. Tracing
   a. Print pupil's name in wet sand tray. Have child trace with fingers, then reproduce name. Transfer to clay tray, following same procedure. Write child's name with Elmer's Glue; when dry, have pupil paint, feel, and reproduce name. Write pupil's name on board; have child trace with fingers and with chalk.
   b. Using primary large-spaced paper and crayons, trace around wood or hardboard letters. Transfer to stencil templates and trace letter and number forms. Prepare pupil's name, letters, and numbers in crayon on heavy sandpaper and have child trace, first with finger, and then again with crayon.
   c. With onionskin, have pupil trace name, numbers, and designs. Child should then go over his tracings with both crayon and pencil. For letter tracings, use arrows to indicate direction of strokes.

3. Copying and Independent Writing
   a. Write name in cursive on chalkboard. First, have pupil copy writing in the air. Then, use finger paint and clay for copying attempts. Transfer to primary paper and copy board work.
   b. On board, introduce letters *L, I, T, H, O*; indicate strokes. Have pupil copy with felt pen and crayons. Gradually introduce entire alphabet and numbers. Have extensive practice and success with each symbol before proceeding to next.
   c. Extend to copying simple sentences from board and sentences written on pupil's paper by teacher. Have pupil dictate words and simple sentences to teacher. Then teacher writes them in cursive and gives to child for copying. Pupil then traces with

finger and writes individual work cards. Transfer exercises to copying sentences from book. Introduce formal handwriting system such as Noble's.

d. For extended activities, teach writing of simple music, foreign words, sign language.

e. Extend to creative writing activities. Have pupils draw cartoon characters and write in conversation. Write special interest stories.

REFERENCES

Arena, John, ed. *Building Handwriting Skills in Dyslexic Children.* San Rafael, Calif.: Academic Therapy Publications, 1970.

Gardner, W. *Text-Manual for Remedial Handwriting.* Danville, Ill.: Interstate Printers and Publishers, 1966.

Gillingham, A., and Stillman, B. *Remedial Training for Children with Specific Disability in Reading, Spelling, and Penmanship.* Cambridge, Mass.: Educators Publishing Service, 1960.

Related Programs

- *Noble's Handwriting for Everyday Use* (manuscript, transition, enlarged regular), Palfrey's Educational Supply Co., 7715 E. Garvey Boulevard, Rosemead, Calif.
- *Beginner's Book in Writing and Spelling* (cursive), Palfrey's Educational Supply Co.
- *Easy Way to Handwriting* (Giant Activity Book), Palfrey's Educational Supply Co.
- *Fun with Writing* (activity series), Palfrey's Educational Supply Co.
- Petty, Walter T., and Plessas, Gus P. *You Can Spell,* Vol. 1. Boston: Allyn and Bacon, 1964–1968.
- Frostig, Marianne, and Horne, David. "Reversals and Rotations" and "Mirror Patterns." *The Frostig Program for the Development of Visual Perception.* Chicago: Follett Publishing, 1964.
- Gardner, Warren. *Text-Manual for Remedial Handwriting.* Danville, Ill.: Interstate Printers and Publishers, 1966.
- Skinner, B. F., and Krakower, S. A. *Handwriting with Write and See Series* (workbooks). Chicago: Lyons and Carnahan, 1968.
- *Language and Study Skills* Program, No. 1 (letter writing) and No. 2 (handwriting masters), Continental Press, Elizabethtown, Pa.
- *Tracing Paper Designs* and *Pre-Writing Designs.* Developmental Learning Materials, 3505 N. Ashland Avenue, Chicago, Ill.
- *Handwriting Demons Program,* Noble and Noble Publishers, 750 Third Avenue, New York, N.Y.

Instructional Materials

- *Picture-Alphabet Wall Charts* (manuscripts and cursive), Palfrey's Educational Supply Co.
- *It Is Fun to Write* (book), Palfrey's Educational Supply Co.
- Metal Insets (form tracing stencils), Teaching Aids, 159 W. Kinzie Street, Chicago, Ill.
- New Felt-riters (large felt pens)
- Two-inch Alphabet Letter Stencils, Palfrey's Educational Supply Co.
- Small chalkboard for individual pupil use
- Play-doh, clay, fingerpaint, cookie trays, crayons, paints, soft pencils
- Wide-lined paper, heavy crayons, broad pencils
- Pencil Grippers, MKM Co., 809 Kansas City Street, Rapid City, S.D.

Further Evaluation

- Writing performance on spelling tests such as the Wide Range Achievement Test
- Direct evaluation of copy work from sequential handwriting workbooks
- Subjective evaluation of pupil work samples
- Slingerland Screening Tests for Specific Language Disability

PRESCRIPTIVE ILLUSTRATION

Priority Teaching Objective: Bobby, ten years old, specific learning disability. Upon completion of the lesson, Bobby will be able to copy a list of five words on regular writing paper while maintaining the correct posture and position for pencil and paper.

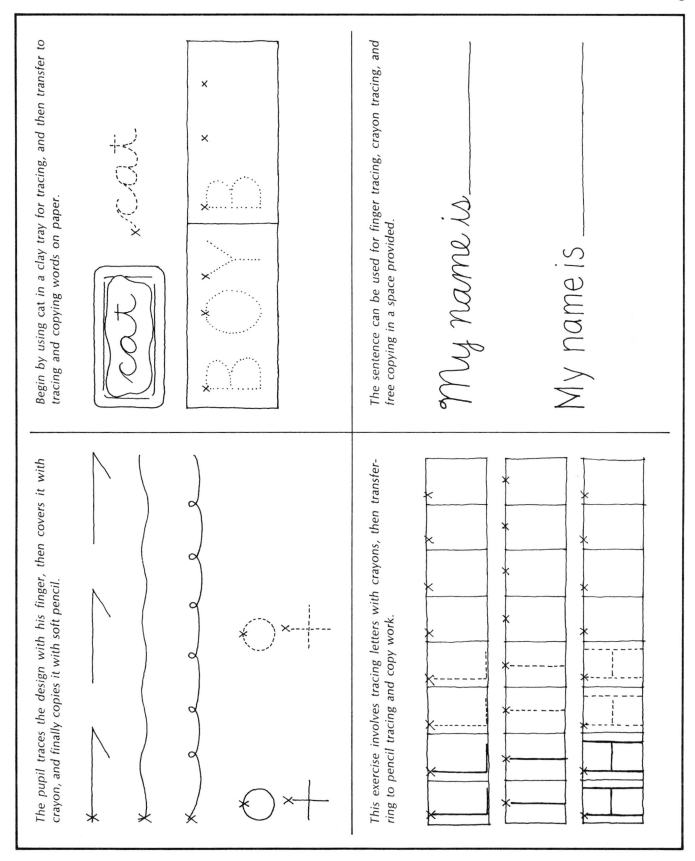

Begin by using cat in a clay tray for tracing, and then transfer to tracing and copying words on paper.

The sentence can be used for finger tracing, crayon tracing, and free copying in a space provided.

My name is _____

My name is _____

The pupil traces the design with his finger, then covers it with crayon, and finally copies it with soft pencil.

This exercise involves tracing letters with crayons, then transferring to pencil tracing and copy work.

All programs should be modified or extended to meet the needs of individual pupils.

Pretest Tasks: Bobby was asked to write his name on a sheet of primary paper with a primary pencil. He could not remember how to spell his last name, was tense, held the pencil very close to the tip, and bent over the paper in an awkward position.

Specific Teaching Procedures: "Bobby, in this lesson you are going to practice how to sit while you write. You will also learn how to hold your pencil correctly as you work. I will write some words for you now to show you how to do it."

"Watch me now; I am holding the pencil here, not down by the point. I am sitting straight with my back against the chair, and I have my paper turned like this. My feet are flat on the floor and I am writing with my right hand and holding my paper with my left, just as you are going to do. Now, Bobby, what are you going to do?"

Pupil: "Hold the pencil like this and sit with my back against the chair, put my feet on the floor, and hold the paper with my left hand."

"Good. Now for each word that you copy without forgetting to sit up straight and hold the pencil correctly, you'll get one point on your card. OK, here are your words to write."

Performance Eavluation: "Good, Bobby! You copied all of the words without forgetting to sit up straight and hold the pencil correctly. Was there anything you forgot to do?"

Pupil: "I forgot to hold the paper once. How many points did I get? Four?"

Analysis and Comments: The lesson was partially appropriate, but Bobby needs much more practice as he has poor writing posture. He also appears to need appropriate exercises to develop prerequisite fine muscle coordination. Future lessons should incorporate reproducing visual-motor tasks such as tracing, string patterns, coloring, and kinesthetic exercises.

For Self-instruction: Devise a teaching procedure and performance evaluation method for this pupil: Jean, twelve years old, educationally handicapped. Jean will be able to complete a four-frame cartoon story sequence by writing simple sentences in the space provided.

Language Development

43/Spelling

DEFINITION: The ability to spell in both oral and written form.
ILLUSTRATION: Pupil spells within general age expectancy.
EDUCATIONAL RATIONALE: Spellng is a higher-order skill requiring visual-motor integration together with basic vocabulary knowledge and phonic awareness. Correct spelling develops through good habits and practice, proceeding from simple to complex words that are meaningful to the pupil.

SUGGESTED PROGRAM IDEAS

1. Small Muscle Control
   a. Begin with exercises for gross hand and finger control. Have pupil scribble on chalk-board and primary paper, gradually confining movement between wide lines. Introduce pupil to finger painting, clay and sand marking, and tracing of designs such as circles, squares, diamonds.
   b. Give pupil crayons and large soft pencils for coloring book work to gain proficiency in holding and manipulating markers. Have child draw pictures (family, teacher, home, school, etc.), beginning with crayons and gradually moving to felt pens and soft pencils.
   c. Introduce controlled drawing of forms using stencils, letter and number forms, etc. Show pupil how to hold pencil properly and position paper at correct angle for writing. Play finger game of turning pencil around in circles with fingers—both forward and backward—to develop control. If necessary, wrap tape around pencil to give pupil greater control. Extend exercises to mastery of alphabet and number series.

2. Development of Word Image
   a. Introduce limited number of basic words (pupil's name, *boy, love, ghost,* etc.) on board in cursive. Slowly pronounce word, use it in a simple sentence, pronounce word again. Have pupil pronounce word and trace over board model or word written on paper by teacher. Child should trace word first with finger, then with crayon, and last with pencil.
   b. Have pupil close eyes and try to imagine the word, following tracing. Pupil then traces word in the air with finger. If pupil has difficulty, have him open his eyes, again view word, close eyes, and trace in air again until successful.
   c. Next, have pupil copy word on paper and slowly say the word as he writes it. For handicapped pupils, cursive is the method of choice (because of its unified characteristics); manuscript may be introduced later. Model word is then covered and pupil spells it in written form from memory. Each word should be written until success is achieved at least five times.

3. Spelling Reinforcement
   a. Trace, copy, and write spelling words from memory, using basic words from Dolch list or readers. For difficult words, extend tracing techniques by using clay trays, raised words made with Elmer's Glue, rope words, walking patterns, etc.
   b. Extend spelling list with words provided by pupil. Have child use his own words in sentences. Begin "word box" for constant reference and use in sentence construction.
   c. Follow procedure of having pupil correct all words by blotting out incorrect spelling and then writing correctly; reward pupil for correction. Always file words missed

and corrected. Have frequent practice with these words. Have pupil make dictionary of his own word list.

d. Extend program to include *written* spelldowns and use of words in simple stories. Oral spelldowns or tests should only be used as a review technique after words have been mastered in written form. Utilize formal spelling textbook program supplemented by occasional lists of special interest words from pupil projects, newspapers, other assignments, etc. Provide daily practice, correction, and reinforcement of success.

e. Use crossword puzzles, Scrabble, and other spelling games for reinforcement. Use Scrabble letters to spell out words chosen by the pupil.

REFERENCES

Dolch, E. W. *Better Spelling.* Champaign, Ill.: Garrard Press, 1942.

Fernald, Grace. "Spelling." *Remedial Techniques in Basic School Subjects,* pp. 181–210. New York: McGraw-Hill, 1942.

Related Programs

- *Introduction to Spelling Sense* (record), Educational Record Sales, 157 Chambers St., New York, N.Y.
- *Spelling for Word Mastery* (spelling and writing, manuscript and cursive), Palfrey's Educational Supply Co., 7715 E. Garvey Boulevard, Rosemead, Calif.
- *The Magic World of Dr. Spello* (filmstrip), Webster Division, McGraw-Hill Book Co., Manchester Road, Manchester, Mo.
- Activity Series: *Spell and Play; More Spelling,* Palfrey's Educational Supply Co.
- Petty, Walter T., and Plessas, Gus P. *You Can Spell,* Vols. 1–7. Boston: Allyn and Bacon, 1964–1968.
- *Key Lab: A Self-Correcting Spelling Program,* Houghton Mifflin Co., 110 Tremont Street, Boston, Mass.
- *Teach Key Reading and Spelling,* 3M Co., Box 9905, St. Paul, Minn.
- *Cyclo Teacher,* 3020 Spelling Cycles, Field Enterprises Education Corporation, Merchandise Mart Plaza, Chicago, Ill.
- *The Spell of Words* (workbook for dyslexics), Educators Publishing Service, 75 Moulton Street, Cambridge, Mass.

Instructional Materials

- *The Picture Dictionary for Children,* Palfrey's Educational Supply Co.
- *Color ABC* (book), Palfrey's Educational Supply Co.
- *My First Crossword Puzzle Book, Junior Crossword Puzzle Book, The Sports Crossword Book,* Palfrey's Educational Supply Co.
- Anagrams
- Scrabble for Juniors
- Milton Bradley Aids: Dial 'n Spell, Palfrey's Educational Supply Co.
- Judy Alphaforms, The Judy Company, 310 N. Second Street, Minneapolis, Minn.
- Child Guidance Magnetic Alphabet Board
- Dolch Basic Sight Cards, Lakeshore Equipment Co., 1144 Montague Avenue, San Leandro, Calif.
- Toss Words, Palfrey's Educational Supply Co.
- Alphabet children's blocks
- Spelling Key-Kits, Childcraft Equipment Co., Inc., 155 E. 23rd Street, New York, N.Y.

Further Evaluation

- Wide Range Achievement Test: spelling
- California Achievement Tests: spelling
- Subjective analysis of spelling performance in letters and general class work

Tracing and copying words improves hand-eye control in reproducing integrated symbols.

Mom

teacher

Batman

Santa

Sentence completion and meaningful spelling: after the sentence has been completed, the entire sentence should be written again from memory or from the teacher's dictation.

I am a

Today is

This month is

My name is

The dog

I like

Tonight I

After tracing these designs with finger, crayon, and soft pencil, the pupil copies them.

a B 6 R e i

s t d l

Boxed and outlined cues help the pupil to write the words with models covered.

Mom Dad

apple

ghost

spelling

All programs should be modified or extended to meet the needs of individual pupils.

Priority Teaching Objective: Joe, eighteen years old, educable mentally retarded. Upon completion of this lesson, Joe will be able to spell nine out of ten of the following words: *television, turkey, camera, glasses, check, ring, motorcycle, woman, flower,* and *elephant.*

Pretest Tasks: Joe was presented twenty picture word cards for a period of ten minutes. Then these words were taken away from him, and he was asked to spell them individually as I presented the picture to him. He was unable to spell nine out of the twenty words, and these are all to be taught to him.

Specific Teaching Procedures: "Joe, in this lesson I want you to place these plastic sheets on the picture word cards and trace each word five times carefully with your finger while saying each letter out loud. Then you are to trace each word five times with your felt pen without lifting it while saying each letter out loud. After doing this, take off the plastic cover and cover the whole card with this sheet of paper. Next, pull the blank sheet of paper back slowly until you see the first letter. Say that letter and then pull the sheet back to expose the second letter, which you are to say, and so on."

"Watch me now as I demonstrate it for you. See how I trace the word five times with my finger. Now five times with the felt pen and again I say each letter as I trace it. Now I cover the word and slowly expose each letter and say it."

"Now, for each word that you spell correctly you will get one minute free time on your credit card. OK, let's start."

Performance Evaluation: "That was well done, Joe. You earned seven minutes credit time and only made three mistakes. Do you know which mistakes you made?"
Pupil: "I think I missed *motorcycle, elephant,* and *television.*"

On the repetition of the twenty-word pretest, Joe misspelled only one word: *motorcycle.*

Analysis and Comments: Joe was cooperative and well motivated. He learned well by this method, which will be continued with new words.

For Self-instruction: Devise a teaching procedure and performance evaluation method for this pupil: Gina, seven years old, educationally handicapped. Gina will be able to spell orally ten of eleven words using a kinesthetic approach followed by spelling the word in written form.

Conceptual Skills

44/Number Concepts

DEFINITION: The ability to understand and use the concepts of quantity, sets, number, numeral, shape, size, position, and measurement.

ILLUSTRATION: Pupil can arrange objects into sets, can count the number in each set, and can recognize the numeral that represents that number.

EDUCATIONAL RATIONALE: Mathematical understanding begins with manipulating objects, counting them, and comparing the quantity of objects in different sets. The child learns that there are symbols to represent the relationships between numbers ($=$, $>$, $<$, etc.) and other symbols, called numerals, that represent the numbers themselves.

SUGGESTED PROGRAM IDEAS

1. Concepts of Quantity and Sets
   a. Form a wide variety of sets for the child by using the objects at hand, such as the people in the room, the books on the desk, the square blocks in a box. Be certain that some of the sets have elements that are dissimilar. Have the child form a wide variety of sets of his own choice.
   b. Introduction to quantity: Using the sets formed in "a," introduce the concepts of many/few, more/less/same, and not any, as they apply to the sets. Have the children discuss these concepts and demonstrate them by citing concrete examples.
   c. The concept of quantity applied to sets: Place six identical candies in two piles in front of the child. Have the child pair each of the candies in one pile with one of the candies in the second pile until all of the candies are paired. Are there any candies that can't be paired? Do both sets have the same amount of candy? These are called "equivalent sets." Have the child identify other equivalent sets. Point out that the kind of objects is not important; only their quantity is important. Have the child identify sets that do not have the same quantity. Point out that, when the objects in these sets are paired, there are always some left over in one of the sets. Have the child describe the relationships between these different quantities.
   d. The empty-set concept: Arrange a string in the shape of a large circle on the child's desk. Place two blocks in it and ask the child how many are in the set. Then remove them and say, "Now there are not any blocks in the circle. Now you have an empty set." Reinforce by discussion and comparison with sets that are not empty.

2. Concept of Number and Numeral
   a. Learning to count: Provide concrete experiences by counting the objects in many different sets so that the child learns that, as he counts higher, the number of objects increases by one more each time he says another number. When possible, count for a purpose—to see how many children are present, or how many crayon boxes there are. Move from counting objects to counting pictures of objects.
   b. Learning the quantity of each number and the numeral that represents that quantity: Use some systematic method of introducing each number and numeral, allowing the child enough time to master the relationship. You might, for example, introduce a set of two wooden beads and ask, "How many beads are in this set?" When the child responds, "Two," tell him that he has identified a number. Then show him the numeral 2 and tell him that it is the numeral that represents the number 2. Ask him to place the beads in a small can; have him paste the numeral to the side of the

173

can. Proceed until the child has nine cans with the appropriate number of beads in each can and the appropriate numerals on the outside.

c. Learning the meaning of zero: Repeat the procedure of arranging a string in the shape of a large circle on the desk to indicate an empty set. When he says there are not any beads in it, show him "0" and tell him it is the numeral that represents that set. Have him paste the 0 on an empty can.

d. Understanding place value and base ten. Before proceeding to written numerals greater than 9, the child must acquire some concept of place value. Since we have only ten numerals, we must combine them in a sensible way to represent quantities greater than nine. Ask the child to count 23 toothpicks. Then tell him that, in order to know which numerals represent that number, he must arrange them into sets of ten. Let him use a rubber band to hold each set. When he sees that he has two sets of ten, with three single ones left over, show him a place-holder chart, ask him to put the single toothpicks in the "ones" pocket and the two sets of ten in the "tens" pocket. Now he will see that he has three ones and two tens. Show him how to write this numeral as 23. Discuss the difference between the numeral 23 and the digits 2 and 3. Introduce "hundreds" and show their place on the chart. Discuss the importance and meaning of zero as a place holder.

3. Understanding the Relation Symbols

a. Have the students count the elements in a variety of sets to determine the number associated with the quantity of each set. Use several examples to show that when two sets have the same number, they are equivalent sets. Point out that the numbers associated with equivalent sets are equal. Introduce the symbol $=$. Be certain the child understands that equivalence relates to sets while $=$ relates to numbers. Point out that counting is an easy way to show sets equivalent without having to pair all of the elements.

b. Now use sets whose numbers are not equal to introduce the symbol $\neq$. Have the student tell you how to use counting to tell if two sets are not equivalent. Point out that the numbers associated with these sets are $\neq$. Now introduce the symbols for greater than ($>$) and less than ($<$). Use these to describe the relationships between the numbers representing nonequivalent sets.

c. Gradually change the emphasis from sets to numbers so that in the end the child can use the symbols ($=$, $\neq$, $>$, $<$) to describe relationships between numbers. Write many pairs of numerals and have the child insert the correct relation symbol between them.

4. Concepts of Shape, Size, and Position

a. Shape: Introduce the square, rectangle, triangle, and circle. Have the child use templates and later draw and cut his own shapes. Gradually introduce more complicated geometric shapes. Encourage comparison of shapes.

b. Size: Introduce concepts of big/little, long/short, wide/narrow, fat/thin, tall/short. Use concrete examples and have the child make comparisons. Let him cut different sizes from scrap paper.

c. Distinguish between size as a measure of area and size as a measure of circumference or perimeter. Using a length of string, have the child form a wide variety of simple closed figures and notice how the shape changes the area even though the perimeter remains constant. Ask the child to enclose the largest possible area (a circle) and the smallest possible area (a figure with zero area). Point out that the two ends of the string must touch, and the string must not overlap itself, so that you deal only with simple closed figures. Have the child make figures that have the same area but different perimeters, such as a 1×4 rectangle and a 2×2 square. Have the child cut the rectangle up and fit it into the square. Reexamine the concepts of big/little, long/short, wide/narrow, fat/thin, tall/short in terms of area, perimeter, and shape.

d. Position: Introduce concepts of over/under, high/low, beside/between, bottom/top, in front of/behind, above/below, and middle. Have the children place objects in these positions and draw diagrams of objects in various positions. Does the size or shape change when the position is changed?

5. Concept of Measurement
   a. Time: Teach the concepts of late/early, now/later, yesterday/today/tomorrow. Discuss the days of the week and months of the year. Use a calendar to keep track of time. Use a time-line to show passage of time and relationship of events. Teach the use of clocks and recognition of seconds, minutes, hours, half- and quarter-hours. Discuss sun dials and hour glasses as instruments to measure time.
   b. Distance: Pace off distance in the classroom and make estimates. Measure, using feet, inches, and yards. Introduce the metric measurement system of meters, decimeters, and centimeters. Introduce miles and kilometers. But do not attempt to convert from one measure to the other. Objects to be measured in the metric system are best measured with metric instruments. Conversion factors can be left to intuition. Measure the circumference of objects and the waistlines and heights of the students.
   c. Liquids and solids: Teach the use of English and metric units such as teaspoons, tablespoons, cups, pints, quarts, gallons, milliliters and liters. Have the children measure liquids and solids and compare amounts to discover relationships. Use recipes for practical measuring experiences.
   d. Weight: Teach the concept of light/heavy. Teach the use of ounces and pounds, grams and kilograms. Have the children weigh themselves and others. Weigh objects, discuss differences, and make comparisons.

REFERENCES

Collier, Calhoun, and Lerch, Harold. *Teaching Mathematics in the Modern Elementary School.* New York: Macmillan, 1969.

Montessori, Maria. "Arithmetic." *Dr. Montessori's Own Handbook.* New York: Schocken Books, 1965.

Trivett, John V. *Mathematical Awareness.* New Rochelle, N.Y.: Cuisenaire Company of America, 1962.

Related Programs
- *Number Readiness I* and *Number Concepts II* (filmstrips), Educational Record Sales, 157 Chambers Street, New York, N.Y.
- *More or Less (record),* Educational Record Sales
- *ABC and One to Ten* (record), Educational Record Sales
- *Counting Games and Rhythms* (record), Educational Record Sales
- *Science Research Associates Mathematics Program* (kindergarten book), SRA, Inc., 259 E. Erie Street, Chicago, Ill.
- *Numbers in Color Cuisenaire Rods,* Cuisenaire Company of America, Inc., 9 Elm Avenue, Mt. Vernon, N.Y.
- *U.S. Money, Level 1* and *Number Concepts, Levels 1–2,* Continental Press, Elizabethtown, Pa.
- *Math Concepts* (record), Curtis Audio-Visual Materials, Independence Square, Philadelphia, Pa.
- *Inquisitive Games* (exploring number and space), Science Research Associates, Inc.
- *Arithmetic—Step by Step,* Kit A, Continental Press
- Proportional Number Blocks, Milton Bradley Co., Springfield, Mass.
- Ryder, Ruth T.; Allmond, Phyllis P.; and Mock, Valerie. *Pacemaker Arithmetic Program.* Belmont, Calif.: Fearon Publishers, 1973.

Instructional Materials
- Milton Bradley Aids: Memory Arithmetic Game, Link Numbers, Number Concept Cards, Beginner's Number Poster Cards, Modern Mathematics Kindergarten Kit, Palfrey's Educational Supply Co., 7715 E. Garvey Boulevard, Rosemead, Calif.
- Colored Counting Cubes, One Hundred Chart, Number Concept Chart, Number Readiness Posters, Place Value Charts, Ideal School Supply Co., 11000 S. Lavergne Avenue, Oak Lawn, Ill.

These problems deal with the pairing of objects in sets.

Pair the objects by drawing lines between them.

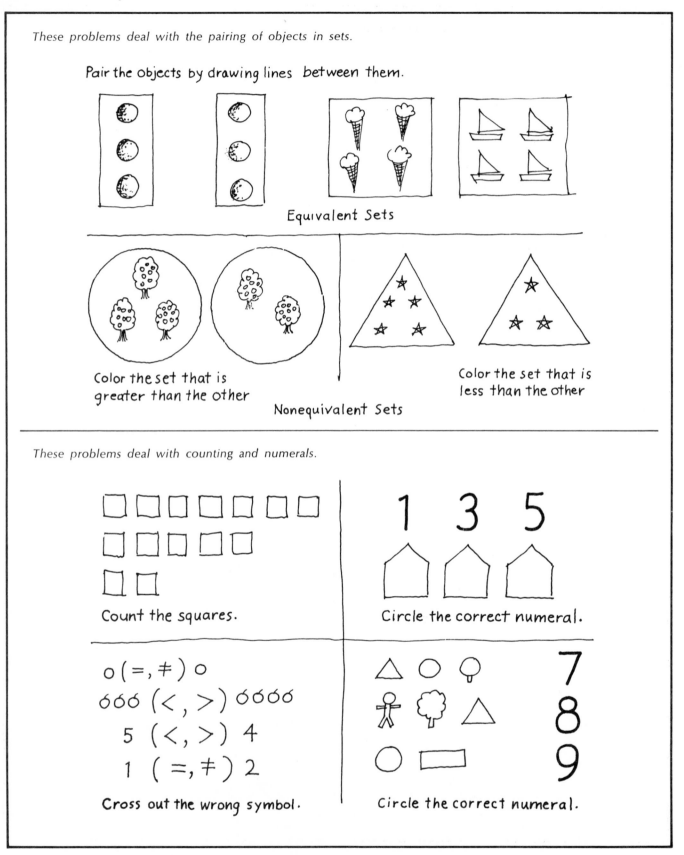

Equivalent Sets

Color the set that is greater than the other

Nonequivalent Sets

Color the set that is less than the other

These problems deal with counting and numerals.

Count the squares.

Circle the correct numeral.

1 3 5

o (=, ≠) o
óóó (<, >) óóóó
5 (<, >) 4
1 (=, ≠) 2

Cross out the wrong symbol.

7
8
9

Circle the correct numeral.

These problems deal with the place-value system.

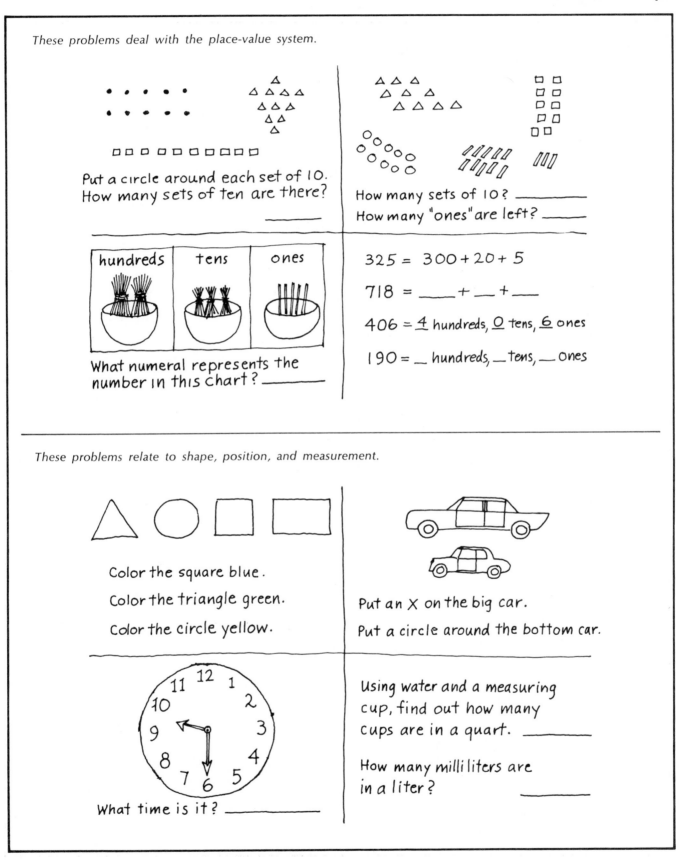

Put a circle around each set of 10.
How many sets of ten are there? _____

How many sets of 10? _____
How many "ones" are left? _____

hundreds	tens	ones

What numeral represents the number in this chart? _____

325 = 300 + 20 + 5

718 = ___ + __ + ___

406 = _4_ hundreds, _0_ tens, _6_ ones

190 = __ hundreds, __ tens, __ ones

These problems relate to shape, position, and measurement.

Color the square blue.
Color the triangle green.
Color the circle yellow.

Put an X on the big car.
Put a circle around the bottom car.

What time is it? _____

Using water and a measuring cup, find out how many cups are in a quart. _____

How many milliliters are in a liter? _____

All programs should be modified or extended to meet the needs of individual pupils.

- Pegboards and pegs
- Beaded Number Cards, Ben-G Number Concept Puzzles, Fret-Cut Plywood Numbers, Metal Chalkboard and Magnetic Numerals, Palfrey's Educational Supply Co.
- Judy Numberite, Hundred Pegboard, Bead Abacus, Hundred Vari-Bead, The Judy Company, 310 N. Second Street, Minneapolis, Minn.
- Dolch First Arithmetic Game, Lakeshore Equipment Co., 1144 Montague Avenue, San Leandro, Calif.
- Activity Series: Beginning Arithmetic, Count, Color and Play, Palfrey's Educational Supply Co.
- Hayes Pre-Primer Number Play, Lakeshore Equipment Co.
- Touch to Learn (numbers), Systematic Learning Corp., 52 Hook Road, Bayonne, N.J.

Further Evaluation
- Wide Range Achievement Test: counting
- Stanford-Binet L-M: number concepts
- Simple counting and grouping problems

PRESCRIPTIVE ILLUSTRATION

Priority Teaching Objective: Charlene, eight years old, educationally handicapped. When presented five different sets of paper circles, frogs, and owls, Charlene will be able to identify the sets with "more" objects as opposed to "less" objects.

Pretest Tasks: Charlene was presented five different pairs of sets enclosed within red yarn loops. The objects were green paper circles and she was asked to point out the loops with "more." She got two of the five correct.

Specific Teaching Procedures: "Charlene, I want you to match the circles I am placing in this loop on the flannel board. See how I place, one, two, three, four circles in the loop. Now you take some circles and place them in this loop. For each one I have, you place one inside your loop."

"Both loops have the same number of circles. There are four circles in each loop. They are the same. Neither one has more than the other."

"Now watch what I will do. I take one more circle and put it in my loop. Now my loop has more and your loop has less. Put your hand on the loop that has more circles."

"That's right. Now we will remove them and try again. I am going to give you these frogs to put in your loop. Go ahead and put them in. Now I will put these frogs in my loop. Look at them carefully and point to the one that has more."

"Fine. This time we are going to use small owls. I will put these owls here and you put those owls over there in that loop. Which loop has more?"

Pupil: "Mine has more. I have four owls and you have three."

Performance Evaluation: On the posttest, Charlene got four of the five sets correct. She missed the set with nine owls saying that the loop with eight had more.

Analysis and Comments: Although there was fair performance, the classroom was too noisy, and this bothered Charlene. Maybe she needs a less distracting work place to aid her concentration.

For Self-instruction: Devise a teaching procedure and performance evaluation method for this pupil: Lottie, twenty-five years old, chronic schizophrenic. Lottie will be able to play a game of Scrabble with me, taking at least four turns at forming words, counting them up by points, and writing down her points earned. She needs to use her conceptual abilities, and in this lesson concentration on number concepts, to help her cut through auditory hallucinations and as a means of interrrelating with people.

Conceptual Skills

45/Arithmetic Processes

DEFINITION: The ability to add, subtract, multiply, and divide whole numbers, fractions, and decimal fractions.

ILLUSTRATION: Pupil can demonstrate knowledge of basic mathematical operations within relation to his level of understanding of mathematical concepts.

EDUCATIONAL RATIONALE: The ability to perform mathematical operations accurately is a necessary skill in order for the child to solve the many problems in his day-to-day life that deal with number concepts.

SUGGESTED PROGRAM IDEAS

1. Addition and Subtraction
   a. Present addition as a convenient means of determining the number associated with a set formed by combining two sets that have no elements in common. Have the child construct his own addition table. Discuss the need for counting in order to form the table.
   b. Provide concrete experiences in combining sets, using blocks, buttons, clothespins, candy, pegboard, abacus, and Cuisenaire Rods. Allow the student to manipulate these materials to demonstrate addition.
   c. Present subtraction as undoing addition. Show how subtraction reverses the addition process. Provide concrete experiences similar to those in "b" above emphasizing the word "inverse" to describe this relationship. Show the child how to subtract by using the addition table.
   d. After the teaching the symbols $+$ and $-$, introduce numerals in problems by systematically writing each "family of facts" to sum $9 + 9$. (Example: $4 + 3 = 7$, $3 + 4 = 7$, $7 - 4 = 3$, $7 - 3 = 4$) so that the relationship between addition and subtraction is further established. Use flash cards and drill to assist in memorization.
   e. Continually refer back to the addition table as the source for addition facts and to addition as the source for subtraction.
   f. When the concept of place value has been taught, teach addition and subtraction of numbers greater than 9. Begin with addition problems in which the addends have a sum less than 10 (*Figure A*) and subtraction problems in which the subtrahend is less than the minuend (*Figure B*). Gradually extend the program to include the addition and subtraction of three-, four-, and five-place numerals.
   g. Again using the concept of place value, teach the addition of columns in which the sum is greater than ten and the subtraction of columns in which the ones digit in the subtrahend is greater than the ones digit in the minuend. Begin by using the three-step "long method" of renaming numerals (*Figure C*).
   h. When the above concept is firmly established, teach the "short method" of renaming in one step (*Figure D*). Although the terms "carrying" and "borrowing" are no longer commonly used, for some children they help to clarify the concept.

Fig. A		*Fig. B*		*Fig. C*		*Fig. D*		
	24		97		38		$\overset{1}{38}$	$\overset{7\ 16}{\cancel{86}}$
	$+ 35$		$- 25$		$+ 24$		$+ 24$	$- 37$
					12 $(8 + 4)$		62	49
					50 $(20 + 30)$			
					62 $(50 + 12)$			

2. Multiplication and Division

   a. After some degree of skill has been acquired in addition and subtraction, introduce multiplication as repeated addition, which is a faster, more efficient way to add equal numbers. Division should be taught as the inverse of multiplication or as repeated subtraction.

   b. Using blocks, marbles, beads, and pegboard, give concrete experiences in multiplying and in dividing. Using concrete objects, demonstrate how there can be a remainder in division.

   c. Teach the meaning of the symbols $\times$ and $\div$. Introduce numerals in problems that systematically present each "family of facts" (Example: $3 \times 4 = 12$, $4 \times 3 = 12 \div 4 = 3$, $12 \div 3 = 4$) so that the relationship between multiplication and division is established.

   d. Have the child construct his own multiplication table to 9×9. Point out the use of addition in forming such a table. Show how to use the table for division. Again emphasize the word "inverse" as an undoing process.

   e. Introduce multiplication charts and wheels as aids, along with flash cards. Provide drill to assist in memorization.

3. Fractions and Decimals

   a. To introduce fractions, have the child divide a whole piece of paper into parts. After defining "numerator" and "denominator," demonstrate how to write the fractions that represent these parts. Have the child cut a piece of paper in half, in fourths, etc., as he writes each fraction. He will see that (since the numerator remains the same) the denominator gets *larger*, but the fraction represents an increasingly *smaller* part of the whole. This concept is difficult but necessary.

   b. By shading areas of a whole, demonstrate equal-valued fractions (Example: $\frac{1}{2}$ and $\frac{2}{4}$ and like fractions (Example: $\frac{1}{4}$ and $\frac{2}{4}$.)

   c. In order to teach reduction of fractions to lowest terms, again use shaded areas to demonstrate (Example: $\frac{3}{6} = \frac{1}{2}$). Give many examples to demonstrate clearly, by shading, that multiplying both numerator and denominator by the same number results in an equal-valued fraction. Next ask the child to reverse the process. Suggest that he use the inverse operation to multiplication. The child should see that dividing both numerator and denominator by the same number will also result in an equal-valued fraction. This is called reducing fractions to lowest terms. Provide many examples.

   d. Introduce multiplication of fractions by shading or cutting paper (Example: shade $\frac{1}{3}$ of $\frac{1}{2}$ to show $\frac{1}{6}$.) Define multiplication of fractions as finding the fraction whose numerator is the product of the numerators of the given fractions and whose denominator is the product of their denominators. Require that the answers be in lowest terms; then demonstrate how this can be done before multiplying. Point out that you are reducing the fraction by division before it is actually multiplied (*Figure E*).

Fig. E Since $\dfrac{5}{8} \times \dfrac{7}{5} = \dfrac{35}{40} = \dfrac{7}{8}$ the same result can be obtained by $\dfrac{\cancel{5}^{1}}{8} \times \dfrac{7}{\cancel{5}_{1}} = \dfrac{7}{8}$

Introduce division as an inverse process and show how multiplying by the reciprocal of a fraction reverses the multiplication (*Figure F*).

Fig. F $\dfrac{3}{5} \times \dfrac{2}{7} = \dfrac{6}{35}$ so $\dfrac{6}{35} \div \dfrac{2}{7} = \dfrac{3}{5}$ or $\dfrac{\cancel{6}^{3}}{\cancel{35}_{5}} \times \dfrac{\cancel{7}^{1}}{\cancel{2}_{1}} = \dfrac{3}{5}$

Reinforce with many examples.

e. Teach addition and subtraction of like fractions by using shading and other devices. Indicate the importance of having the same denominator. Show by shading that $\frac{1}{2} + \frac{1}{3} \neq \frac{2}{5}$. Review like fractions and show how to find equal-valued fractions (common denominators). Teach subtraction as the inverse of addition. Reinforce each step with many examples. Require all answers to be in lowest terms.

f. Introduce mixed numbers by shading and show how to change to an improper fraction by addition (*Figure G*). ·

Fig. G
$$2\frac{3}{5} = 2 + \frac{3}{5} = \frac{2}{1} + \frac{3}{5} = \frac{10}{5} + \frac{3}{5} = \frac{13}{5} \text{ or } 2\frac{3}{5} = \frac{2 \times 5 + 3}{5} = \frac{13}{5}$$

The child should see that the second method is the first method with steps missing. Show how to add, subtract, multiply, and divide mixed numbers by changing to fractions when necessary. Reinforce with many examples. Talk about improper fractions and show how to change them to mixed numbers by division. Point out that improper fractions are easier to reduce if they are changed to mixed numbers first.

g. Decimals should be compared to fractions (Example: $\frac{3}{10} = .3$.) Define the decimal point and emphasize its importance by reviewing the place value system and extending it to show tenths and hundredths. Use the number line to show the meaning of numerals to the right of the decimal. Demonstrate the significance of zero as a place holder. Teach addition, subtraction, multiplication, and division of decimals, stressing the importance of keeping the decimal point in the correct place. Teach how to round off decimals and how to change decimals to fractions and fractions to decimals.

REFERENCES

Fernald, Grace. "Arithmetic." *Remedial Techniques in Basic School Subjects*. New York: McGraw-Hill, 1943.

Gattengno, C. *For the Teaching of Elementary Mathematics*. New Rochelle, N.Y.: Cuisenaire Company of America, 1963.

Related Programs

- *Math Made Meaningful,* Vols. 1 and 2 (records), Educational Record Sales, 157 Chambers Street, New York, N.Y.
- *Primary Arithmetic* (filmstrip series), Educational Record Sales
- *Cuisenaire Rods,* Cuisenaire Company of America, Inc., 9 Elm Avenue, Mt. Vernon, N.Y.
- *Number Concepts,* Level 3, and *U.S. Money,* Level 2 and 3, Continental Press, Elizabethtown, Pa.
- *We Work with Numbers* and *Learning New Skills in Arithmetic,* Continental Press
- *Science Research Associates Mathematics Programs,* SRA, Inc., 259 E. Erie Street, Chicago, Ill.
- *The Learning Skills Series: Arithmetic,* Webster Division, McGraw-Hill Book Co., Manchester Road, Manchester, Mo.
- *Teach Key Math,* 3M Co., Box 9905, St. Paul, Minn.
- *Sullivan Mathematics Laboratory,* Behavioral Research Lab., Box 557, Palo Alto, Calif.
- *Opening Doors in Mathematics* (primary program), Cuisenaire Company of America

Instructional Materials

- Dolch Materials: The 10 Game; Say It Addition, Subtraction, Muliplication, Division; Popper Numbers: Addition, Subtraction, Multiplication, Division; Make One (simple fractions), Lakeshore Equipment Co., 1144 Montague Avenue, San Leandro, Calif.
- Link Numbers, Quizmo: Add-Subtract/Multiply-Divide, Number Line, Lakeshore Equipment Co.
- Puzzle Plans: Addition, Subtraction, Multiplication, Fractions, Palfrey's Educational Supply Co., 7715 E. Garvey Boulevard, Rosemead, Calif.
- Activity Series: First Steps in Understanding Arithmetic, Vols. 1–4, Palfrey's Educational Supply Co.

Addition and Subtraction

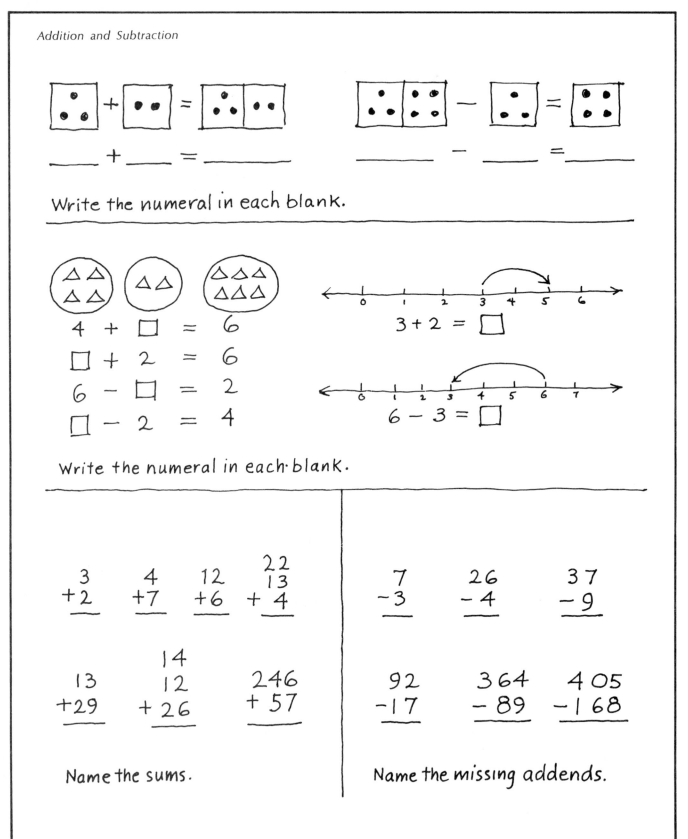

Write the numeral in each blank.

___ + ___ = ___   ___ − ___ = ___

4 + □ = 6

□ + 2 = 6

6 − □ = 2

□ − 2 = 4

3 + 2 = □

6 − 3 = □

Write the numeral in each·blank.

| 3 | 4 | 12 | 22 13 + 4 |
| +2 | +7 | +6 |

| 13 | 14 12 | 246 |
| +29 | + 26 | + 57 |

Name the sums.

| 7 | 26 | 37 |
| −3 | − 4 | −9 |

| 92 | 364 | 4 05 |
| −17 | − 89 | −1 68 |

Name the missing addends.

All programs should be modified or extended to meet the needs of individual pupils.

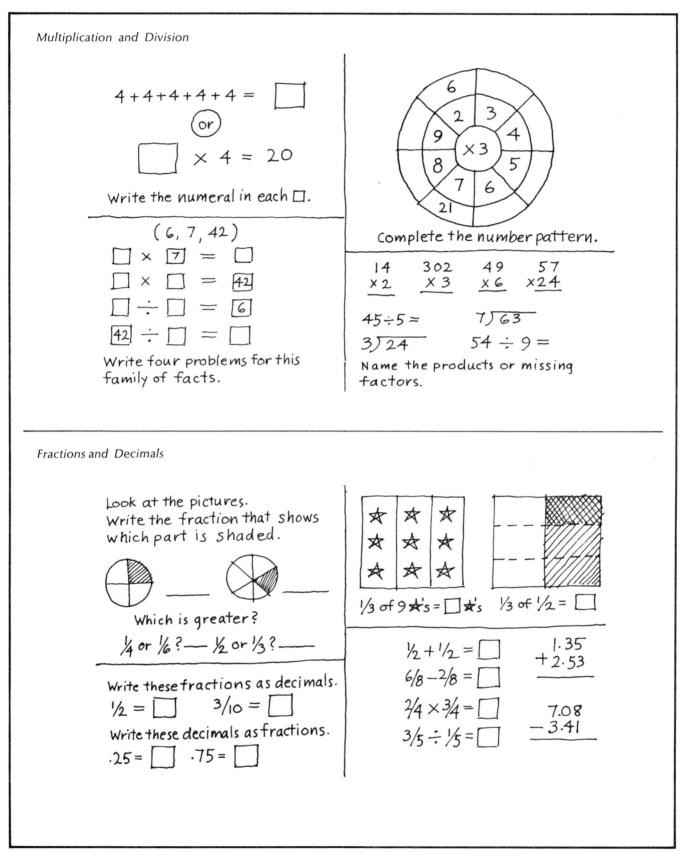

Multiplication and Division

$4 + 4 + 4 + 4 + 4 =$ ☐

(or)

☐ $\times 4 = 20$

Write the numeral in each ☐.

$(6, 7, 42)$

☐ $\times$ 7 $=$ ☐

☐ $\times$ ☐ $=$ 42

☐ $\div$ ☐ $=$ 6

42 $\div$ ☐ $=$ ☐

Write four problems for this family of facts.

Complete the number pattern.

14	302	49	57
×2	×3	×6	×24

$45 \div 5 =$ $7\overline{)63}$

$3\overline{)24}$ $54 \div 9 =$

Name the products or missing factors.

Fractions and Decimals

Look at the pictures.
Write the fraction that shows which part is shaded.

Which is greater?

¼ or ⅙ ? ___ ½ or ⅓ ? ___

Write these fractions as decimals.

½ $=$ ☐   3/10 $=$ ☐

Write these decimals as fractions.

.25 $=$ ☐   .75 $=$ ☐

⅓ of 9 ✬'s $=$ ☐ ✬'s   ⅓ of ½ $=$ ☐

½ + ½ $=$ ☐ $\begin{array}{r} 1.35 \\ + 2.53 \\ \hline \end{array}$

6/8 − 2/8 $=$ ☐

2/4 × 3/4 $=$ ☐ $\begin{array}{r} 7.08 \\ - 3.41 \\ \hline \end{array}$

3/5 ÷ 1/5 $=$ ☐

All programs should be modified or extended to meet the needs of individual pupils.

- "Magic Squares" Teaching Aids, A. R. Davis and Co., 15216 Charlotte Avenue, San Jose, Calif.
- TUF—A New Game of Mathematics, Cuisenaire Company of America
- Computational Skills Development Kit, SRA, Inc.

Further Evaluation
- Wide Range Achievement Test: arithmetic
- California Achievement Tests: arithmetic fundamentals
- Wechsler Intelligence Scale for Children: arithmetic reasoning

PRESCRIPTIVE ILLUSTRATION

Priority Teaching Objective: Bill, nine years old, educationally handicapped. Bill is having difficulty understanding and working multiplication problems in class. He will be able to show me how to do five of the six given multiplication problems, using Cuisenaire Rods.

Pretest Tasks: Bill was taught how to use the Cuisenaire Rods for addition and multiplication. He was then asked to show me what $r \times g$, $g \times y$, and $p \times d$ are and say what each problem stood for numerically. He demonstrated understanding of the rods sufficient to begin training.

Specific Teaching Procedures: "Bill, I'm going to give you six multiplication problems, which I want you to show me how to do, using the Cuisenaire Rods."

"Watch me now. The problem is 2×3. First I find a rod equal to 2 and one equal to 3, then I cross them like this. Now I find all the g rods which will fit under the r rod. The r is finished and put aside and I put the g rods end to end. Then I measure how long the two g rods are by using either the w which equals 1, or the o which is equal to 10. I find the answer is 6, so I write the answer to the problem on this sheet of paper."

"Now show and tell me what you are to do."

Pupil: "Find a rod equal to 2 and one that equals 3 and cross them like this. Then I find all the rods that will fit under the top rod—2 g. The answer is 6."

"Good! You sure are catching on to this hard stuff fast."

"Now show me how to do the following problems:

4×5	9×3	$(2 \times 3) + (4 \times 2)$
3×6	8×2	$(7 \times 3) + (4 \times 7)$

Performance Evaluation: "Great. You got all of them correct except the last problem. Do you see where you went wrong there? What is 7×3? What is 4×7? Would $21 + 28$ add up to 14? See if you can show me how to do the last problem again."

Analysis and Comments: The posttest was given the following day, and Bill only made one error, which involved adding two parts together. Bill had never used the rods before, and they proved to be a real challenge to him. We will continue with more Cuisenaire problems using charts from the workbook.

For Self-instruction: Devise a teaching procedure and performance evaluation method for this pupil: Martina, eleven years old, slow learning. Martina will be able to use concrete objects (paper clips) to solve nine of the following ten multiplication problems within eight minutes:

6	6	0	4	6	3	6	4	6	6
$\times 2$	$\times 6$	$\times 6$	$\times 6$	$\times 5$	$\times 6$	$\times 5$	$\times 6$	$\times 3$	$\times 1$

Conceptual Skills

46/Arithmetic Reasoning

DEFINITION: The ability to apply mathematical concepts to problem solving in personal and social situations.

ILLUSTRATION: Pupil can purchase goods and account for funds, can demonstrate knowledge of coinage and exchange, can calculate time differentials, and can understand weights and measures.

EDUCATIONAL RATIONALE: The purpose of learning mathematical concepts is to be able to apply this understanding to the solution of every-day problems. Educational programs should provide ample opportunity for the pupil to test his skill in practical situations.

SUGGESTED PROGRAM IDEAS

1. Money
   a. Review decimal system and basic coinage with pupil. Using toy store or play situations, have pupil develop reasoning problems around simple purchases. Use newspaper food store advertisements. Have pupil list and total purchases, then subtract from given dollar denomination. Include problems involving purchase of gifts, clothes, etc.
   b. Show the pupil how to make change by adding rather than subtracting (Example: $3.00 − $2.75 is $2.75 + .25 = $3.00).
   c. Develop wage problems. Begin with pupil working part-time at given rate per hour. Calculate weekly and monthly wages. Have pupil develop wage problems from experience. Use "Help Wanted" ads and figure hourly, weekly, monthly, and annual wages for positions advertised.
   d. Introduce simple taxation problems, such as sales tax at five cents to the dollar. Generalize to simple interest problems at 8 percent rates using purchase of automobile, motorcycle, or items suggested by pupil. Compute sample short-form (1040 A) of Federal Income Tax.
   e. Present problems of writing simple checks and balancing accounts. For older, advanced pupils, extend program to writing checks for utilities, credit accounts, housing, etc. Design simple family budgets.

2. Time and Fractions
   a. For young pupils, review hour and half-hour concepts. Have pupil make clock faces. Extend program to quarter-hour and A.M.–P.M. concepts. Gradually teach precise time counting, including minutes and seconds. Apply time concepts to time zones in this country and different parts of the world.
   b. Teach calendar awareness. Select outstanding dates in history, such as Columbus' discovery of the "New World," and build time lines. Project time lines into the future with estimated dates of natural resources depletion, space travel, etc.
   c. Discuss parts of hours in fractional equivalents. Relate fractions to money and purchase problems (buying a half-dozen eggs, three-quarters pound of meat, pound and one-quarter of potatoes, etc.). Also, figure similar problems in grams and kilograms. Introduce addition and multiplication of fractions using pictorial and concrete aids. Use fractions in following simple cookie recipes.

3. Weights and Measures
   a. Present basic measurement concepts such as inch, foot, yard, and mile. Also introduce metric system equivalents. Keep the two systems separate. Avoid use of con-

version factors. Problems should be stated either in English units or in metric units. Develop practical problems requiring actual measurements (size of room, book, table, etc.). Introduce map work including city, state, and federal highway maps for calculating distances.

b. Review ounces, pounds, pints, quarts, and tons. Also introduce metric measures. If possible, involve pupils in cooking programs, comparison of varied weights of products, such as canned goods and produce. Calculate miles per gallon for various cars and compute costs for trips to various destinations.

c. Use scales and weights and measures to weigh different products, determine combined weights, cost per weight unit, etc. Consider advanced problems of cost per ton of coal, animal feed, and foodstuffs. Transfer to advanced arithmetic reasoning problems using puzzle books and games.

REFERENCES

Bereiter, Carl. *Arithmetic and Mathematics*. San Rafael, Calif.: Dimensions Publishing, 1968.

Heddens, James. *Today's Mathematics*. Greater Cleveland Math Program. Chicago: Science Research Associates, 1971.

Related Programs

- *Measurement,* Level 3, and *Learning New Skills in Arithmetic* series, Continental Press, Elizabethtown, Pa.
- *Science Research Associates Mathematics Program,* Science Research Associates, Inc., 259 E. Erie Street, Chicago, Ill.
- *Giant Golden Book of Mathematics* and *The Wonderful World of Mathematics,* Palfrey's Educational Supply Co., 7715 E. Garvey Boulevard, Rosemead, Calif.
- *Arithmetic Games and Activities* and *Building Arithmetic Skills with Games,* Palfrey's Educational Supply Co.
- *Let's Look at Children: A Guide to Understanding and Fostering Intellectual Development in Young Children* (beginning mathematical concepts), Educational Testing Service, Princeton, N.J.
- *How Far?* Rand McNally and Company, Chicago, Ill.
- *Modern Mathematics, Unit II, Mark-away Program,* Paul S. Amidon and Associates, Inc., 1035 E. C. Plymouth Building, Minneapolis, Minn.
- School Mathematics Project, Cuisenaire Co. of America, 9 Elm Avenue, Mt. Vernon, N.Y.
- Drilltapes: Audio Reinforcement for Modern Math, Science Research Associates
- *Fitzhugh Plus Program,* Book 206, Allied Education Council Distribution Center, Galien, Mich.
- Piaget Number Measurement and Space Conservation Program, Learning Research Associates, Inc., 1501 Broadway, New York, N.Y.
- Games for Thinkers, WFF'N PROOF Publishers, 1111 Maple Avenue, Turtle Creek, Pa.
- Kahn, Charles H., and Hanna, J. Bradley. *Pacemaker Practical Arithmetic Series.* Belmont, Calif.: Fearon Publishers, 1972.

Instructional Materials

- Playstore Cash Register, Toy Money (grades 1–4), Palfrey's Educational Supply Co.
- World Time Dial, Solar Year Wheel, *Tell Time Quizmo,* Educational Thermometer, Weather Station, Palfrey's Educational Supply Co.
- Monopoly game
- Pay the Cashier game, Memory Arithmetic game, Palfrey's Educational Supply Co.
- Spring Balance Scale, Palfrey's Educational Supply Co.
- Single Beam Balance Scale and Weights, Palfrey's Educational Supply Co.
- Mathematics in Living Series (buying, wages and budgets, banking, credits, loans and taxes), P.O. Box 1560, Boulder, Colo.
- Dominoes

Further Evaluation

- Wechsler Intelligence Scale for Children: arithmetic
- Stanford-Binet L-M: arithmetic reasoning items
- California Achievement Tests: arithmetic reasoning
- Subjectively developed arithmetic reasoning items

This exercise introduces simple money problems.

If one apple costs six cents, how much change would you get back from a dime? _____

How much would three candy bars cost at nine cents each? _____

Estimate what a person might pay to complete the following shopping list and then total the cost:

- two pounds hamburger ___ $1.78
- One candy bar ___ .10
- One loaf of bread ___
- One quart of milk ___ _____

TOTAL $ _____

These problems require more advanced money and time calculations.

Larry weeded a lawn for 80 cents an hour. If he worked 4½ hours, how much would he earn?

If Mrs. Brown earns $3.75 an hour, how much is her paycheck for a forty hour week?

If the sales tax is 5% on the dollar, how much tax will Billy have to pay if he buys a basketball costing $8.50?

Such questions enable the teacher to determine, for instructional purposes, the pupil's concept of time.

Approximately how many years old is the United States of America? _____

About how long ago did Abraham Lincoln live? _____

If it is 3 p.m. in New York City, what time is it in San Francisco? _____

These problems involve measurement and comparison of distance.

If a mountain is 5 miles high, how many feet high is it? _____

Which is the shorter distance: New York to Chicago or Chicago to San Francisco? _____

If car X gets 25 miles to a gallon of gas, how many miles farther can it travel with ten gallons than car Y, which gets only 20 miles to the gallon?

All programs should be modified or extended to meet the needs of individual pupils.

Priority Teaching Objective: Reed, eight years old, educationally handicapped. This lesson is to provide practice with interest in developing measurement skills; Reed is interested in his father's occupation of masonry, which involves some measuring of this type. When he has finished the lesson, Reed will be able to measure correctly the following distances:

1. Length and width of the room in feet and yards.
2. Home plate to first base.
3. First to second base.
4. Second to third base.
5. Third to home plate.
6. The length of the sidewalk in front of the classroom in yards and feet.

Pretest Tasks: I gave a ruler and a yardstick to Reed and asked him to do seven problems. He answered correctly the following three: How many inches in a foot? What is the length of your pencil in inches? What is the length of your Afro comb in inches?

Specific Teaching Procedures: "Reed, in this lesson we are going to learn to measure off distances in feet and yards. This is a 'measurement wheel' that measures yards, and this one measures feet."

"This foot wheel is twelve inches long—exactly one foot around. When the wheel rolls around once, you hear a click, and you have measured one foot." (The wheel was rolled along the ruler to show the same number of inches. A similar explanation was given for the yard wheel.)

"Now on these cards we have some problems. They tell us what to measure with the foot and yard wheels. Now tell me what you are going to do."

Pupil: "I'm going to roll this thing around for feet and this one for yards and do the measurements on the cards."

"Good! If you work hard, you can help Mr. Lee chalk the baseball diamond for the next game."

Performance Evaluation: "That was good work, Reed. You really concentrated and worked hard. You missed only one measurement. Do you remember what it was?"

Pupil: "Yep, I flubbed my numbers [counting of yards] when I was watching those kids."

An additional five problems were given as a posttest, and Reed got four of them correct; he missed the measurement of the perimeter of the baseball diamond.

Analysis and Comments: The task was appropriate and demanding for Reed. He has trouble concentrating on what he is doing. The measurement wheel helped him attend and think about what was happening. His motivation was good throughout the lesson.

For Self-instruction: Devise a teaching procedure and performance evaluation method for this pupil: Jack, twenty-two years old, rehabilitation training center. Jack is able to count to 100 and can recognize the value of coins. However, he has not yet been able to apply this understanding to making change from purchased amounts less than $1.00, which is currently a primary vocational handicap. Upon completion of this lesson, Jack will be able to give back correct change from six of seven simulated purchases.

Conceptual Skills

47/General Information

DEFINITION: The ability to acquire and utilize general information from education and experience.

ILLUSTRATION: Pupil is aware of major local and national current events, knows local geography, has concept of city, state, and nation.

EDUCATIONAL RATIONALE: A child's fund of information is acquired through a variety of experiences and formal education. Early preschool and childhood opportunities for exploring the immediate environment may aid in the development of interest and motivation essential to the acquisition and retention of general information.

SUGGESTED PROGRAM IDEAS

1. Home and Family
   a. Introduce pupil to playhouse and furniture, doll house, and family dolls. Have child name and describe members of his family and draw a family picture; request parents to send photographs of family members and the home to school. Talk about family activities, interests and hobbies, occupations, and trips or vacations.
   b. Arrange field trip to visit several different homes or to fathers' offices during work hours. Follow up trips with discussion of observations. Show primary films of family life in other countries. Discuss housing, occupations, interests, etc.
   c. Use primary social studies worksheets and pictures depicting family life. From magazine cutouts, develop picture book on different kinds of families in different parts of the city, state, and country. Put on pupil-developed play or puppet show about family life and feelings.

2. Neighborhood and School
   a. Take field trips around school and pupil's neighborhood and discuss observations; draw pictures of neighborhood and school, and compare varied pupil perceptions. Have principal and other teachers visit class and discuss homes, families, and neighborhoods.
   b. Develop pet projects in class, such as caring for rats, snakes, turtles, chipmunk, etc. Visit pet shop, zoo, and neighborhood store. Discuss class and pupil responsibilities to pets and one another. Introduce seasonal pictures, holiday plays and activities, together with discussion of what they represent and how they might be celebrated in different homes and areas.
   c. Read school and neighborhood stories. Tell folk and fairly tales about other lands, people, and make-believe neighborhoods. Discuss story meanings.

3. Community
   a. Visit police, fire station, supermarket, department store, local industries, zoo, parks, and recreation areas. Have follow-up activities. Arrange bus and/or train trip to neighboring city or town. Take boat ride. If possible, arrange for overnight camp-out with parent sponsors. Teach use of telephone and community resources.
   b. Extend use of stories to national heroes (Lincoln, Washington, Kennedy, etc.). Show films of community and state or travel films about the nation. Request policeman, physician, carpenter, etc., to visit class and tell about their jobs and families. Use selected television shows for discussion, together with folk songs, records, and picture displays.

c. Make arrangements for class or pupil visitations to local concert, theater, art show, and museum with appropriate follow-up activities, such as tape recording personal experiences and observations. Introduce junior encyclopedias and source books as reference material for general information. Tour school and community library and point out shelves where different books and informational materials are available. Have pupil select library book of his choice on some general topic and begin simple book reports.

d. Government: Tour city hall and governmental centers. Discuss governmental organization and elections. Invite councilmen to visit class and discuss government.

e. World Community: Have pupils plan trips to foreign countries and develop individual study projects on world affairs, U.N., etc.

REFERENCES

Sullivan, N. "Making History in Prince Edward County." *Saturday Review*, October 17, 1964.

Related Programs

- *Let's Look at Children: A Guide to Understanding and Fostering Intellectual Development in Young Children* (general signs of development—general knowledge), Educational Testing Service, Princeton, N.J.
- *Living Things: Science Obstervations, Day by Day, Holidays and Playdays*, Continental Press, Elizabethtown, Pa.
- *Patriotic Holidays* (filmstrip series), Educational Record Sales, 157 Chambers Street, New York, N.Y.
- Judy Puzzle series: Mother Goose, Folk Tales, Holidays and Seasons, Community Helpers, The Judy Company, 310 N. Second Street, Minneapolis, Minn.
- Extended field trip experiences
- Selected use of films and educational television to supplement class work
- *Community Helpers Series* (filmstrips), Educational Record Sales
- *Our Working World Series*, Science Research Associates, 259 E. Erie Street, Chicago, Ill.
- *Your World*, Series I and II for kindergarten-primary, Taylor Publishing Co., P.O. Box 597, Dallas, Texas
- *Information* (audio flashcard set), Electronics Futures, Inc., 57 Dodge Avenue, North Haven, Conn.
- *The Thinking Box—A Program for Developing Critical Thinking Skills*, Benefic Press, 10310 W. Roosevelt Road, Winchester, Ill.
- Hudson, Margaret W., and Weaver, Ann A. *The Young American Series.* Belmont, Calif.: Fearon Publishers, 1973.

Instructional Materials

- *Holiday Dances: Holiday Rhythms* (record), Educational Record Sales
- Hayes Classroom Pictures, Sets 1–4, Lakeshore Equipment Co., 1144 Montague Avenue, San Leandro, Calif.
- Hayes Seasonal Poems and Decorations, Lakeshore Equipment Co.
- Social Studies 1 and 2 (family, farm, village, community life), Lakeshore Equipment Co.
- Toy farms and zoos
- Doll house and plastic family, Constructive Playthings, 1040 E. 85th Street, Kansas City, Mo.
- *Kindergarten-Primary Art Activities, Nature Quiz Book, At Home in Our Land, The Golden Book Encyclopedia, Giant Activity Book Series*, Palfrey's Educational Supply Co., 7715 E. Garvey Boulevard, Rosemead, Calif.
- *The Answer Book* and *Answers and More Answers*, Palfrey's Educational Supply Co.
- Community Mapping—Basic Set, The Learning Center, Inc., Princeton, N.J.
- What Am I? (ETA puzzle cards), A. Daigger Co., 159 W. Kinzie Street, Chicago, Ill.

Further Evaluation

- Wechsler Intelligence Scale for Children: general information tests
- Subjective questions regarding home, neighborhood, community, and fund of information acquired from present education

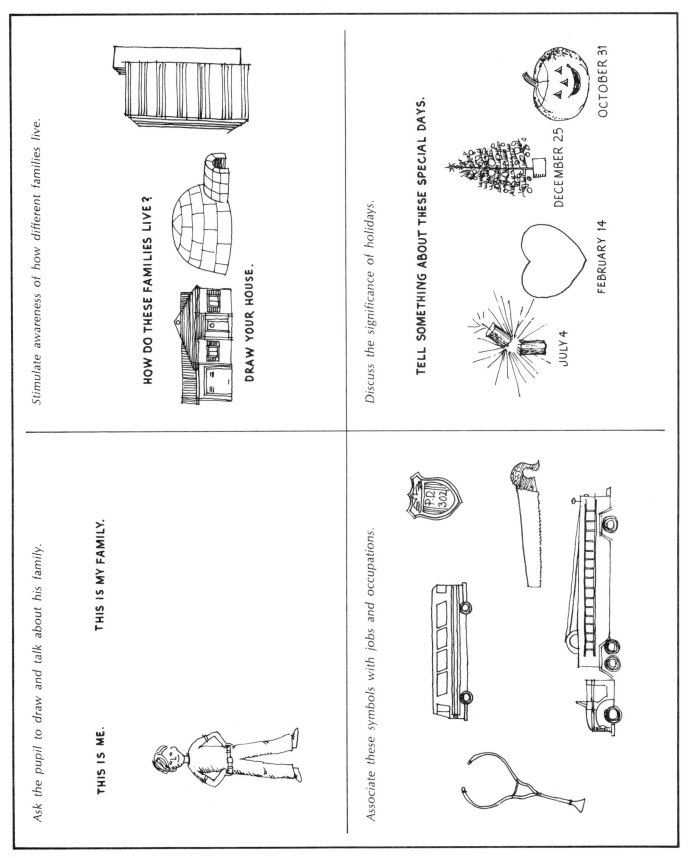

Stimulate awareness of how different families live.

HOW DO THESE FAMILIES LIVE?

DRAW YOUR HOUSE.

Discuss the significance of holidays.

TELL SOMETHING ABOUT THESE SPECIAL DAYS.

OCTOBER 31

DECEMBER 25

FEBRUARY 14

JULY 4

Ask the pupil to draw and talk about his family.

THIS IS MY FAMILY.

THIS IS ME.

Associate these symbols with jobs and occupations.

All programs should be modified or extended to meet the needs of individual pupils.

- Pupil-written stories about personal experiences
- *What I Like to Do* (personal interest inventory), Science Research Associates

PRESCRIPTIVE ILLUSTRATION

Priority Teaching Objective: Shirley, ten years old, educationally handicapped. Because Shirley is new to the city, I thought an awareness of her neighborhood would be immediately useful. I hoped the lesson on exploring her immediate environment might stimulate her interest and motivation in applying this information. Following the lesson, Shirley will be able to find seven specified locations in her general neighborhood without assistance.

Pretest Tasks: Shirley was asked to take me to seven different places. She was successful in guiding me to Cal's Market, Edison High School, and her home.

Specific Teaching Procedures: "Shirley, I'm glad to visit you at your home today and to be able to show you around the neighborhood on our bicycles. I was also glad to be able to meet your mother and to tell her about our next school program."

"Now, here is a map I have drawn of the neighborhood. We are going to ride our bikes to those places marked with an X. I will show you the shortest way to go because you will probably want to get to them at times to meet some of your new friends."

"What are we going to do now, Shirley? Can you tell me?"

Pupil: "Yep. We are going to look at these places and ride around on our bikes."

"Good! Now stay behind me and watch out for the traffic. Here are the places on the map we will go to in this order: Hinton Center, Frank H. Playground, Library, Medical Center, Shopping Center. OK, let's go."

Performance Evaluation: "You did very well; after we found one place, you were able to point in the direction of the next location. What was the hardest to find?"

Pupil: "The library was the hardest."

On the posttest, the same locations were used but in no specific order. She used the map for three of the places and went directly to all of them. A total time of one hour and forty-five minutes was spent on the lesson and posttest·

Analysis and Comments: Shirley was eager to explore the community and ran into three school friends at different locations. Although she would have eventually learned to get to all of the places, I felt that this speeded her adjustment to the neighborhood.

For Self-instruction: Devise a teaching procedure and performance evaluation method for this pupil: Winston, eight years old, remedial reading. Winston will be able to answer orally eight specific questions about San Francisco after reading a selected book, looking at photographs, and viewing a film about the city.

48/Classification

DEFINITION: The ability to recognize class identities and to use them in establishing logical relationships.

ILLUSTRATION: Pupil can sort objects by classification, recognize subclasses, verbalize common elements in class identity.

EDUCATIONAL RATIONALE: A child's mental development is gradual, progressing from sensory-motor and concrete stages to recognizing relationships inherent in groupings and classification systems. Experience in dealing with likenesses and differences in many varied sequential learning situations provide the foundation for later development of formal logical thought.

SUGGESTED PROGRAM IDEAS

1. Matching Identical Elements
   a. Begin with simple matching of color, using same-sized paper cutouts, sticks, etc. Next, match color, using varied objects and sizes such as clothes, beads, and blocks. Using circles, triangles, and squares of different sizes and colors, extend exercise to matching first by color and then by form.
   b. Develop toy box for matching identical objects. Have pupil find identical objects in the room, such as pencils, textbooks, desks, chairs, papers, etc.
   c. Use picture cards for generalizing programs from identical color and form to identical function: pictures of transportation, food, clothes, housing, books, television sets, and instruments. Then have pupils group and describe class qualities by function.
   d. Extend program to identification and matching of identical symbolic elements such as large and small letters, numbers, and abstract symbols. Develop discrimination to include slight color differences, formulas, signs, and nonsense words.
2. Categorization of Similar Elements
   a. Using toys, have pupil group similar objects such as airplanes, automobiles, boats, bicycles, and explain distinctive functions. Introduce pictures of similar objects for sorting. Have pupil develop cutout card file from magazines by grouping objects with similar functions.
   b. Introduce classification by position in time and space, including taller/shorter, up/down, first/last, more/less, young/old. Use sticks and coins of different sizes for concrete reference and grouping. Classify pictures into groups of young and old people, animals, automobiles, etc. Sort up/down objects such as kites, airplanes, smoke, submarines, rain, snow, etc.
   c. Generalize to identification of symbolic elements, including grouping letters, numbers, and designs of various sizes. Group by length of number or letter series. Extend to nonsense words and symbols beginning with the same letter or having other similar characteristics.
3. Verbal Classification and Association
   a. Verbally identify relationship in complex categories, such as varied, same-colored forms involving similar size or area. Discuss nature of subclasses and have pupil make subgroups such as Animals/Dogs/Collies. Complete functional sentences: "Knives are to cut; clothes are to wear."

b. Discuss concept of opposites. Then arrange picture representations such as day/night, sun/moon, morning/evening, A.M./P.M. Develop and write lists of opposites from memory and experience.

c. Extend classification to aesthetics and emotional qualities, including pretty/ugly, happy/sad, good/bad, etc. Use pictures of humans for emotional judgments, stories of social situations for comparison problems, pictures of merchandise of various qualities. If possible, visit museums, courts, and stores to provide meaningful experiences in developing judgmental skills.

REFERENCES

Engelmann, Siegfried. *Conceptual Learning.* San Rafael, Calif.: Dimensions Publishing, 1969.

Levi, Aurelia. "Treatment of a Disorder of Perception and Concept Formulation in a Case of School Failure." *Journal of Consulting Psychology* 29 (1965): 289–295.

Related Programs

- *Let's Look at Children: A Guide to Understanding and Fostering Development in Young Children* (beginning logical concepts units), Educational Testing Service, Princeton, N.J.
- *Reading Readiness Series* (filmstrips), Educational Record Sales, 157 Chambers Street, New York, N.Y.
- *Taller? Shorter? Larger? Smaller?* (filmstrip), Educational Record Sales
- *Seeing Likenesses and Differences,* Level 1–3; *Thinking Skills,* Level 1–2, Continental Press, Elizabethtown, Pa.
- *Reading-Thinking Skills,* Level 1–2 (grade 2), Continental Press
- *The Frostig Program for the Development of Visual Perception* (position in space, similarities and differences), Follett Publishing Co., 1010 W. Washington Boulevard, Chicago, Ill.
- *Learning to Think Series,* Red and Blue Books, Science Research Associates, Inc., 259 E. Erie Street, Chicago, Ill.
- *Color Concepts* (record), Curtis Audio-Visual Materials, Independence Square, Philadelphia, Pa.
- Colors (audio flashcard set), Electronics Futures, Inc., 57 Dodge Avenue, North Haven, Conn.
- *A Reading Readiness Workbook in Concepts* by Herbert Goldstein and Edith Levitt, Parkinson Program for Special Children, Follett Publishing Company
- *Inquisitive Games: Exploring Number and Space,* Science Research Associates
- *Classification and Seriation Kit,* Learning Readiness System, 2500 Cranford, Evanston, Ill.
- Attribute Games and Problems, McGraw-Hill, Webster Division, Manchester, Mo.
- Classification Program (Piaget), Learning Research Associates, Inc., 1501 Broadway, New York, N.Y.

Instructional Materials

- Judy Color-Shapes, Judy Matchettes, The Judy Company, 310 N. Second Street, Minneapolis, Minn.
- The Classification Game (Instructo), Lakeshore Equipment Co., 1144 Montague Avenue, San Leandro, Calif.
- Go Together Lotto, Teach Me Observation Lotto, How We Live, Palfrey's Educational Supply Co., 7715 E. Garvey Boulevard, Rosemead, Calif.
- Ideal Pictures for Pegboard (classification), Magic Cards, Opposites Concepts (Instructo material), Lakeshore Equipment Co.
- Classification (flannelboard kit), Palfrey's Educational Supply Co.
- Discovering Opposites, Let's Learn Sequence, Childcraft Equipment Co., Inc. 155 E. 23rd Street, New York, N.Y.
- Concepto-Sort, Mafex Associates, 111 Barron Avenue, Johnston, Pa.

Further Evaluation

- Kasanin-Hanfmann Concept Formation Test, C.H. Stoelting Co., 424 N. Homan Avenue, Chicago, Ill.
- Columbia Mental Maturity Scale
- Detroit Verbal-Opposites
- Torrance Tests of Creative Thinking

The pupil should identify similar symbols by circling each set with a distinctive color.

The pupil is asked to identify "longer" and "shorter" lines and concepts of "young" and "old."

The pupil should mark each set of identical designs with the same color.

A color code can be used to classify these objects by function.

All programs should be modified or extended to meet the needs of individual pupils.

- Piaget-like tests of concrete operational thought
- Englemann Concept Inventory, Follett Publishing Co.

PRESCRIPTIVE ILLUSTRATION

Priority Teaching Objective: Maurice, six years old, transitional kindergarten. Upon completion of the lesson, Maurice will be able to group eighteen objects into the following groups:

Large squares (3)	Squares (6)
Large circles (3)	Blue pieces (6)
Large triangles (3)	Orange pieces (6)
Small squares (3)	Yellow pieces (6)
Small triangles (3)	Circles (6)
Small circles (3)	Triangles (6)

Pretest Tasks: Maurice was asked to arrange the eighteen pieces in as many groups as he could. He made three piles dividing the objects by colors but failed to make any groups by size or shape.

Specific Teaching Procedures: "Maurice, today we are going to play with all of these pieces of wood. Look at this piece I am holding. It is blue. Let's work together and put all of the blue ones in this pile."

"That was good. Now let's take all of the orange ones like this and put them here."

"Fine. This time we will place the yellow ones over here."

"Very good. Our next game will start by mixing them all up again. This time we will look for all of the large pieces with the same shape. This one is called a triangle. See, there is a blue, a yellow, and an orange triangle—but they all have the same shape and size. We will call this group large triangles and place them one on top of another in this pile."

"Now you pick another piece. Fine. Do you know what that is called?"

Pupil: "A yellow circle—a big one."

"OK, go ahead and make a group of them over here. Oh, I see you have put all of the circles together; is there another way you could do it?"

Pupil: "I could put big circles here and little circles here [pointing]."

"That's right. Now go ahead and make as many other groups as you can but tell me what you are thinking as you do it."

Performance Evaluation: On the posttest, Maurice made all twelve possible groupings without hesistation.

Analysis and Comments: Maurice was well motivated and responded quickly to the materials. The task was somewhat easy for him. More advanced classification tasks should now be used.

For Self-instruction: Devise a teaching procedure and performance evaluation method for this pupil: Max, twelve years old, educationally handicapped. When Max has completed this lesson, he will be able to identify eight words of a ten-word series in logical groups or classes.

Conceptual Skills

49/Comprehension

DEFINITION: The ability to use judgment and reasoning in common sense situations.

ILLUSTRATION: Pupil responds to factual reasoning when situation is explained to him, can recognize alternatives in situations and can judge actions accordingly, can identify logical reason for given action.

EDUCATIONAL RATIONALE: Comprehension develops through experience resulting in increasing attention and in the understanding of varied situations and their implications for problem solving. General exploration, directive instruction, and practice in making inferences and behavioral responses are essential to any relevant educational program.

SUGGESTED PROGRAM IDEAS

1. Common Sense Understanding
   a. Present simple paper maze puzzles. Gradually introduce more difficult Judy Senior Puzzles, See-Quees, wire-form puzzles, and picture puzzles. From newspapers and magazines, collect pictures of problem situations (accidents, building construction, etc.); discuss picture interpretation. Practice verbal interpretation of simple and complex pictures to develop communication of ideas.
   b. Develop list of cause-and-effect relationships, such as heavy clouds/rain, gun/shoot, firemen/put out fires, rockets/outer space. Have pupils discuss and extend possible relationships. Have them write stories and draw pictures about cause and effect relationships.
   c. Discuss simple social situation or concrete picture situations and free associate with possible solutions. Role-play possible solutions. Have class write and put on play demonstrating understanding of a class project.

2. Following Directions and Demonstrating Insight
   a. Give simple commands such as: "jump," "bend over," "open the door," etc. Gradually extend to include more complex and involved directions, taking pupil through each step if necessary. Have pupil repeat directions before complex series of actions, follow through, then review steps.
   b. Extend program to using number directions, such as "Take seven steps, counting as you walk, jump twice, climb over the box, and crawl under the table." Have pupil explain rules of simple games such as tag, hopscotch, and checkers.
   c. Teach rules of new games and have pupil explain them in detail to others. Require pupil to bring in hobby or project of interest and explain it in detail to others so they can understand.
   d. Have pupils create new games and explain them to others.

3. Comprehending Abstractions
   a. Teach a simple word code and then give pupil several problems requiring decoding. Extend activity to crossword puzzles. Play two-person games requiring strategy; discuss all possible moves in advance to develop anticipation.
   b. Stop during oral reading of paragraphs or sections and discuss anticipated events and alternative action in stories. Consider logical inferences of stories and events: e.g., "Wolf wants to eat three pigs"; "In the evening we eat dinner and go to bed."

c. Use folklore, fairy tales, and *Aesop's Fables* to discuss abstractions and their logical or illogical happenings. With older pupils, introduce discussion of proverbs ("bird in hand . . . ," "stitch in time . . . ," etc.). Play Twenty Questions game using animal, vegetable, or mineral classification. Discuss social and personal implications of recent local and world news.

d. Have pupils write illogical stories and present them for class discussion. Cut out dialogue from easy comic strips and have pupils write in the story.

e. Have pupils bring in commercials, advertisements, stories, etc., that contain illogical elements.

REFERENCES

Cronbach, Lee. "Improving Understanding and Thinking." *Educational Psychology*, pp. 349–395. New York: Harcourt, Brace and World, 1963.

Fowler, William. "Cognitive Learning in Infancy and Early Childhood." *Psychological Bulletin* 59 (1962): 116–152.

Related Programs

- *Let's Look at Children: A Guide to Understanding and Fostering Educational Development in Young Children* (growth of reasoning skills), Educational Testing Service, Princeton, N.J.
- *Imagination and Insight* (record), Children's Music Center, Inc., 5373 W. Pico Boulevard, Los Angeles, Calif.
- *Independent Activities 1 and 2, Thinking Skills 1 and 2*, Continental Press, Elizabethtown, Pa.
- *The Frostig Program for the Development of Visual Perception* (Position in Space: Shortest Path to Goal, 18–24; Assembly of Parts, 69–85), Follett Publishing Co., 1010 W. Washington Boulevard, Chicago, Ill.
- *Learning to Think Series*, The Green Book, Science Research Associates, Inc., 259 E. Erie Street, Chicago, Ill.
- Myers, R. E., and Torrence, E. Paul. *For Those Who Wonder*. Boston: Ginn and Co., 1966.
- *Developing Cognitive Skills in Young Learners* (filmstrips), Educational Activities, Inc., Freeport, L.I., N.Y.
- *Concepts* (record), Curtis Audio-Visual Materials, Independence Square, Philadelphia, Pa.
- *Creative Thinking Activities* and *Tricks and Teasers*, Highlights Handbook, Highlights For Children, Inc., 2300 W. Fifth Avenue, Columbus, Ohio
- *The Productive Thinking Program*, Educational Innovation, Box 9248, Berkeley, Calif.

Instructional Materials

- See-Through Puzzles, Creative Playthings, Princeton, N.J.
- *Listening Games* (listening and comprehension), Palfrey's Educational Supply Co., 7715 E. Garvey Boulevard, Rosemead, Calif.
- *Folklore of the World: The Illustrated Book of American Folklore*, Palfrey's Educational Supply Co.
- Proverb books
- Dominoes
- Chinese checkers, chess, checkers
- Monopoly game
- Rhyming Pictures (flannel board kits), Palfrey's Educational Supply Co.
- Art and craft projects
- Model building
- World About Us Lotto, Go Together Lotto, Childcraft Equipment Co., 155 E. 23rd Street, New York, N.Y.
- Judy Senior Puzzles and See-Quees, The Judy Company, 310 N. Second Street, Minneapolis, Minn.
- *Science Games and Activities* by Guy Wagner, et al., Teachers' Publishing Corp., 866 Third Avenue, New York, N.Y.
- Dr. Nim Game, Ed-U-Cards, Lakeshore Equipment Co., 1144 Montague Avenue, San Leandro, Calif.

Incomplete sentences that portray general comprehension and logical inference may be completed orally or in writing.

Mary had _____

The cow jumped over _____

If I am late for school, _____

Elephants are big animals and must eat _____

During the winter, _____

Simple crossword puzzles introduce this type of activity and help to develop comprehension skills.

Across:
1. Has whiskers and drinks milk.
Down:
2. Flys at night.

Across:
1. Has long ears and hops.
3. Short for "bicycle."
Down:
2. Sound made by dog.

Discuss alternate approaches to a common problem.

This girl is three years old.

Billy found her walking in the street.

What should he do?

The code teaches abstraction from basic facts. Completed, it reads, "It is fun to learn a code."

1	2	3	4	5	6	7	8	9	0	X	X̄	X̄
T	F	U	N	I	O	L	E	A	S	C	D	R

5	0
I	T

| 2 | 3 | 4 |

| 1 | 6 |

7	8	9	X̄	4

| 9 |

| X | 6 | X̄ | 8 |

All programs should be modified or extended to meet **the needs of** individual pupils.

- Picture Sequence Cards, and What's Funny Cards, Speech and Language Materials, Inc., P.O. Box 721, Tulsa, Okla.
- *Beginning Science—A Modern Approach,* Holt, Rinehard and Winston, Inc., New York, N.Y.
- *Thinking and Writing: An Inductive Program in Composition,* Prentice-Hall, Englewood Cliffs, N.J.
- *The Fundamentals of Thinking* (filmstrips and manual), Eye Gate House, Inc., 146-01 Archer Avenue, Jamaica, N.Y.
- *The Thinking Book,* Open Court Publishing Co., Box 599, LaSalle, Ill.

Further Evaluation

- French Intellience Test
- Porteus Maze Tests
- Stanford-Binet L-M: general comprehension items
- Valett Developmental Survey of Basic Learning Abilities: conceptual development
- Wechsler Intelligence Scale for Children: comprehension subtests
- Subjective evaluation of pupil responses to concrete directions and commands
- Rosenzweig Picture Frustration Test
- The Basic Concept Inventory, Follett Publishing Co.

PRESCRIPTIVE ILLUSTRATION

Priority Teaching Objective: Cheril, fifteen years old, educationally handicapped. Cheril will demonstrate her knowledge of basic chess moves by playing a game with the teacher and correctly moving each selected piece without asking for help.

Pretest Tasks: Cheril could identify the king by name. She did not know the names of any other chess pieces or how they moved.

Specific Teaching Procedures: "Cheril, you have done very well, so far, in learning chess. You have learned the names of all of the pieces. You also know how the pawn, bishop, king, and queen move."

"Today, we will learn how the rook and the knight may move. Look at the empty chess board. Pick up the knight and place it on its position—either the black or white knight will do. Fine. Now place a white rook where it belongs."

"Now the rook can move forward, backward, or sideways like this [demonstrate] any number of squares that he wishes as long as the squares are empty; that is, he cannot jump over any men in front of him. Now you show me the kind of moves the rook can make."

"That was good. Now the knight, here, is the only chess piece that can jump over other men to occupy an empty space or to take another piece. He moves two spaces forward and one space to the left like this. Or the knight can move two spaces backward or sideways, but never diagonally, before he moves one space either to the right or left. Let me show you the possibilities. Now you make some of the moves."

Performance Evaluation: A chess board set up with the black rook, black pawn, and white knight, were presented as in the diagram. Cheril was asked to demonstrate all possible moves for each piece on the board, which she did without difficulty.

Analysis and Comments: On the posttest, Cheril demonstrated her knowledge of all moves, except castling, which had not yet been introduced.

For Self-instruction: Devise a teaching procedure and performance evaluation method for this pupil: Jack, eight years old, specific learning disability. Following this lesson, Jack will be able to read five problem cards, such as that below, and explain what will happen into a tape recorder.

Mother bought a box of ice cream at the store. She put it in the car. When she got home, she forgot to bring it into the house. What do you think will happen?

50/Social Acceptance

DEFINITION: The ability to get along with one's peers.
ILLUSTRATION: Pupil can relate meaningfully to others and is accepted in both one-to-one and group situations.
EDUCATIONAL RATIONALE: To become socially acceptable, children must be taught self-control, cooperation, and good manners. The school must cooperate with the home in both direct and indirect teaching of these important personal habits and the related skills of social behavior.

SUGGESTED PROGRAM IDEAS

1. Self-acceptance
   a. Using several pictures of the child, have him associate to the various ages presented and reflect on feelings about himself at that time. Use baby pictures and photographs of the pupil in different activities for purposes of exploring and developing pupil insight into his behavior. Discuss his views of his place in the family, personal strengths, limitations, and interests.
   b. Develop picture book of drawings, cutouts, and pupil-made stories entitled "Who I Am," "I Am a Boy (Girl) Named _____," etc. Discuss pupil aspirations, problems, concerns, and related feelings regarding failures, mistakes, successes, and awards.
   c. Generalize discussion to include pupil's views of personal, home, and family responsibilities and obligations. Discuss the importance of recognizing and expressing personal feelings in socially acceptable ways. Ask the pupil to share feelings about his birthday and special holidays.

2. Family Acceptance
   a. With basic social studies discussion pictures, discuss family roles, rules, and responsibilities. Explore the necessity for having family and social rules. Discuss how they are made by parents, teachers, councils, committees, and legislators. Write stories on family issues and alternate means of solving problems.
   b. Consider parental roles, responsibilities, work, interests, appropriate birthday gifts, and how to get along with family members. List various family problems and have pupils write short plays or role-play problem situations to develop insight and to consider possible resolutions.
   c. Discuss the importance of good manners in home and school. Teach use of social amenities including: "excuse me," "thank you," "I'm sorry," "please," "you're welcome," and "how are you?" Read stories about family concerns and discuss implications.

3. School and Community
   a. Investigate need for social regulations and rules of school and city council, firemen, policemen, auto license requirements, etc. Discuss sportsmanship, including appropriate behavior for winners and losers. Have pupils explain rules of games to one another. Teach pupils the skills required for success in table games, individual and team sports.
   b. Develop class rules, council, or officers. Have pupils organize a party or activity such as a field trip. Write invitations, thank-you notes, etc. Use filmstrips, movies, etc., to explore social graces and etiquette.

> c. Organize class projects to meet, play, and work with another cultural or racial group. Develop pen pals with children in other countries or states. Take class photographs, make tape recordings, etc., for exchange purposes. Use related stories and films to broaden social acceptance.
> d. Pupils keep journals of feelings about self and others—include photos, sketches, etc.

REFERENCES

Campbell, John. "Peer Relations in Childhood." *Review of Child Development Research,* Vol. 1, edited by Martin L. and Lois W. Hoffman, pp. 289–321. New York: Russell Sage, 1964.

Ross, Sheila. "Effects of Intentional Training in Social Behavior on Retarded Children." *American Journal of Mental Deficiency* 73 (1969):912–919.

Related Programs
* *Good Manners Through Music* (record), Educational Record Sales, 157 Chambers Street, New York, N.Y.
* *Good Manners* (filmstrip series), Educational Record Sales
* *People Live Together,* 1 and 2, Continental Press, Elizabethtown, Pa.
* *Basic Social Studies Discussion Pictures,* Harper and Row Publishers, 2500 Crawford Avenue, Evanston, Ill.
* *Good Manners Books,* Palfrey's Educational Supply Co., 7715 E. Garvey Boulevard, Rosemead, Calif.
* *Unfinished Stories for Pupils,* National Education Association, 1201 16th Street, N.W., Washington, D.C.
* *How Five Students Found the Way* by Judith M. Anderson, Mafex Associates, Inc., 111 Barron Avenue, Johnston, Pa.
* *You and They: Taking Stock,* You and Your Needs, Accent/Social Contact Books, Follett Educational Corp., 1010 W. Washington Boulevard, Chicago, Ill.
* *Words and Action: Role Playing Photo-Problems for Young Children,* Holt, Rinehart and Winston, Inc., New York, N.Y.
* *Developing Understanding of Self and Others,* American Guidance Service, Inc., Publishers Building, Circle Pines, Minn.
* *ESP "Grandpa Says" Stories,* G. W. School Supplies, 5626 E. Belmont, Fresno, Calif.
* Emotions and Social Attitudes, Mafex Associates, Inc.

Instructional Materials
* *What Do You Do, Dear?* (book), Educational Record Sales
* *My Home and Family Kit* (Instructo materials), Lakeshore Equipment Co., 1144 Montague Avenue, San Leandro, Calif.
* *Manners Can Be Fun* (record), Educational Record Sales
* *The Three Bears, Cinderella, Pollyana, Pinocchio,* Little Golden Books, Golden Press, New York, N.Y.
* *Our Friend the Policeman,* McGraw-Hill Book Co., New York, N.Y.
* *What Do You Say, Dear?* by Sesyle Joslin, Scholastic Book Services, New York, N.Y.
* *The Person You Are,* Turner-Livingston Reading Series, Follett Publish Co., 1010 W. Washington Boulevard, Chicago, Ill.
* *Who Would You Like to Be?* (cartoon manners book), Hightlights for Children, Inc., 2300 W. Fifth Avenue, Columbus, Ohio
* *Getting Along Together,* Coronet Special Education Film Series, 65 E. South Water Street, Chicago, Ill.
* *Tell It Like It Is* (game), Au Vi Inc., P.O. Box 964,, Garden Grove, Calif.

Further Evaluation
* Incomplete Sentences
* Sociograms
* Spraing's Behavior Rating Scale and teacher evaluation of peer group acceptance
* Michigan Picture Test
* Pupil self-rating scales such as California Test of Personality
* My SELF Check List

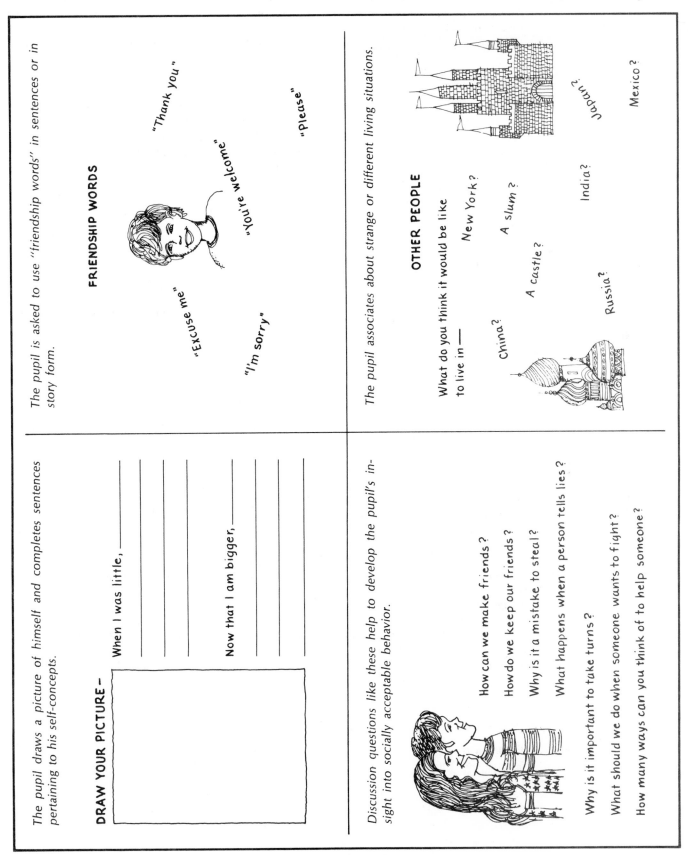

The pupil is asked to use "friendship words" in sentences or in story form.

FRIENDSHIP WORDS

"Thank you"

"You're welcome"

"Please"

"Excuse me"

"I'm sorry"

The pupil associates about strange or different living situations.

OTHER PEOPLE

What do you think it would be like to live in —

New York?

China?

A castle?

A slum?

Russia?

India?

Japan?

Mexico?

The pupil draws a picture of himself and completes sentences pertaining to his self-concepts.

DRAW YOUR PICTURE —

When I was little, _____

Now that I am bigger, _____

Discussion questions like these help to develop the pupil's insight into socially acceptable behavior.

How can we make friends?

How do we keep our friends?

Why is it a mistake to steal?

What happens when a person tells lies?

Why is it important to take turns?

What should we do when someone wants to fight?

How many ways can you think of to help someone?

All programs should be modified or extended to meet the needs of individual pupils.

Priority Teaching Objective: Shawn, twelve years old, educationally handicapped. The long-range objective is for Shawn to be able to relate to and be accepted by his peers; the immediate priority is for him to arrive in the class relatively clean and presentable. At present, Shawn seems to be unable to relate to male peers, and he relates in a silly manner to girls. He doesn't seem to care about himself or his appearance and is unaware of the effect he has on others.

Pretest Tasks. Shawn comes to school with his hands, face, neck, and ears dirty. Most days, his clothes are also dirty and he has a strong body smell. His general appearance is very unkempt.

Specific Teaching Procedures: I talked with Shawn about his problem, the objectives we had in mind, and how his general appearance affects his acceptance by the group. We discussed ways to improve his appearance and made up a "good appearance chart" that he could check off daily as a personal guide.

Shawn said he understood his appearance was poor. He also said he would come with his clothes clean, even if it meant borrowing from his brother. He thought that he might have difficulty showering every day as there are nine other children at home and poor facilities. We agreed that if he comes to school dirty, arrangements will be made for him to take a shower; he was also told that we would wash and dry his clothes if necessary.

Next a meeting was arranged with Shawn's mother. The concerns and objectives were explained as was the program discussed with Shawn. His mother was evasive and noncommittal, but did appear to understand our concern.

Other procedures involved integrating Shawn into group activities as soon as he appeared in a presentable manner. Class discussions were used to explore feelings about appearance, and from comments that Shawn made about his situation, the group appeared to gain some understanding of his problem.

Performance Evaluation: The program continued for eight weeks. Shawn's appearance changed after the first three days, with his clothes being clean, as were his hands, face, and neck. His showers became regular and body odor disappeared. This opened the gate to social acceptance. Although first ignored by others, he is now accepted by classmates in games and learning activities. He has even begun to use after-shave lotion!

Analysis and Comments: A successful start has been made with Shawn. We now need to work on specific social skills to enable him to gain greater acceptance.

For Self-instruction: Devise a teaching procedure and performance evaluation method for this student: Grant, seventeen years old, educable mentally retarded. Upon completion of the social training lessons, Grant will be able to act properly during an employment interview arranged at the C. K. Jones Company. Specifically, Grant will dress appropriately, demonstrate poise and respond to interview questions regarding his experience, interests, and training work-experience program.

51/Anticipatory Response

DEFINITION: The ability to anticipate the probable outcome of a social situation by logical inference.

ILLUSTRATION: Pupil can predict the consequences of his own behavior and that of others in given situations.

EDUCATIONAL RATIONALE: Children must be taught to consider alternate behavioral responses in specific learning situations and to judge the consequences and desirability of possible choices. The development of foresight is essential in social learning and should be emphasized throughout the curriculum.

SUGGESTED PROGRAM IDEAS

1. Developing Basic Anticipatory Skills
   a. First, discuss with pupil the importance of learning what to expect from breaking the rules in playing games. Discuss rules in checkers, play the game, discuss alternate possible moves and their implications in advance. Discuss the value of flexibility of personal response dependent upon actions of others; illustrate through checker moves and strategy. Using simple erector set, have pupil build model, followed by *planning* and constructing his own design.
   b. Introduce use of simple magic set materials and card tricks with discussion of what the magician anticipates from the audience. Teach tricks, have pupil put on a show, then discuss his feelings.
   c. Play listening games with *advance* notification that if instructions are followed in correct sequence, a reward (such as candy, etc.) will be given. Introduce simple craft projects with advance instructions; reward correct completion of projects with no further instruction. Present simple Judy See-Quee Puzzles with detailed discussion as to alternate solutions. Discuss rules of team games and sports and encourage pupil participation and evaluation of plays.

2. Home and Family
   a. Using Basic Social Studies Discussion Pictures (Harper and Row), consider alternate solutions of family problem situations. Use selected guidance films and filmstrips permitting discussion of behavioral patterns. Have pupil list social problem situations with follow-up role-playing of possible resolutions.
   b. With play village toy material, have pupil *plan* and lay out town, then explain reasons for his plan and its consequence on community life. Discuss home chores, responsibilities to family, and the consequences of doing jobs poorly or not at all. Create puppet shows around various ways of approaching family issues such as, "How to teach Johnny to make his bed every day"; "How to teach Mary not to fight"; etc.
   c. Read children's stories such as "The Little Red Hen' and "Cinderella," and discuss the social anticipation problems involved. Generalize to discussion, recognizing what things need to be done (picking up clothes, etc.), and doing them *without being told*.

3. Community Implications
   a. Have pupils make "those wishes that could come true" and follow up with discussion of personal and community implications. Develop oral and written stories around the theme, "What Could Be Done to Make This School (Town, City, etc.)

Better?" Have pupils make separate plans for class party, school dance, etc., and then discuss differences in the plans and arrive at the best compromise through anticipation of outcomes and values of each.

b. Select sequential cartoon strips such as "Louie" and "Ferdinand"; cut and paste on separate paper frames, and then arrange in varied sequential orders. Follow with story writing of the plot and outcome. Have pupils develop their own cartoon or story sequences.

c. Discuss reasons for pupils' being tardy, suspended, or in legal difficulty (probation, etc.). Then discuss other alternate behavior that would have been more appropriate. Generalize to court cases from newspaper with discussion of possible alternate behavior. Extend to speculating projects such as, "What if . . . Columbus had not discovered America?" " . . . Billy does not hand in his homework?"

REFERENCES

Cronbach, Lee J. "Healthy Adjustment to Difficulties." *Educational Psychology,* pp. 574–615. New York: Harcourt, Brace & World, 1963.

Valett, Robert E. "A Social Reinforcement Technique for the Classroom Management of Behavior Disorders." *Exceptional Children,* November, 1966.

Related Programs

- *Guidance Stories* (filmstrip), Educational Record Sales, 157 Chambers Street, New York, N.Y.
- *The Family You Belong To,* Turner Livingston Reading Series, Follett Publishing Co., 1010 W. Washington Boulevard, Chicago, Ill.
- *Basic Social Studies Discussion Pictures,* Harper and Row Publishers, 2500 Crawford Avenue, Evanston, Ill.
- Bullis, H., and O'Malley, E. *Human Relations in the Classroom,* Course I & II. Wilmington: Delaware Society for Mental Hygiene, 1947.
- Sugarman, D., and Hochstein, R. *Seven Stories for Growth.* New York: Pitman Publishing, 1965.
- Learning Experience Units in "Mental Health in the Classroom," *The Journal of School Health,* Vol. 33, No. 7a, Sept. 1963.
- "Goofus and Gallant," *Highlights for Children,* 2300 W. Fifth Avenue, Columbus, Ohio
- *Critical Incidents* by James Hoffman, Instructional Fair, Inc., 1225 Bowers Street, Birmingham, Mich.
- *Social Perception Training Kit for Community Living,* Educational Activities, Freeport, Long Island, N.Y.
- *Peer Mobilization Program,* King Film Lab, 1501 S.W. Jefferson Street, Portland, Oreg.

Instructional Materials

- Magic Set, Creative Playthings, Princeton, N.J.
- Erector sets
- Miniature Village, Creative Playthings
- Checkers
- Chess
- Clue (game), Sears, Roebuck and Co.
- *Fortunately* by Remy Charlip, Scholastic Book Services, 906 Sylvan Avenue, Englewood Cliffs, N.J.
- Le Sieg, T. *I Wish That I Had Duck Feet.* New York: Random House, 1965.
- Mother Goose Stories (for group discussion)
- *Cinderella, Little Red Hen, Gingerbread Man, Three Little Pigs*
- Judy See-Quee Puzzles, The Judy Company, 310 N. Second Street, Minneapolis, Minn.
- Six Card Games (Old Maid, etc.), Sears, Roebuck and Co.
- Sequential Pictures, Developmental Learning Materials, 3505 N. Ashland Avenue, Chicago, Ill.
- Moods and Emotions (color study prints), The Child's World, P.O. Box 681, Elgin, Ill.
- *The Road Game* (competition and cooperation), Herder and Herder, 232 Madison Avenue, New York, N.Y.

Anticipatory sequencing: The pupil is required to number the pictures in logical order.

Common problems can be used for discussion of behavioral consequences.

WHAT WOULD HAPPEN IF —

– you put your hand on the stove ?

– you got up late in the morning?

– you play in the street?

– you swear at your parents?

– you hit someone at recess ?

The sentences may be completed in oral or written form and used for follow-up discussion.

If I eat too much candy,

When people are not polite,

It pays to tell the truth because

The three little pigs should have

The pupil projects possible alternate outcomes to varied situations.

WRITE A STORY ABOUT—

–Why everyone should finish school.

–If President Kennedy had not died.

–If we went to other planets.

–When I grow up.

–Sometime in the future.

All programs should be modified or extended to meet the needs of individual pupils.

- *Projective Techniques with Children* by A. Robin and M. Haworth (Madeline Thomas Stories, incomplete sentences, Despert Fables), Grune and Stratton, New York, N.Y.
- Rosenzweig Picture-Frustration Study
- Thematic Apperception pictures

PRESCRIPTIVE ILLUSTRATION

Priority Teaching Objective: Bobby, ten years old, socially maladaptive. Bobby is socially immature and does not realize the effects of his own behavior. Upon completion of this lesson, Bobby will be able to give at least three logical alternative solutions to three different social problem situations presented in photographs.

Pretest Tasks: Bobby was presented five photographs depicting varied social problem situations. He was asked to give as many possible outcomes as he could think of. All of his answers were short and stereotyped, without thought as to probable results.

Specific Teaching Procedures: "Bobby, today we are going to begin to think about different ways that people have to solve problems. There are many ways to do things, and I want to see how many ways you can think of for some problems I will present to you."

"These problems are all about things that happen to boys and girls. For example, if you were in a very noisy classroom and it was disturbing you, there would probably be several different things that you could do. For instance, you might ask the teacher to get it quiet. Or you, yourself, might ask the noisy children to quiet down so you could study. Or you might even yell "QUIET!" if you thought this would help. Can you think of anything else that you might do?"
Pupil: "Maybe move to a quieter place in the room."
"Yes, that might work too. Now which of these do you think might be best to try first?"
Pupil: "Ask the teacher for help."
"Maybe so. Now let's practice with some of these story cards. We will read them together, and for each different solution you can think of, you will get five points on your credit card for free time. Here is the first one:

> There is a boy in your class who is teased and laughed at whenever he raises his hand to say something.
>
> How could you help him?

Performance Evaluation: At first Bobby had difficulty thinking of possible solutions, but he seemed to get better as he went along. The lesson was appropriate, and he did well on the posttest, giving eleven possible solutions to the three photographs.

Analysis and Comments: Much of what Bobby does is given little thought. He needs much more practice with varied experiences, which will help him consider solutions to everyday problems he encounters in school.

For Self-instruction: Devise a teaching procedure and performance evaluation method for this student: James, seventeen years old, work-study program. Upon completion of this program, James will be able to give and explain at least two different possible ways to complete seven different work contracts. He will also be able to judge the alternatives and suggest the most feasible approach.

52/Value Judgments

DEFINITION: The ability to recognize and respond to moral and ethical issues.
ILLUSTRATION: Pupil has a sense of right and wrong, controls own actions, demonstrates proper behavior.
EDUCATIONAL RATIONALE: Children need to be taught consistent standards of right and wrong in keeping with their culture so that they may develop respect for the common humanity and dignity of all mankind. Pupils should also be instructed in the respect for individuality and the values of democracy. Character education should enable the child to develop from egocentric to rational-altruistic behavior.

SUGGESTED PROGRAM IDEAS

1. Moral Issues
   a. Since consistency in standards and discipline, together with routine habit training, is essential to sound character development, begin by carefully defining class limits and involve pupils in the formation of rules of conduct. Develop class council to judge behavior. Discuss nature and limitations of authority figures (parents, teachers, judges, etc.) and importance of legal and ethical rules for guiding behavior.
   b. List pupil dilemmas of judging right and wrong and role-play possible solutions. Utilize unfinished stories, such as the NEA material, to stimulate consideration. Read simple poems (Edgar Guest) and expand on morals involved.
   c. Discuss general importance of religion and appropriate behavior in mixed religious groups, i.e., silent meditation, etc. Encourage individual and class participation in school and community welfare projects. From news media, bring in moral problems and issues for discussion of right and wrong behavior.
   d. Discuss problems of drugs, alcohol, venereal disease, crime, poverty, etc. Bring in current events articles to emphasize issues and alternatives.

2. Patriotism and Democracy
   a. Teach the values of democracy, using stories of presidents, heroes, etc. Discuss the divergent makeup of peoples and subcultures in the U.S.; stress respect for individual and cultural differences.
   b. Provide habitual instruction in meaning and respect of the flag and the Pledge of Allegiance. Present the Bill of Rights and Constitution in understandable concepts for the level of pupils being instructed. Explain how laws are made and enforced, and how the school, city, state, and nation are administered. Use *Boy Scout Handbook* and supplementary audiovisual material.
   c. Use holidays such as Lincoln's Birthday, Memorial Day, Labor Day, Thanksgiving, Hanukkah, and Christmas to teach values of unity, sacrifice, work, and cultural and religious heritage. Have pupils make projects, give reports, and present holiday plays.
   d. Have pupils take turns on student court and jury to judge selected problems.

3. Ethical and Rational-Altruistic Behavior
   a. Discuss the dangers of peer group pressure and undue social conformity as illustrated in mob action, scapegoating, school pressures, etc. Stress the importance of a sense of conscience and rational behavior. Study common elements of mankind and how geographical-cultural differences result in behavioral differences.

211

b. Provide opportunities to study proverbs and universal ethics such as those expressed in simple stories like *Aesop's Fables*. Show religious books and writings and discuss literary samples of religious wisdom, such as poetry from Hinduism, Buddhism, Islam, Judaism, and Christianity.

c. Encourage individual reading in the personal philosophies of great men such as from the *This I Believe* series. Provide discussion of values of membership in character-building organizations such as scouts, church groups, YMCA, etc.

d. Develop pen pal program with youth in other countries and encourage altruistic behavior such as volunteer service to community, contributions to UNESCO, VISTA, Peace Corps, etc.

REFERENCES

Gibson, John. *Citizenship.* San Rafael, Calif.: Dimensions Publishing, 1969.

Krathwohl, David; Bloom, Benjamin; and Masia, Bertram. *Taxonomy of Educational Objectives: The Classification of Educational Goals; Handbook II: Affective Domain.* New York: David McKay, 1956.

Montagu, Ashley. *Helping Children Develop Moral Values.* Chicago: Science Research Associates, 1953.

Related Programs

* *Teaching Children Values Through Unfinished Stories* (record), Educational Activities, Box 392, Dept. C10, Freeport, N.Y.
* *Developing Your Personality* (filmstrip), Educational Record Sales, 157 Chambers Street, New York, N.Y.
* *The Friends You Make,* Turner-Livingstone Reading Series, Follett Publishing Co., 1010 W. Washington Boulevard, Chicago, Ill.
* *Unfinished Stories for Use in the Classroom,* National Education Association, 1201 16th Street, N.W., Washington, D.C.
* *Patriotic Holidays* (filmstrip), Educational Record Sales
* The Human Values Series, Grades 1–6, Steck-Vaughn Co., Austin, Tex.
* "For Beginning the School Day," *Highlights for Children,* 2300 W. Fifth Avenue, Columbus, Ohio
* *Paths to Follow* by A. Leavell, M. Friebele, and T. Cushman, Golden Rule Series, American Book Co., 450 W. 33rd Street, New York, N.Y.
* *Seek and Learn Workbooks (sharing, honesty, differences, justice),* Educational Activities, Freeport, Long Island, N.Y.
* Sporel, D. T. *Tensions Our Children Live With.* Boston: Beacon Press, 1959.
* *Methods in Human Development,* by Harold Bersell and Waldo H. Palomares, Human Development Training Institute, 4455 Twain Avenue, Suite H, San Diego, Calif.
* *Let's Get Hip Drug Education Kit,* Mafex Associates, 111 Barron Avenue, Johnston, Pa.

Instructional Materials

* *Aesop's Fables* edited by Louis Untermeyer, Palfrey's Educational Supply Co., 7715 E. Garvey Boulevard, Rosemead, Calif.
* *Folktales Children Love* by Watty Piper, Platt & Munk, Inc., New York, N.Y.
* *Everyday Poems for School and Home* (moral values), Palfrey's Educational Supply Co.
* Book of proverbs for discussion purposes
* *Beauty and the Beast, Black Beauty, The Yearling, Robin Hood*
* Life Magazine Editors. *The World's Great Religions.* New York: Time Incorporated, 1970.
* Guest, Edgar A. *A Heap O' Livin' Along Life's Highway.* Chicago: Reilly & Lee, 1936.
* Swing, Raymond, ed. *This I Believe.* New York: Simon & Schuster, 1954.
* *Boy Scout Handbook,* National Council of Boy Scouts of America, New Brunswick, N.J.
* *Values* (story records), Bowmar Records, 622 Rodier Drive, Glendale, Calif.

Further Evaluation

* Children's Apperception Test
* Michigan Picture Test
* Madeline Thomas Stories

After completing and coloring the picture, the pupils discuss the history and meaning of our flag.

The poem illustrates the kind of material to be read by the class as a basis for follow-up discussion.

The Friend

It matters not to me how rich or poor he be,
Or where he kneels to worship, or the task he does each day,
Or be he black or white, if he will set me right,
And tell me just which road to turn when I have lost my way.

Edgar A. Guest

The problems provide for discussion of value judgments.

One day in school Barbara took Joan's book and wouldn't give it back to her. What should Joan do?

Jack found that David was copying his arithmetic test answers. What should Jack do?

Bill told John his church was not any good. What should John do? Why?

Story-writing activities allow for expression of personal values.

WRITE A STORY ABOUT—

– Our class rules.

– The most important thing in the world.

– My heroes.

– The person I would like to be.

All programs should be modified or extended to meet the needs of individual pupils.

- Survey of Interpersonal Value, Science Research Associates, Inc., 259 E. Erie Street, Chicago, Ill.
- Incomplete story and sentence techniques
- My SELF Check List

PRESCRIPTIVE ILLUSTRATION

Priority Teaching Objective: Jerry, sixteen years old, emotionally disturbed and with history of drug addiction. When Jerry has completed this program, he will be able to express orally and in writing his personal feelings about "shooting up" (injection of hard drugs into the veins) in a concise statement that indicates an awareness of the possibility of overdose and death. His statement will also include several possible emotional reactions to a friend's death from an overdose.

Pretest Tasks: Jerry was given four questions pertaining to drug use (example: "How do you think your friends would feel if you accidentally died from an overdose?"). He responded to all questions with a surprisingly lackadaisical attitude.

Specific Teaching Procedures: "Jerry, this tape recorder has five different songs on it. I'm sure that you will recognize some of the singers and you may even know the words."

"Listen carefully to the words in each song. If you already know them and want to sing along, that is OK. After you listen to each song, I am going to give you a list of questions. I want you to read them and then write the answers. All of the questions pertain to the message in the song, so be sure to listen closely to see if you can get it!"

"Here is the first one: ['The Needle and the Damage Done' by Neil Young on *Harvest*]. And here are the questions: Why do you suppose Neil Young wrote this song? What does he say in it? Write the message in your own words."

(The other songs were: "Billy Dee" by Kris Kristofferson on *The Silver-Tongued Devil and I*; "Been on a Train" by Laura Nyro on *Christmas and the Beads of Sweat*; "Needle of Death" by Bert Jansch, sung by Sylvia Tyson on *Ian and Sylvia*; and "In the Quiet Morning" by Mimi Farina on *Take Heart*.)

Performance Evaluation: Jerry listened carefully to all of the songs and wrote out responses to seventeen questions on the worksheets. He was highly motivated and requested to replay the songs. On a posttest two days later, he was able to respond emotionally and effectively to the questions.

Analysis and Comments: Very effective. Jerry seems to be reached, and this approach should be continued.

For Self-instruction: Devise a teaching procedure and performance evaluation method for this pupil: Otto, eight years old, behaviorally disturbed. Otto repeatedly takes articles that do not belong to him. He is constantly searching for something to take at the most opportune moment. He wants attention, even though it is unpleasant, and he has to steal to get it. I would like him to learn to give examples of someone taking something of his and how he would feel about it, and to make suggestions to the discussion group as to how stealing might be stopped.

53/Social Maturity

DEFINITION: The ability to assume personal and social responsibility.
ILLUSTRATION: Pupil is socially mature and independent, demonstrates appropriate citizenship, and assumes social responsibilities.
EDUCATIONAL RATIONALE: In order to foster social maturity, the school must provide opportunities for pupils to learn social expectations appropriate to their developmental level. Instruction and practice in the acceptance of responsibility and obligations of good citizenship should be planned to guarantee increasing personal success.

SUGGESTED PROGRAM IDEAS

1. Primary School Years
   a. Provide basic instruction in personal responsibility for neatness and cleanliness. Show pupils how to select individual games and projects and pursue interest without disturbing others. Teach sharing and cooperative play and project work.
   b. Discuss proper behavior going to and from school and teach responsibilities of being a good neighbor. Review how to get around in the neighborhood and use stores, buses, parks, etc. Talk about family chores and have each pupil explain his family responsibilities.
   c. Develop class project for improving the school, such as lawn clean-up, Arbor Day plantings, safety patrol, etc. Use indoor plants and gardening with individual responsibilities. Bring in various pets and assign rotating responsibility.

2. Middle School Years
   a. Assign specific class duties and teach the importance of learning to carry out chores and responsibilities without constant reminding. Teach value of waiting in line quietly and taking turns. Discuss skills of how to greet and make new friends in school and neighborhood. Stress participation in school government.
   b. Talk about choosing and selecting proper clothes and simple management of money and allowances. Teach good study habits and how to successfully complete homework assignments and responsibilities. Have pupils consider ways to earn money such as mowing lawns, special home jobs, paper routes, etc., and encourage exploratory work involvement.
   c. Assign pupils to run errands both in and out of school. Instruct in simple repair jobs such as mending books, replacing lost nuts and bolts, emptying vacuum cleaners, fixing flashlights, etc. Use stories (Indian stories, etc.) to investigate different concepts of manhood and maturity. Plan and carry out class picnics or camping trip with individual responsibilities.
   d. Have pupils assist younger pupils as tutors and helpers. Request they keep written record of assistance to others.

3. Adolescence and Young Adulthood
   a. Discuss individual travel arrangements for visiting nearby points and distant areas. Promote vacation reports and planning. Arrange field trips to out-of-town places with specific pupil responsibilities. Write letters of inquiry, newspaper or magazine orders, and simple business correspondence.
   b. Visit industries, businesses, and possible work locations with follow-up prevocational study units. Help pupils investigate steps involved in preparing for actual

215

work experience or specialized schooling (college, technical school, etc.). Encourage independent reading and projects to explore individual interests.

c. Discuss civic responsibilities and visit city council and courts. Explore responsibilities involved in marrage and family life. Consider means of planning and providing for the future, including personal contributions to civic progress and social welfare. Discuss importance of current events and personal responsibilities of citizens in world affairs.

REFERENCES

Doll, E. A. *The Measurement of Social Competence*. Minneapolis: Educational Test Bureau, 1953.
Valett, Robert E. "Curriculum Implications of Psychological Practice." *The Practice of School Psychology*, pp. 253–264. Belmont, Calif.: Fearon Publishers, 1963.

Related Programs
- *The Jobs You Get* and *The Town You Live In*, Turner-Livingston Reading Series, Follett Publishing Co., 1010 W. Washington Boulevard, Chicago, Ill.
- *Pictures in Your Mind* (film), Association Press, New York, N.Y.
- *Who Built America?* (record), Educational Record Sales, 157 Chambers Street, New York, N.Y.
- *What Could I Be?* by Walter Lifton, Science Research Associates, Inc., 259 E. Erie Street, Chicago, Ill.
- Student government activities and programs
- *Early Years of Great Men and Women*, Highlights for Children, Inc., 2300 W. Fifth Avenue, Columbus, Ohio
- Turner Career Guidance Series, Follett Publishing Co., 1010 W. Washington Boulevard, Chicago, Ill.
- *Living and Working Together, Series 1680,* Jim Handy Organization, 2821 E. Grand Boulevard, Detroit, Mich.
- *Living in Your Community Program,* Mafax Associates, 111 Barron Avenue, Johnston, Pa.

Instructional Materials
- *Your Child Grows Up* (for parent education), John Hancock Mutual Life Insurance Co., Boston, Mass.
- *Discoverers of America, Famous Indian Chiefs, Great American Series,* Palfrey's Educational Supply Co., 7715 E. Garvey Boulevard, Rosemead, Calif.
- *Glory of Negro History* (record), Educational Record Sales
- Travel pictures
- Camping equipment for outings
- Animal cages, food, and equipment
- Cameras and tape recorders for field trips
- *Fables* (story record), Curtis Audio-Visual Materials, Independence Square, Philadelphia, Pa.
- *Character Development* and *Personality Development* (filmstrips), International Film Bureau, Inc., 332 S. Michigan Avenue, Chicago, Ill.
- *Retold Fables* by K. Evans, Follett Library Book Co., 1018 W. Washington Boulevard, Chicago, Ill.

Further Evaluation
- Vineland Social Maturity Scale
- Cain-Levine Social Competency Scale (for trainable mentally retarded)
- My SELF Check List
- Sociometric devices

PRESCRIPTIVE ILLUSTRATION

Priority Teaching Objective: Al, fourteen years old, socially maladjusted. Al will accept a term as president of the class self-government council. As president he will aid the council in developing the new behavior code and will lead all council meetings. He will also show some evidence of assisting other council members in carrying out their assigned duties.

The pupil demonstrates personal responsibility through written communication.

WRITE LETTERS —

— To thank someone for a gift.

— To request a tour of a local industry.

— To request a job interview for summer work at a camp.

— To order some new records from a magazine.

— To invite friends to a party.

The story themes encourage the pupil to consider future responsibilities.

WRITE A STORY ABOUT —

— The kind of work I would like to do.

— When I get married.

— When I am a parent.

— When I am able to vote.

Pupils should list family pets and discuss the responsibilities involved in their care.

The class plans a camping trip and assigns individual chores and responsibilities.

OUR CAMPING TRIP

Responsibilities:

food —

dishes —

entertainment —

cooking —

campfires —

cleanup —

Other Duties:

Place:

Date:

Time:

Pretest Tasks: Since he joined the class, Al has slowly and grudgingly gone along with the decisions of the class council. Although he accepted one responsibility (running the movie projector), he was not very reliable and needed prompting from other members of the class.

Specific Teaching Procedures: "Al, I'm glad to see you alone today since our class drew your name to be president or chairman of the class council for the next three weeks. Since you are new to our school and this class, I want to show you some things that should help you when you become president the day after tomorrow. I know you already have a good idea of how the council works because you have watched it every day since you arrived two weeks ago."

"Yesterday, you got another idea of how a president operates here when you went with us to the auditorium to watch the all-school council in action. However, our class makes practically all decisions for planning our activities and handling problems that might come up."

"I want you to watch this videotape. It was made over the last three years and shows parts of about eight different council sessions. All of the sessions deal with different problems."

"There now, you have seen the first two sessions and you have heard the last problem presented to the council. I'm going to stop the tape now and ask you what you think you might do if you were the president chairing the group."

Pupil: (Responds with some suggestions.)

"OK, now let's look again and see what really happened; then we will look at the rest of the sessions in the same way."

Performance Evaluation: Al responded to the videotapes with increasing interest and insight. During his term as class president, he did surprisingly well. At one time he requested that the entire class view the videotape of a council session he had just conducted.

Analysis and Comments: This was a good learning experience for Al. He was intrigued with the videotape, and this should be used more extensively with him in the future.

For Self-instruction: Devise a teaching procedure and performance evaluation method for this student: Herb, eighteen years old, educable mentally retarded. Upon completion of these lessons, Herb will be able to maintain his own job rating card indicating that he has successfully accomplished the following responsibilities: arrived at work on time for two weeks straight; brought the necessary tools with him every day (wristwatch, gloves, apron, hat); stayed on the job for three hours straight every day for two weeks; received *no* penalty marks from his work supervisor for the two-week period.

A PSYCHOEDUCATIONAL EVALUATION OF BASIC LEARNING ABILITIES

Name _____

Date _____ Age _____

Evaluator _____

	Performance Level	Learning Disabilities			Learning Strengths	
		Very Weak	Weak	Average	Strong	Very Strong
		0 5	25	75	95	100
Gross Motor Development						
Rolling (controlled)						
Sitting (erect)						
Crawling (smoothly)						
Walking (coordinated)						
Running (course)						
Throwing (accurately)						
Jumping (obstacles)						
Skipping (alternately)						
Dancing (eurythmy)						
Self-identification (name/awareness)						
Body Localization (part location)						
Body Abstraction (transfer/generalization)						
Muscular Strength (sit-, leg-ups/bends)						
General Physical Health (significant history)						
Sensory-Motor Integration						
Balance and Rhythm (games/dance)						
Body-Spatial Organization (mazes)						
Reaction-Speed Dexterity (motor-accuracy)						
Tactile Discrimination (object identification)						
Directionality (right-left/etc.)						
Laterality (hand-eye-foot)						
Time Orientation (lapse and concept)						
Perceptual-Motor Skills						
Auditory: Acuity (functional hearing)						
A: Decoding (following directions)						
A: Vocal Association (imitative response)						
A: Memory (retention)						
A: Sequencing (patterning)						
Visual: Acuity ("Snellen")						
V: Coordination and Pursuit (tracking)						
V: Form Discrimination (association)						
V: Figure-Ground (differentiation)						

	Performance Level	Learning Disabilities				Learning Strengths	
		Very Weak	Weak	Average		Strong	Very Strong
		0	5	25		75	95 100
V: Memory (visual recall)							
Visual-Motor: Memory (designs)							
VM: Fine Muscle Coordination (designs)							
VM: Spatial-Form Manipulation (blocks)							
VM: Speed of Learning (coding)							
VM: Integration (draw-a-man)							
Language Development							
Vocabulary (word knowledge)							
Fluency and Encoding (use and structure)							
Articulation (initial/medial/final)							
Word Attack Skills (phonic association)							
Reading Comprehension (understanding)							
Writing (expression)							
Spelling (oral/written)							
Conceptual Skills							
Number Concepts (counting)							
Arithmetic Processes ($+ - \times \div$)							
Arithmetic Reasoning (problem solving)							
General Information (fund of knowledge)							
Classification (relationships)							
Comprehension (common sense reasoning)							
Social Skills							
Social Acceptance (friendship)							
Anticipatory Response (foresight)							
Value Judgments (ethical-moral sense)							
Social Maturity (gross problem solving)							

PUPIL PROGRESS REPORT BY TEACHER

Pupil's Name _____ Birthdate _____ Grade _____

Address _____ Telephone _____

Gross Motor Development: Programs and progress in motor activities, physical education, general health, etc.

Sensory-Motor Integration: Programs and progress in motor integration, art, music, etc.

Perceptual-Motor Skills: Programs and progress in perceptual skills, including listening, attention and memory, fine muscle coordination.

Note to teacher: First, on the form entitled, "A Psychoeducational Evaluation of Basic Learning Abilities," evaluate *present* functioning in the basic learning abilities by marking the performance level. Then, in January and June at the end of each school semester, complete the "Pupil Progress Report," indicating the present educational program and progress to date. Make two copies of that report. Place the original in the special cumulative record folder. Send the carbon to the office of the director of special education for inclusion in the pupil's central file.

222 Language Development: Programs and progress in language usage, including functional level of reading, writing, and spelling.

Conceptual Skills: Programs and progress in arithmetic understanding, social studies, fund of information, concept development.

Social Skills: Programs and progress in social and personal development, including self control, responsibility, and general behavior.

General Comments:

What recommendations do you have regarding educational placement and programs for this pupil for the forthcoming semester or year?

Signed: _____   _____
                        Teacher   Type of Special Class

_____   _____   _____
            Principal   School   Date

INDIVIDUAL PRESCRIPTIVE LESSON PLAN OUTLINE

Pupil's Name _____   Date _____

Learning Objectives	Check (x) Each Objective						Specific Learning Tasks and Practice Activities	Learning Materials Needed (Books, Equipment)	Pupil Performance Evaluation (Quality and Quantity)
	Gross Motor	Sensory-Motor	Perceptual	Language	Conceptual	Social			

223

A RECOMMENDED DAILY CLASS SCHEDULE

8:30–8:50 A.M.   Opening activities and pupil selection of priority learning objectives for the day

8:50–9:50 A.M.   **Language Skills**
Vocabulary   Reading Comprehension
Fluency and Encoding   Writing
Articulation   Spelling
Word Attack

9:50–10:20 A.M.   **Gross Motor Skills**
Rolling   Throwing   Body Localization
Sitting   Jumping   Body Abstraction
Crawling   Skipping   Muscular Strength
Walking   Dancing   General Physical Health
Running   Self-identification

10:20–11:10 A.M. **Conceptual Skills**
Number Concepts   General Information
Arithmetic Processes Classification
Arithmetic Reasoning Comprehension

11:10–11:20 A.M. Recess

11:20–12:00 A.M. **Sensory-Motor Skills**
Balance and Rhythm   Directionality
Body-Spatial Organization Laterality
Reaction-Speed Dexterity   Time Orientation
Tactile Discrimination

12:00–12:45 P.M. Lunch

12:45–1:40 P.M.   **Social Skills**
Social Acceptance   ⎫
Anticipatory Response ⎬ Including daily discussion group meetings
Value Judgments   ⎭
Social Maturity

1:40–1:45 P.M.   Recess

1:45–2:40 P.M.   **Perceptual-Motor Skills**
Auditory Acuity
Auditory Decoding
Auditory-Vocal Association
Auditory Memory
Auditory Sequencing
Visual Acuity
Visual Coordination and Pursuit
Visual-Form Discrimination
Visual Figure-Ground Differentiation
Visual Memory

Visual-Motor Memory
Visual-Motor Fine Muscle Coordination
Visual-Motor Spatial-Form Manipulation
Visual-Motor Speed of Learning
Visual-Motor Integration

2:40–2:50 P.M.   Closing activities

3:00–3:30 P.M.   Individual prescriptive teaching with selected pupils as feasible

---

Note:

It should be recognized that this is merely a guide to the development of a class schedule. Time allocations for teaching specific skills will, of course, vary with the needs of each class as determined by the diagnostic-prescriptive teacher.

PRESCRIPTIVE REMEDIAL ACTIVITIES CORRELATED WITH PSYCHOLOGICAL SUBTESTS

Evaluative Instrument		Item Numbers			
Wechsler Intelligence Scale for Children	Information	47	10		
	Comprehension	49	51		
	Arithmetic	44	45	46	
	Similarities	24			
	Vocabulary	37			
	Digit Span	26			
	Picture Completion	27			
	Picture Arrangement	51	32		
	Block Design	34	36		
	Object Assembly	34	36		
	Coding	17	35		
	Bender Visual-Motor Gestalt	32	33		
	Draw-a-Person	12			
Wide Range Achievement Test	Arithmetic	44	45	46	
	Reading	40	41		
	Spelling	42	43	32	
Illinois Test of Psycholinguistic Ability	Auditory Decoding	23			
	Auditory-Voc. Automatic	25	38		
	Auditory-Voc. Association	24			
	Auditory-Voc. Sequencing	26			
	Vocal Encoding	38			
	Visual Decoding	27			
	Visual-Motor Association	36			
	Visual-Motor Sequencing	32			
	Motor Encoding	32			
Frostig	Position in Space	29	32		
	Spatial Relations	33	34		
	Form Constancy	29			
	Visual-Motor Coordination	33			
	Figure Ground	30			
	Vineland	53			
	PMA-Fluency	38			
	Wepman Auditory Discrimination	23			
	Keystone	27			
	Sentence Completion	50	51		
	Sociogram	50	53		
	Thematic Apperception	51			
	Lincoln-Oseretsky	4	6	7	15

COMMONLY USED DIAGNOSTIC-PRESCRIPTIVE TESTS AND SUPPLIERS

Ayres Southern California Perceptual Tests—Western Psychological Services, 12031 Wilshire Boulevard, Los Angeles, Calif.

Bender Gestalt Test for Young Children—Grune & Stratton, Inc., 111 Fifth Avenue, New York, N.Y.

Cain-Levine Social Competency Scale—Consulting Psychologists Press, 577 College Avenue, Palo Alto, Calif.

Columbia Mental Maturity Scale—Harcourt Brace Jovanovich, Inc., 757 Third Avenue, New York, N.Y.

Detroit Verbal Opposites Test—Bobbs-Merrill Co., 4300 W. 62nd Street, Indianapolis, Ind.

Dolch Basic Sight Words—Lakeshore Equipment Co., 1144 Montague Avenue, San Leandro, Calif.

Frostig Developmental Test of Visual Perception—Consulting Psychologists Press

Gesell School Readiness Tests—Harper & Row, Publishers, 10 E. 53rd Street, New York, N.Y.

Gilmore Oral Reading Test—Harcourt Brace Jovanovich, Inc.

Goodenough-Harris Draw-a-Person Test—Harcourt Brace Jovanovich, Inc.

Gray Oral Reading Tests—Psychological Corporation, 304 E. 45th Street, New York, N.Y.

Hiskey-Nebraska Test of Learning Aptitude—Marshall S. Hiskey, 5640 Baldwin, Lincoln, Neb.

Illinois Test of Psycholinguistic Ability—University of Illinois Press, Urbana, Ill.

Lincoln-Oseretsky Motor Development Scale—C. H. Stoelting Co., 424 N. Homan Avenue, Chicago, Ill.

Mecham Verbal Language Development Scale—American Guidance Service, Inc., Publishers Building, Circle Pines, Minn.

Peabody Picture Vocabulary Test—American Guidance Service, Inc.

Porteus Maze Tests—Psychological Corporation

Purdue Perceptual Motor Survey—Charles E. Merrill Co., 1300 Alum Creek Drive, Columbus, Ohio

Riley Articulation and Language Test—Western Psychological Services

Slingerland Tests of Specific Language Disability—Educators Publishing Service, 75 Moulton Street, Cambridge, Mass.

Spache Diagnostic Reading Scales—California Test Bureau, Del Monte Research Park, Monterey, Calif.

Spraings Bender Recall Test—Violet Spraings, Northern California School for Neurologically Handicapped Children, Lake Merced Boulevard and Winston, San Francisco, Calif.

Stanford Binet L-M—Houghton Mifflin Co., 110 Tremont Street, Boston, Mass.

Strauss Marble Board Test—Appendix I in *Psychopathology and Education of the Brain-Injured Child* by Alfred Strauss and Newell C. Kephart, Grune & Stratton, Inc.

Valett Developmental Survey of Basic Learning Abilities—Consulting Psychologists Press

Vineland Social Maturity Scale—American Guidance Service

Wechsler Intelligence Scale for Children—Psychological Corporation

Wepman Auditory Discrimination Test—Joseph Wepman, 950 E. 59th Street, Chicago, Ill.

Wide Range Achievement Tests—Guidance Associates, 1526 Gilpin Avenue, Wilmington, Del.

DIAGNOSTIC-PRESCRIPTIVE RESOURCES

The Remediation of Learning Disabilities is a resource book of developmental learning tasks, activities, and programs for use in prescriptive teaching and psychoeducational therapy. Its use presumes that a diagnostic evaluation of learning or behavior problems has been completed prior to the selection of remedial or developmental learning objectives.

It is recommended that this resource book be used in conjunction with other materials developed by Dr. Valett and published by Pitman Learning, Inc.

- *The Psychoeducational Inventory of Basic Learning Abilities* (with *Workbook*): This is the basic evaluation instrument designed to correlate with the resource programs presented in this book.
- *A Basic Screening and Referral Form for Children with Suspected Learning and Behavioral Disabilities*
- *Developmental Task Analysis*
- *An Inventory of Primary Skills*
- *Determining Individual Learning Objectives*
- *My Goal Record*
- *My Self Checklist*